HUMAN MEMORY

Paradigms and Paradoxes

HUMAN MEMORY

Paradigms and Paradoxes

Robert L. Greene
Case Western Reserve University

LEA LAWRENCE ERLBAUM ASSOCIATES, PUBLISHERS
1992 Hillsdale, New Jersey Hove and London

Lawrence Erlbaum Associates, Inc., Publishers
365 Broadway
Hillsdale, New Jersey 07642

Library of Congress Cataloging-in-Publication Data

Greene, Robert L. (Robert Leo), 1956–
Human memory : paradigms and paradoxes / Robert L. Greene.
p. cm.
Includes bibliographical references and index.
ISBN 0-8058-0996-1. – ISBN 0-8058-0997-X (pbk.)
1. Memory. I. Title.
BF371.G669 1992
153.1'2–dc20 91-32065
CIP

Printed in the United States of America
10 9 8 7 6 5

This book is dedicated to my parents,
Edward J. Greene and Therese Greene.

Contents

Preface

Many commentators have noted a disturbing aspect of research in cognitive psychology. Work in this field becomes more and more driven by a limited number of experimental tasks. Initially, these tasks are designed to illuminate some important aspect of cognitive functioning. However, over time, the tasks themselves become the chief concern. Researchers try to understand every little detail of such tasks with little regard for whether these details are relevant to important general issues.

I use the term *paradigms* to refer to these tasks that form the core of research and knowledge in the field. The famous philosopher of science, Thomas Kuhn (1962), popularized this term. My use of it is only one of many possible ways in which this term is commonly employed. In fact, Kuhn himself used this term in at least 21 different ways (Masterman, 1970). As a result of this multiplicity of usages, there are disputes as to whether cognitive psychology has a paradigm, whether it is a paradigm, whether it will eventually develop a paradigm, or whether it already has many (and probably too many) paradigms. However, my usage is probably the most common way in which the term ''paradigm'' is employed by cognitive psychologists, although it seems to bear little relationship to what Kuhn usually had in mind.

How should one react to the fact that cognitive psychology has become largely concerned with a handful of laboratory tasks? Most commentators have understandably reacted with expressions of concern, as well as suggestions as to how to place the field on a more solid footing. On the other hand, my reaction is to embrace the status quo with undisguised glee. Each of these classic cognitive paradigms has become a fascinating puzzle on which some of the best minds of our field have labored. An examination of the development of research in these areas yields many examples of the scientific method at its most sophisticated. I don't know whether these tasks have helped us truly understand vague abstractions like "remembering" and "thought." However, they have all been impressive examples of how theories and data can interact.

This book deals with human memory, but it is not intended to be a standard textbook. There is no attempt to discuss every isolated experimental finding, however important. Rather, it is intended as a review of the major paradigms that have been used by experimental psychologists to study human memory. I chose to write a book in this way for three reasons. The first was that this approach seemed to allow a more accurate depiction of the field than other approaches. What we know about memory stems overwhelmingly from a handful of paradigms, and we may as well admit it. Since such a large proportion of effort in our field has been devoted to these classic paradigms, it appeared reasonable to devote a book to them. A second reason was motivated by my general sympathy for the proceduralist approach to memory (Kolers & Roediger, 1984), which sees memory as a by-product of the particular procedures carried out while analyzing a stimulus. An implication of this approach is that there may be about as many kinds of memory as there are mental procedures. Trying to draw general conclusions across experimental situations thus becomes a hopeless task. Finally, I wanted to write this book because I was frustrated with how most texts (and many journal articles) describe these memory paradigms. Too often, authors have felt content to stick with the original interpretation of a paradigm even though the researchers working in that area may have obtained strong evidence that this interpretation is false. Thus, it seemed useful to try to gather in one place descriptions of the current states of these paradigms.

How does one decide which experimental tasks are the most classic and important ones? I would like to think that there would be little quibbling about most of my choices. The paradigms described in the first five chapters are all fixtures of the research literature and would be covered at length in any serious book on memory. Those were easy choices. All five of those chapters dealt with tasks that demand retention of events that are at most a few seconds old. The last four chapters dealt with longer-term retention. Curiously, there is less agreement here as to what are the central paradigms. However, I have included work on encoding, repetition, and forgetting, which certainly seem to be dominant themes in long-term memory research. The final chapter deals with implicit-memory tasks. These implicit tasks are too new to be considered genuine paradigms yet. However, there has been so much fascination with these tasks that they undoubtedly are becoming a part of the core of our discipline.

There are certainly other paradigms that I could have included. Some paradigms (such as serial learning, paired-associate learning, and the verbal-discrimination task) I have omitted because they have not been the focus of much work in the last few decades. There are other paradigms that may be interpreted as memory tasks (such as the Stroop task and the mental-rotation task) but have been omitted because they have had their primary influence in other areas in cognitive psychology. Finally, although there are probably enough short-term memory paradigms to fill a book of their own, I wanted to cover the whole temporal range of memory experiences. Thus, there are some short-term paradigms (such as the memory-span task and the research on acoustic-confusability effects) that easily could have been included here but were not so that a greater variety of tasks could be discussed.

Each of these chapters is written as an independent tutorial on a separate memory paradigm. They can easily be read in any order. There are some references between chapters, but these are few and are not central to understanding major points. I have not assumed any particular background in these chapters, though undoubtedly some familiarity with experimental methods or cognitive psychology would prove helpful.

I am grateful to many people for their assistance. Judith Amsel at Lawrence Erlbaum Associates was tremendously helpful. Most of all, I would like to thank my family. My wife, Karen Goda, and my two children, Matthew and Charlotte, have had to put up with a lot as I was writing this book, and I love them for their understanding.

CHAPTER ONE

Iconic Memory: The Partial-Report Paradigm

One of the most important concepts in cognitive psychology is that human information-processing capacity is limited. That is, people are not able to process an infinite amount of information at any one time. A number of errors that people make on cognitive tasks may reflect the limitations that are present on human information processing.

There are perhaps three classic sources for the presence of limitations on information-processing capacity. One would be Miller's (1956) demonstration that immediate recall rarely exceeds 7 $\pm$ 2 items. A second would be the work on monitoring several simultaneous auditory inputs (i.e., *shadowing*; Broadbent, 1958). The third classic source would be the topic for this chapter—the partial-report paradigm developed by Sperling (1960). This paradigm illustrated the limitations that are present on visual information processing. Moreover, Sperling's work in this area established one of the most famous and influential paradigms to be found in cognitive psychology. The account typically offered for this paradigm is breathtakingly elegant. Unfortunately, the truth as revealed by more recent findings is far more complex, as we shall see.

THE WORK OF GEORGE SPERLING

Psychologists have long been interested in the study of reading and visual perception. A natural question to ask in these areas is "How much information is a person able to see in a single glance?" A number of experimenters, dating back to the early days of psychology, addressed this question. Typically, these investigators would flash a large amount of information to subjects for so brief a time that eye movements would not be possible. Then, subjects would be asked to recall the information flashed to them. Early researchers, such as Erdmann and Dodge (1898), established that people could usually report about four stimuli (letters, numbers, or short words).

George Sperling (1960), in his doctoral dissertation at Harvard University, verified these claims. He would flash an array of numbers or letters to subjects. He found that subjects usually would report four items. It mattered little how many other items were in the array or how the items were distributed spatially. It also mattered little how long the display was flashed for, from a range of 15 milliseconds (ms: thousandths of a second) to 500 ms. In this whole-report procedure, recall seemed to be limited to around four items.

Subjects in these experiments often reported being able to see the whole array. In fact, they claimed to continue having information about the items in the array even for a time after the array was turned off. However, this information quickly faded away, so that by the time about four items had been reported, it was no longer present. Sperling's contribution was to develop a procedure for determining whether people really did have access to more information than they were able to report with this procedure. He developed the *partial-report procedure,* in which he used people's ability to recall part of the display as an indication of how much information they had about the whole display.

In his first experiment on this topic, Sperling presented two rows of letters (either three or four letters in each row). The letters were flashed briefly. Immediately after the display was turned off, a tone was sounded. The tone could be either low or high. If the tone was high, subjects were required to report the letters that had been present on the upper row of the display. If it was low, subjects were to report the letters in the bottom row. Because the tone was not sounded until after the display was turned off (and since subjects had no way of knowing what tone was going to be given until it occurred), they could only apply the tone to some form of memory for the items. The items themselves were no longer physically being shown. The most important finding was that the proportion of items reported was much higher in this partial-report procedure than in the situation where all of the items had to be recalled (the whole-report procedure). Sperling took this as evidence that the whole-report procedure led to underestimates as to the number of items that subjects were able to see in a display.

Sperling used the partial-report results to estimate the minimum number of letters that subjects must have available to them at the time the tone sounded. He calculated this estimate by multiplying the average number of items correctly recalled from the cued row by the number of rows. This estimate was considerably higher than the number of items recalled in whole report. Sperling believed that this estimate derived from a partial report was the minimum number of items available to the subject. Since subjects have to spend some time interpreting the tone and determining the correct row, some items available when the tone was presented could be lost by the time that subjects are ready to respond.

Sperling argued that subjects used a rapidly decaying trace of the visual display in this task. Some primitive memory for the items remained after the display was turned off. When asked to report the letters, subjects read them from this brief visual memory trace. During the time this trace is present, subjects have a high proportion (perhaps all) of the items available to them. However, this trace fades quickly so that it is gone by the time subjects have read out about four items. Sperling obtained evidence for the rapidly decaying nature of this trace in a later experiment where he varied the amount of time that passed between the offset of the display and the presentation of the tone. By the time a second had passed, the proportion of items recalled in the partial-report procedure was approximately the same as in the whole-report procedure. Sperling interpreted this finding to suggest that the visual trace of the display had decayed in under a second.

The partial-report task has been used by countless investigators on different populations. For example, a superiority of partial over whole report has been reported in both children (Haith, 1971) and the elderly (Gilmore, Allen, & Royer, 1986). The brief visual trace described by Sperling is typically called *visual sensory memory,* the *visual sensory register,* or, after Neisser (1967), the *icon* (or *iconic memory*). This concept now occupies a prominent place, both in our textbooks and in our theories of visual cognition.

A procedure similar to that of Sperling (1960) was developed independently by Averbach and Coriell (1961). In their procedure, an array of letters is presented for a brief period of time. At some point after the array goes off, a visual marker is presented near a location that had been occupied by a letter in the array. Subjects have to name the letter that occupied the position designated by the marker. Thus, unlike Sperling's task, subjects only have to recall one stimulus. However, like Sperling's task, subjects do not know what has to be reported until the signal is presented sometime after the array has been turned off. Averbach and Coriell often used a bar as their marker. They would show it under the position that had to be recalled. For this reason, the Averbach and Coriell task is sometimes called the *bar-probe task.*

Using their procedure, Averbach and Coriell found results that were consistent with those of Sperling. When the signal is presented immediately after the offset of the array, subjects are usually able to name the letter that occupied the cued location. It is as if subjects retain considerable information about the visual characteristics of the display. However, this information decays quickly. On trials where more time is allowed to pass between the offset of the array and the presentation of the visual marker, performance gets worse. Averbach and Coriell found that the performance of their subjects bottomed out at around 30% correct when 300 ms separated the display and the marker. Extending the time between the display and the marker past 300 ms had little effect on performance. Averbach and Coriell, in agreement with Sperling, viewed their results as evidence for a quickly decaying source of visual information.

A Model for the Partial-Report Paradigm

Sperling (1967) developed a complete model for how subjects performed the partial-report task. This model is presented in Fig. 1.1. Following the convention of such diagrams, mental structures are depicted in boxes and mental processes in circles. A pattern of light stimulation from the outside world enters the system. Information regarding this light pattern first enters into iconic memory (which Sperling called Visual Information Storage at the time). Iconic memory is indicated by the box labeled VIS in the figure. Information decays from this stage in less than a second. Information at this stage is *precategorical*; that is, there is no contact between the light patterns as they are represented in the icon and the categories contained in long-term memory. The information at this point is still raw and physical and does not contain any information about the meaning of the stimuli.

Subjects extract information from the icon through the use of a rapid scanning process. It creates a visual image for each of the stimuli. This scanning process is notable chiefly for its speed. Sperling estimated that at least the first few items in the icon are scanned at a rate of 10 ms per item. (In other words, if this scan continued at this rate, subjects would

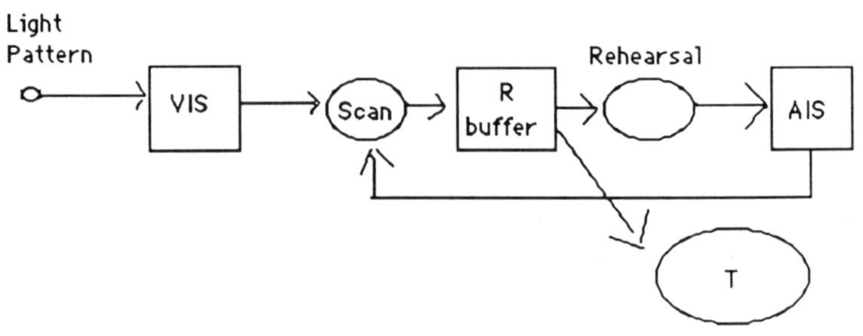

FIG. 1.1. Sperling's (1967) model of performance in the partial-report paradigm.

be able to scan 100 items per second.) Sperling assumed that this scanning process happened in a serial fashion; that is, subjects did not process all the stimuli at once but rather scanned one stimulus at a time. Although Sperling himself had little evidence on this point, subsequent research has tended to support this conjecture (e.g., Pashler, 1984).

The images from the scanning process are still meaningless; they are simply representations of light patterns. However, they are placed in a recognition buffer. It is this buffer that "recognizes" each of the items; that is, it is in this buffer that each stimulus is given a name. Sperling (1960) had noticed that many of the errors that subjects made when identifying letters were based on the sounds of the letters. That is, subjects were more likely to confuse the letter B with the letter V than with physically similar letters, such as F. (The presence of speech-based errors in recall was studied more systematically by Conrad, 1964, and many subsequent researchers.) Thus, Sperling assumed that items were stored in the recognition buffer in terms of their sounds. More specifically, he imagined that the recognition buffer converts the visual image created by the scanner into a "program of motor instructions," a listing of the mouth movements that would be needed to say the item aloud.

The next stage is a rehearsal stage. Subjects attempt to maintain the items by rehearsing them. Rehearsal is a much slower process than the earlier stages. Typically, it takes well over 100 ms to rehearse a single item. Rehearsal may be either aloud or silent. Sperling believed that it made no difference in memory whether items were rehearsed aloud or silently, a belief that we now know was mistaken (Crowder, 1970; this work is discussed in chap. 2).

Whether rehearsal is aloud or silent, Sperling saw the information as flowing into Auditory Information Storage, an auditory analogue of the Visual Information Store (or icon). (The terms *auditory sensory memory, auditory sensory register, echo,* or *echoic memory* have since become more popular terms for this concept.) Subjects scan this auditory store in a way analogous to the way the icon is scanned.

When subjects want to write down items they saw in the display, they have to translate the stimuli (as they are contained in the recognition buffer) into a series of muscular movements that would let them write down the correct items. Sperling professed ignorance as to the details of this stage but realized that such a process was necessary. This translation stage is indicated by the symbol T in Fig. 1.1. Information at this translation stage is now ready to be reported.

To summarize the main aspects of this model, information is stored in raw unanalyzed form in the icon. It is rapidly scanned and then maintained through rehearsal until subjects have a chance to write all the items down.

How could a model such as this be used to explain Sperling's (1960) results? In a whole-report condition, subjects form an icon of the display, scan the icon, and recognize the items (that is, assign them the correct names). They begin rehearsing the items and writing them down. However, performance is limited at several stages. Subjects may not be able to scan and recognize all of the items before the icon has faded away. They are only able to maintain the items by rehearsing them. However, since rehearsal is such a relatively slow process, only a few items are able to be maintained this way. The result of these limitations is that subjects are only able to recall about four items or so in whole report.

When subjects are placed in a partial-report situation, they are able to use the partial-report signal to determine which locations in the icon to scan. Assuming that the signal was presented so close to the offset of the array that the icon is still present, subjects should be able to scan the necessary locations. Then, subjects will have to recognize and recall the cued items. Since there are only a few cued items, the icon should persist long enough to allow the subjects to recall a higher proportion of items than in whole report.

Although the exact details of this model did not get unanimous support, the general approach did gain general acceptance. Theoretical accounts of this sort constitute the classical explanation of performance in the partial-report paradigm.

COMMENTS ON THE CONCEPT OF ICONIC MEMORY

Alternative Procedures for the Study of Iconic Memory

In the years since Sperling's (1960) initial research, a number of other investigators using very different approaches have supported the idea that visual stimulation persists in the nervous system for a brief time period after the end of a stimulus. Some of these approaches involved asking participants for subjective judgments as to the presence of visual persistence. These approaches are often called *direct methods,* because the logic for determining the presence of the icon seems far simpler and more direct than the partial-report procedure. For example, one kind of approach involves flashing a stimulus until it appears to the observer to be continuous in time (e.g., Haber, 1970; Haber & Standing, 1969; Purcell & Stewart, 1971). Another approach required asking subjects to adjust the occurrence of some signal so that it coincided with the offset of a target stimulus (e.g., Efron, 1970; Sakitt & Long, 1979). Approaches such as these have been useful in confirming the existence of iconic memory. Therefore, the concept of the icon (at least as a subjective persistence of light stimulation) is not dependent solely on evidence from the partial-report paradigm.

Initially, many researchers assumed that these direct approaches tapped exactly the same stage of visual processing that was tapped by Sperling's partial-report paradigm. However, subsequent research has proven that assumption false. Particular emphasis has been placed on energy effects on these paradigms. The energy present in a stimulus can be manipulated by altering its luminance or duration. A large number of studies have been performed. The literature as a whole suggests that not all of these paradigms are tapping the same stages of information processing. The literature does contain enough contradictions so that two reviewers, discussing the same experiments, can reach exactly opposite conclusions (Coltheart, 1980, 1984; Long, 1980). However, it is fair to say that the partial-report paradigm is much less likely to be influenced by stimulus energy than are the direct approaches (Coltheart, 1980, 1984). The picture is complicated by the fact that energy effects do appear in the partial-report paradigm for certain combinations of target and background luminance: Under these limited conditions, the rate of decline for partial report as a function of cue delay is slower for bright displays than for dimmer ones (e.g., Adelson & Jonides, 1980; Long & Beaton, 1982). The circumstances under which partial report is affected by stimulus energy seem to be far more constrained than the circumstances under which the direct procedures exhibit energy effects. Moreover, the direct procedures often exhibit inverse energy effects; that is, the estimate for the duration of the icon decreases as the energy in the stimulus increases (e.g., Efron, 1970; Haber & Standing, 1969; Sakitt & Long, 1979). This is contrary to the findings from the partial-report paradigm where either no effect or positive effects on iconic persistence are found as stimulus energy is increased. Thus, it seems likely that performance in the partial-report procedure is not determined by the same processes as determine performance in the direct paradigms. Although these direct approaches are certainly relevant to an overall understanding of visual information processing, there is no need to consider these direct measures further in our discussion here of the partial-report procedure.

The Locus of the Icon

There has been considerable interest in determining the place in the visual system where iconic memory takes place. For example, is the icon in the eye (specifically, on the retina, that part of the eye where the visual image of a scene is projected), or does it reside deeper in the nervous system? Sakitt (1976) attracted considerable attention by suggesting that the icon represents the persistence of activity at the level of the *rods,* one type of receptor cell located in the retina. However, Banks and Barber (1977) presented evidence against this claim by showing that subjects could perform a partial-report experiment when required to select items on the basis of color. In this experiment, subjects were shown a display containing items in several different colors. The partial-report cue would indicate the color of the items that subjects had to report. (Although earlier investigators had used color in this task, they had not controlled all other factors carefully and were therefore not considered definitive by Sakitt, 1976). A normal partial-report curve was found, with an initial high level of recall and a gradual decline on trials where the cue was delayed. Since rod cells do not perceive color but only respond on the basis of the brightness of a stimulus, Sakitt's proposal could not explain these results.

Banks and Barber's (1977) findings did not end the dispute over the locus of the icon in the nervous system. Much of the subsequent research used procedures other than the partial-report paradigm, so their relevance for the present chapter is unclear. As we have seen, not all iconic procedures tap the same processes, so one should hesitate to generalize from one procedure to another. On the basis of the fact that energy effects are not usually found in the partial-report paradigm under most circumstances, it seems that performance in this paradigm at least is based on the persistence of information more central than the retina.

Ecological Validity and the Icon

An interesting (and controversial) argument has been made by Haber (1983). Essentially, he criticized the attention paid to the icon in our theories, research, and textbooks. He maintained that the icon (as presented, for example, in Sperling's model) could play no useful role in visual perception outside the laboratory.

The icon has often been presented as if it were a static image. However, Haber (1983) points out that the maintenance of a static image for a period of less than a second could play no useful role in perception. When we are gazing at a scene, two things could happen: The scene could change, or it could stay the same. If the scene is changing, then the icon would no longer be an accurate picture of what the scene looks like at that immediate point of time; rather, it would be a picture of what the scene looked like a little while ago. Not only would the icon be an inaccurate description of the present scene, it might also serve to disrupt our processing of the current state of the scene. When scenes change, we might be better off without an icon. What about when the scene isn't changing? When there is no change in the scene, the icon would do no harm but would be useless. If we want to spend more time processing the scene, we simply have to look at it for a longer period of time. We do not need the icon to preserve a picture of the scene for us.

Haber (1983) maintained that psychologists have been deceived by reliance on equipment such as the tachistoscope, a machine that allows experimenters to present bright scenes for brief periods of time. In the standard visual-perception experiment, single, unchanging scenes are presented very briefly. Under these circumstances, one can imagine how an icon would be useful: It would allow the subject to process the scene even after the brief presentation has been completed. However, in our everyday life, we can observe a scene as long as we need to. The only real-life situation comparable with tachistoscopic experiments would be trying to read outside at night in the middle of a lightning storm: You are in complete darkness, punctuated by a brief, bright flash, followed by the return of darkness. This is not at all similar to how we perform most of our visual perception.

It should be emphasized here that Haber (1983) was not questioning either the existence of iconic memory or the claim that the partial-report paradigm measures iconic memory. Rather, he was questioning the assumption that the icon plays a major role in visual perception outside the laboratory. He believed that psychologists had a tendency to believe that any phenomenon that they discovered in laboratory experiments must play a useful role in our everyday lives.

Haber's (1983) article was followed by a number of commentaries. Some of these commentaries agreed with his reasoning, and others disagreed. Obviously, this is not a topic about which there is anything resembling a consensus. Some of the commentators suggested that current theories assume a much more sophisticated version of iconic memory than the one that Haber was criticizing. For example, the icon could be seen as being dynamic, that is, carrying information about motion and change. Indeed, Treisman, Russell, and Green (1975) used the partial-report procedure with a display of six moving dots and found that partial report of motion was superior to full report of motion (for a review of other methods used to study iconic memory for motion, see Farrell, 1984). This study does indeed suggest that the information that underlies the partial-report advantage must be more complex than the simple picture seemingly envisioned by Sperling. However, one could wonder whether such a more complicated account would not be bending the concept of the icon into such a new form that the old name is not really applicable anymore. (After all, the term "icon" means "picture.") Moreover, studies such as the Treisman et al. study do not address Haber's chief concern, which is whether the icon could be shown to play a role in perception experiments under conditions more closely resembling normal, everyday scene perception.

Haber's (1983) article, which actually echoed the earlier concerns of Neisser (1976), raised important issues about the concept of iconic memory and the usefulness of paradigms such as the partial-report task. These issues are not yet settled and indeed may never be comprehensively settled, but they are important to keep in mind when one is thinking about the concept of iconic memory.

THE PARTIAL-REPORT TASK IN OTHER SENSORY MODALITIES

Sperling (1960) interpreted his results as evidence for a visual sensory memory store. Presumably, however, vision would not be the only sense with such a store. Why shouldn't there be comparable stores for each of our other sensory modalities? It was only a matter of time before psychologists tried to apply Sperling's tasks to the other senses.

Auditory Versions of the Partial-Report Task

Treisman and Rostron (1972) and Rostron (1974) devised one way to alter the partial-report paradigm to the auditory sense. In these experiments, subjects heard six tones over three loudspeakers placed in different locations. At some point after presentation of the tones, subjects heard another tone (called a *probe*) and had to indicate whether that probe matched any of the tones presented over the loudspeakers. Recognition accuracy dropped as a function of the delay of the probe. (The point where performance bottomed out differed as a function of exactly how the experimenters scored accuracy.) These authors assumed that echoic memory (an auditory analogue of iconic memory) must be the basis of performance here. They believed that there were too many tones for the subjects to be able to classify all of them and encode them into long-term memory. Therefore, subjects would only be able to perform this task with high accuracy for as long as they retained a literal copy of the tones in echoic memory. Unfortunately, these experiments are rather hard to interpret or to compare with Sperling's visual experiments. These authors did not use a partial-report recall task (as Sperling did), but rather a recognition task. Moreover, by using a recognition task, these authors made it impossible to use a whole-report procedure as a control condition. Since the essence of Sperling's procedure is to compare partial report with whole report, these experiments could not be said to apply his paradigm successfully to the auditory domain. The absence of a whole-report condition is a criticism that could be made of several other studies (Eriksen & Johnson, 1964; Glucksberg & Cowan, 1970; Norman, 1969).

Moray, Bates, and Barnett (1965) used a somewhat different and more effective procedure. They had their subjects wear headphones and receive four different messages over these headphones. The messages (each containing one or more auditory items) were constructed so that subjects would feel that they came from different locations. As soon as the messages were completed, a visual signal indicated which of the messages to report. Performance in this partial-report condition was compared with performance in a whole-report condition where subjects had to report all of the messages. The estimated number of items available in partial report exceeded the number of items recalled in the whole-report condition.

Darwin, Turvey, and Crowder (1972) extended the Moray et al. (1965) study by varying the delay of the partial-report cue. They found that the advantage for partial report over whole report was eliminated when the partial report cue was delayed for more than a few seconds. Darwin et al. (1972) concluded that results from this paradigm supported the notion of an echoic memory. Moreover, since delays of several seconds were needed to eliminate the partial-report advantage in the auditory case, compared with the fractions of a second needed in the visual case, these authors also concluded that echoic memory persisted for a longer time than did iconic memory. The Darwin et al. study stands as the best evidence that the partial-report paradigm can be successfully applied to auditory stimuli.

Tactile Versions of the Partial-Report Task

The sense of touch can be used as one more example of a sensory modality to which the partial-report task has been applied. Bliss, Crane, Mansfield, and Townsend (1966) performed an experiment requiring whole report or partial report of sensations on people's fingers. Each of four fingers on each hand was considered to have three regions: top, middle, and bottom. (Thumbs were always excluded.) There were thus 24 regions, and subjects were trained to use a letter of the alphabet to name each of these regions. On each trial, subjects placed their hands in a device that could direct a puff of air at each of these regions. The number of regions stimulated on each trial varied. In the whole-report condition, subjects had to name each of the regions that had been stimulated. On partial-report trials, subjects were given a visual cue to report either the top regions that had been stimulated, the middle regions, or the bottom regions. This parallels the Sperling task, if you imagine the 24 regions on the fingers as corresponding to three rows on eight fingers. Bliss et al. found a small but significant advantage of partial report over whole report as long as the partial report cue was not given more than 800 ms after the termination of the stimulation.

One interesting sidelight of this research is that two blind subjects were included in the study. These subjects were tested either for whole report or for partial report (with high, medium, or low tones used as partial-report cues). One subject, an adult who had become blind at age 14, performed identically to the sighted subjects. However, the other blind subject, who had been born blind, was much more accurate at this task than other subjects (Hill & Bliss, 1968). The authors interpreted this as evidence that tactile sensory memory could be improved by long experience in relying on the sense of touch.

ARGUMENTS AGAINST THE SENSORY–MEMORY INTERPRETATION OF THE PARTIAL-REPORT PARADIGM

So far, we have not raised any challenges to Sperling's (1960) interpretation of the advantage of partial report over whole report. Indeed, as has been already mentioned, this approach became the standard. However, there is mounting evidence against this interpretation.

On the Comparability of Whole and Partial Report

Perhaps the most fundamental axiom of experimental design is that, when one is varying a certain independent variable, all other aspects of the experimental situation must be held constant. One can only meaningfully interpret a comparison between two conditions if they differ only by a single factor.

Since the heart of the Sperling (1960) paradigm is a comparison between whole report and partial report, one might imagine that experimenters would make these conditions be as comparable as possible and have them differ only by the number of items that have to be reported. However, this is not true. Experimenters have habitually allowed whole- and partial-report conditions to vary in a large number of uncontrolled ways.

For example, when experimenters want to compare two conditions, it is customary for them to intermix those conditions randomly. Intermixing has the advantage of ensuring that subjects begin each trial with the same strategy and thereby prevents strategy selection from being confounded with condition. It is disconcerting to find therefore that researchers, starting with Sperling (1960), habitually present whole- and partial-report conditions in different blocks. This allows subjects to employ entirely different strategies in the two conditions. The whole point of the Sperling paradigm is to compare the estimates of items available under conditions of whole and partial report. How can one make this comparison meaningfully when entirely different strategies are being followed in the two cases?

Paradoxically, some investigators emphasize the importance of allowing subjects to follow different strategies in the two conditions. For example, Chow (1985) stresses that experimenters should be sure to give subjects extensive practice in separate blocks of each condition to ensure that they are mastering a strategy suitable for a particular condition. He then goes on to compare whole and partial report as if such comparisons are meaningful when entirely different (and unknown) strategies are being followed in the two cases.

Of course, it is not impossible to mix the whole- and partial-report conditions randomly. This can be done by presenting a signal that may either indicate whole report or else indicate which part of the array should be given in partial report. A few investigators, starting with Dick (1969, 1970), have done exactly that. When this is done, however, the results do not seem to support the existence of a sensory memory store, as will be discussed.

Cuing on Postcategorical Dimensions

The essence of the concept of a sensory memory store is that it is supposed to be *precategorical,* that is, that information in such a store is believed to be raw and to have not yet made contact with any of the learned categories held in memory. In other words, visual sensory memory would not contain letters or numbers but rather patterns of light stimulation that had yet to be interpreted. The crucial evidence for this interpretation rests on the fact that cuing items for partial report is so effective when the dimension used for cuing is physical (e.g., location, color) and is not dependent on learned categorical information.

Of course, if the information is truly precategorical, then one would expect that cuing on the basis of learned dimensions would be entirely ineffective. Early evidence on this point was somewhat ambiguous. Sperling (1960) performed an experiment in which subjects were shown displays consisting of letters and digits. In the whole-report condition, subjects were asked to recall all the stimuli. In the partial-report condition, subjects were told that a tone of a certain frequency would indicate that letters had to be reported and a tone of a different frequency would indicate that digits had to be reported. Although performance was better in partial report than in whole report, the difference was small and statistically nonsignificant. Similar results were reported by von Wright (1968). Although Sperling's and von Wright's data are often cited as evidence for the precategorical nature of the partial-report paradigm, one should interpret them cautiously. Even though the partial-report superiority did not reach statistical significance with categorical cues, there was a consistent slight advantage over whole report. Moreover, these studies presented partial- and whole-report conditions in different blocks, thereby allowing subjects to employ greatly different strategies in the two conditions. This makes comparison between the two conditions difficult.

Merikle (1980) studied categorical selection in an experiment where the partial- and whole-report conditions were randomly mixed. The visual array consisted of both letters and digits. A male voice would say 1, 2, or 3, with these numbers corresponding to the conditions of partial report (letters), partial report (digits), and whole report. Merikle found that there was a significant advantage for the partial-report conditions over the whole-report condition. Moreover, the partial-report superiority declined as a function of cue delay at approximately the same rate as it did when partial report was based on the location of the stimuli. This pattern suggests that the categorical selection and location selection processes are based on the same source of information. If this is true, then partial report cannot be taken as evidence for a precategorical sensory store.

A skeptic might suggest that perhaps subjects could use a physical dimension to select between letters and digits. For example, curved lines seem to occur more often in digits than in letters, while straight lines occur more often in letters than in digits. It might be possible for subjects to select members of a certain category based on their physical appearance, in which case Merikle's (1980) findings would not be inconsistent with the idea that partial report involves selection from a precategorical iconic memory. However, Duncan (1983) ruled out this possibility in a study that controlled for physical differences between letters and digits. Thus, the existence of a partial-report superiority based on semantic category does not seem to be due to an artifact.

It should be noted in passing that a significant advantage for categorical partial report over whole report is by no means limited to visual stimuli. Darwin et al. (1972), in their study of the auditory partial-report task, included a condition where subjects were asked to report items based on their semantic category (in this case, letters or digits). The authors were presumably hoping to find no advantage of partial report over whole report here, which would have allowed them to argue that the auditory store that they were tapping was truly precategorical. To the authors' chagrin, however, they found that categorical partial report was significantly better than whole report and that this partial-report advantage declined as a function of the delay of the cue. In other words, cuing a category worked the same way as cuing a physical dimension would work. Massaro (1976) subsequently showed that partial report was equivalent in accuracy whether a category or a location was cued.

To summarize this section, theorists have typically followed Sperling (1960) and assumed that the partial-report task was a measure of information from a precategorical store, one that contained raw, unanalyzed information. If this assumption were true, it should be possible for subjects to select items from this store on the basis of some physical dimension (e.g., location) but not on the basis of the meaning of the stimuli. This prediction has been falsified both in the visual and auditory domains. Therefore, whatever information subjects are using to perform the partial-report task is far more meaningful than most theorists have believed.

The Role of Output Interference

There is a basic law in memory experiments: The more things you have to remember, the lower will be the proportion of things you are able to recall. This is often called *output interference.* It is assumed that the act of maintaining an item in memory and recalling it involves considerable effort. As you try to keep a particular stimulus in your mind and recall it, you are interfering with your memory for the other stimuli. As you are asked to recall more and more stimuli, you would suffer more and more interference, and your memory will be impaired. This observation is important here for one simple reason: A person has to remember a lot more stimuli in a whole-report condition than in a partial-report condition. For that reason alone, one would expect a subject to remember a lower proportion of items in whole report than in partial report.

The importance of output interference in this task has been documented in several ways. For example, Dick (1971) reported accuracy of responses as a function of position in a response sequence. Dick recorded how often each subject was right in the first stimulus reported in whole report and in the first stimulus reported in partial report. Dick went on to examine the second, third, and fourth stimuli recalled. (In these experiments, subjects would have to report four stimuli in partial report.) When this sort of response-by-response analysis was performed, which has the effect of controlling for number of previous responses, there was no sign of an advantage of partial report over whole report.

A similar point was made by Sakitt and Appelman (1978). They showed that the amount of information that the subject had to retain and recall greatly influenced both the magnitude of the difference between whole and partial report and also the shape of the decay function for partial report. Sakitt and Appelman concluded, "Since nonvisual factors also can affect partial report superiority, we suggest that partial report superiorities be used as being consistent with the presence of an icon, but not as a definite indicator of the presence of an icon" (p. 566).

In short, at least a part of the difference between whole and partial report cannot be considered sensory (or perhaps even visual) at all. Rather, it just reflects the greater overloading of the system that occurs in whole report. This leads to more of a breakdown and thus a lower proportion of items remembered.

Forgetting as the Loss of Location Information

We have seen so far that the difference between whole and partial report does not necessarily represent what it initially seems. It is often confounded with the different strategies that subjects employ in the two tasks. Output interference makes at least some contribution to this difference. Moreover, meaningful categories can be used to select items in the same way that location was used by Sperling. However, even as we challenge the cause of the difference between whole and partial report, we have not discussed an important question: Why does this difference get smaller as the partial-report cue is delayed? The answer will not be consistent with expectations from traditional iconic-memory explanations.

Let us assume that a traditional iconic-memory model, such as that of Sperling (1967), were correct. What kinds of errors should people make? Reporting three or four items (or one, in the Averbach & Coriell bar-probe task) is quite easy. Such a number is well within the memory span of almost all individuals. Therefore, the chief problem in this task will be whether there is still enough information in the icon to identify the items when the partial-report cue is presented. If the icon has decayed by the time the cue is presented, subjects will have to guess. Sometimes, they will guess right but, more often, they will guess wrong. Even if the decay process of the icon was not complete when the cue was presented, subjects might not have time to read out all of the items on the cued row before the icon decays. Again, subjects would have to guess what the remaining letters on the cued row are.

If this view is correct, then subjects would be more likely than not to guess stimuli that were not shown in the display. (This is simply because there would be more letters not shown in the display than letters shown.) This might be called an item error or an intrusion error. Of course, there is always the possibility that subjects might by chance name a stimulus that was shown on the display but on a row different than the one that had been cued. This could be called a location error. The response is wrong not because the stimulus was absent from the display but rather because it was not in the location that had been cued. Of course, there is also always a small probability that subjects might guess a stimulus that actually had been shown at the cued position, in which case the response would not be classified as an error at all.

How often each of these three possibilities would happen as a result of random guessing would depend on the particular experiment. Let us use the Averbach and Coriell bar-probe task as an example. Imagine that any letter of the alphabet is equally likely to be included on the display and that any letter is shown no more than once on each display. Say that there are nine letters in all shown on a display and that the experimenter uses a bar to indicate the position that has to be reported. If one were guessing randomly, one would only have 1 chance in 26 of guessing the correct letter. You would have eight chances out of 26 of making a location error and 17 chances out of 26 of making an item or intrusion error.

The evidence on errors contradicts this kind of reasoning. The early experiments examining errors in this way used the Averbach and Coriell bar-probe task. Typically, subjects make far more location errors than item errors (e.g., Dick, 1974; Eriksen & Rohrbaugh, 1970; Mewhort, Campbell, Marchetti, & Campbell, 1981; Townsend, 1973). In other words, the difficulty in this task involves not so much knowing what items were shown in the display but rather in knowing where they were shown. Even more striking were the effects of delay of the probe. As the probe was delayed, item errors hardly increased at all. Rather, it was the number of location errors that were most clearly affected by delay of the probe. In other words, there is little evidence for an icon that is fading away and becoming harder to read as more time passes. Rather, subjects know basically what letters were shown on the display and simply have trouble remembering where they occurred as more and more time passes.

Although the majority of studies examining location errors and item errors used the Averbach and Coriell bar-probe task, the same conclusion holds true for Sperling's version of the task where whole rows are cued. Yeomans and Irwin (1985) showed that most errors came from rows that were not cued and that it was predominantly such location errors that increased as a function of delaying the cue.

A Potential Problem: Are Subjects Mislocating the Probe? There is one troublesome aspect of the experiments that should be mentioned and eliminated now. Is it possible that subjects are not forgetting where the items were shown in the display but rather that, as the icon fades, it is becoming harder and harder for subjects to know exactly which location is being cued by the probe? Perhaps the icon may bounce around a little as it decays so that, when the probe comes on, the subject has a hard time matching up the probe with a particular location. This would be one way to reconcile the error data with the traditional iconic-memory interpretation of this task. By this view, the large number of location errors arises not from forgetting where the items were shown in the display but rather from being unable to tell exactly which location is being cued.

There seems to be strong evidence against this alternative explanation. Eriksen and Rohrbaugh (1970) presented all of their letters in a circle and used a bar probe to cue a particular location. As with the other studies cited here, the errors that subjects made were likely to be location errors, and it was the number of location errors that was most affected by delaying the probe. Eriksen and Rohrbaugh checked to make sure that their subjects were able to align the bar probe with the display. Sometimes, subjects had to report the location that was being probed (e.g., a 3 o'clock position around the circular display). Subjects were always able to do this even though they often reported a letter from a different location. (Data reported by Chow, 1986, also suggest that subjects have little difficulty in aligning a probe and a display.) In short, location errors really do reflect a process whereby subjects forget where the items were shown in a display.

Converging Evidence for the Forgetting of Location Information. Whenever one is trying to make an important conclusion, it is always good to seek different lines of evidence that lead to the same conclusion. Mewhort and Lepmann (1985) sought converging evidence for the claim that it was location information and not item information that was being forgotten in this sort of task. In one of their experiments, subjects were shown a row of letters for 50 ms and had to indicate whether a particular named letter was in the display. The letter began to be spoken either 150 ms before the display of letters was turned on, at exactly the same time that the display was turned on, or 50, 100, or 200 ms after the display was turned on. Subjects simply had to indicate whether the named letter was in the display. Accuracy was good (but not perfect). More importantly, accuracy was not affected by the timing of the display and the named letter. In a second experiment, the named letter was always in the display, and subjects had to indicate the location of the letter in the row. There was a statistically significant drop in accuracy as a function of the delay of the named letter. Information about the identities of the items in a display is not quickly forgotten. Information about where in the display particular letters were located is forgotten quickly.

In other words, the pattern of errors that you find in Sperling's (1960) partial-report task or in the Averbach and Coriell (1961) bar-probe task does not conform with predictions that would be made on the basis of a straightforward iconic-memory theory. There is little evidence for a decaying icon that becomes harder to read as time passes. Rather, we see evidence for a process whereby letters are quickly identified but subjects have trouble remembering their locations. In short, why is it that the advantage for partial over whole report diminished over time? Contrary to the expectations of an approach such as Sperling's (1967), it is not because subjects are relying on an icon that is fading away over time. Rather, partial report requires both location information and item information while whole report requires only item information. Since location information is lost quickly as a function of time, partial report is hurt greatly by delaying the cue.

All of our discussion so far has centered on why partial report declines as a function of cue delay in the procedure typically used, where the cue indicates the location that has to be recalled. Unfortunately, much less research has been done on situations where the partial-report cue indicates some other dimension on which to report items (e.g., color, semantic category), so our knowledge is still very incomplete at this point. However, the information that we do have about the decline in partial-report superiority using location is inconsistent with expectations derived from traditional iconic-memory accounts.

ALTERNATIVE ACCOUNTS OF THE PARTIAL-REPORT PARADIGM

We have seen that the standard account for performance in the partial-report task (e.g., Sperling, 1967) has numerous difficulties. It is clear that the memory information that forms the basis of partial report is far more interpreted and meaningful than initially imagined by Sperling and others. The fact that subjects are able to select items on the basis of semantic category and the fact that errors are not random but rather reflect misjudgments of location suggest that this task is tapping far more than the fading away of an uninterpreted picture.

Many alternative accounts that have been proposed share a similar structure. Perhaps the account that has gotten the most attention is the dual-buffer model of Mewhort, Marchetti, Gurnsey, and Campbell (1984; Mewhort et al., 1981), a theory that has also been endorsed by Coltheart (1984). According to this model, visual information processing begins with the extraction of physical features (e.g., circles, curved lines, straight lines) from the display. These features are recorded in a precategorical store called the *feature buffer*. To reiterate, when we call such a store precategorical, we mean that this information has not yet made contact with any of the categories we have learned throughout our lives. When features have been extracted from the display, a process called a *recogni-*

tion mechanism is applied to the feature buffer. This recognition mechanism first sorts features into coherent units and then uses the features to make an ordered list of possible stimuli for each unit. (In other words, it makes up a list in order of what each unit is most likely to be.) The recognition mechanism includes knowledge of how often letters occur in everyday English, so that more common letters are always considered more likely. (Ironically, this information may lead a subject into error if in reality the letters in a display have been chosen randomly; however, it is assumed that our years of reading English have installed knowledge of English frequencies so deeply that we are unable to turn it off.) Using the letter-frequency information, the recognition mechanism decides on the most likely stimulus at each position. It then places an abstract representation of that stimulus in a postcategorical store called the *character buffer.*

The character buffer is not at all like a picture, in the way that Sperling's icon has typically been envisioned. Rather, it contains an abstract representation of each character and information about the spatial location of that character. Although the characters themselves do not show much decay in the character buffer, the spatial information becomes more and more inexact over time, leading to problems in locating particular stimuli in the buffer. If a partial-report cue is given after a long delay, subjects may have a hard time knowing what stimuli were presented in the location indicated by the cue.

A few comments may be made here. Unlike traditional iconic-memory theories, selection is from a postcategorical store that contains already-identified items. This could thus easily explain why one can find a partial-report superiority using semantic category as a basis for report. In addition, the nature of the character buffer would explain why localization errors are so common in this paradigm and why they increase as a function of delay of the cue.

The dual-buffer model is actually just one of a number of models that have been proposed that are surprisingly similar (e.g., DiLollo, 1977; Duncan, 1982; van der Heijden, 1981; Yeomans & Irwin, 1985). All of these models assume that this paradigm involves several discrete stages and that selection of items for partial report involves retrieval of items from a postcategorical store. All of these models thus reject the precategorical visual store envisioned by Sperling (1960).

This convergence of theories upon a single approach is encouraging and suggests that these theorists are on the right track. In psychology, problems are best considered solved not when one theory is determined to be correct but rather when the possible theories become so similar to each other as to be difficult to distinguish. However, there is at least one property that these theories share with Sperling's (1960) original model, and that may in the long run prove to be incorrect. These models tend to be standard stage theories, with each stage representing a static form of information in the mind. As has been pointed out by Merikle (1980) among others, such an approach is rather unrealistic. Visual information is accumulating over time, with different types of information arriving at different times. For example, high and low spatial frequencies contain different sorts of information about a stimulus and are processed at different rates by the perceptual system (Breitmeyer & Ganz, 1976). There is no static representation following the presentation of a stimulus that can be accurately characterized as having certain properties. Rather, visual perception is dynamic, with a number of processes being initiated by a stimulus and with information from these processes accumulating continuously though at different rates. In other words, any stage theory in this area is likely to be at best an oversimplified metaphor for the continuous accumulation of information that actually underlies visual information processing.

Still, not all stage theories are equally good metaphors for what is happening in this paradigm. We now know that Sperling's (1960, 1967) iconic-memory theory is a rather poor metaphor for the processes used in the partial-report task. Far more promising are models that see selection as occurring from a postcategorical store containing all sorts of information about the stimuli shown in a display. Such models may lack the elegant simplicity of Sperling's original approach but appear to come closer to the complexities involved in visual perception.

CHAPTER TWO

The Modality-Effect/ Suffix-Effect Paradigm

Marshall McLuhan uttered the widely quoted saying, "The medium is the message." The point of this statement was that the way a piece of information is communicated is quite important. Although McLuhan certainly had far grander implications in mind than the mundane concerns of memory researchers, there is abundant evidence that how a piece of information is presented will affect how well it is remembered. For example, Kolers (1979) has shown that information presented in an inverted typeface is remembered better than information presented in a normal typeface. Information presented in pictures may be better remembered than pictures presented in words (e.g., Shepard, 1967).

This chapter will deal with one heavily studied example of how the format of presentation affects memory. Two closely related phenomena will be discussed: the *modality effect* and the *stimulus suffix effect.*

THE MODALITY EFFECT

The modality effect is a straightforward phenomenon that has been demonstrated many times. I will illustrate it with an unpublished experiment conducted in my laboratory.

Sixteen subjects were tested in this experiment. They went through 40 trials. On each trial, they received a list of eight digits arranged in random order. Immediately after the last digit was presented, subjects had to type the sequence in order on a computer keyboard. They had to start with the first list position and work their way through the sequence without backtracking. (This sort of ordered recall is often called *serial recall* to indicate that a series is being recalled; it should be distinguished from *free recall,* where items may be recalled in any order.) A couple seconds after subjects were finished recalling one list, the next list began.

The crucial manipulation here is the sensory modality used to present the items. On half of the lists, the items were presented visually (in this case, one digit at a time on the computer screen at a rate of a digit every 500 ms). On the other lists, all of the items were presented auditorily: An experimenter simply read the lists aloud to the subjects, again at a rate of a digit every 500 ms.

The results are presented in Fig. 2.1. Memory performance is measured by the proportion of items correctly recalled at the right place and is shown as a function of presentation modality (visual or auditory) and serial position (that is, what place did an item occupy on the list?). A few general facts about the data may be noted. Performance is better on the first few items than on the middle items (a phenomenon called the *primacy effect*). Performance also rises again at the end of the list (the *recency effect*).

We shall not be concerned in this chapter with aspects of the data that are true for both visual and auditory lists. Rather, we will focus on contrasting the two presentation modalities. Notice that, for most of the items on the list, there is little, if any difference, between visual and auditory presentation. However, for the last one or two items on a list, people are much more accurate if they heard the items than if they saw them. This advantage for auditory items at the end of a list is called the *modal-*

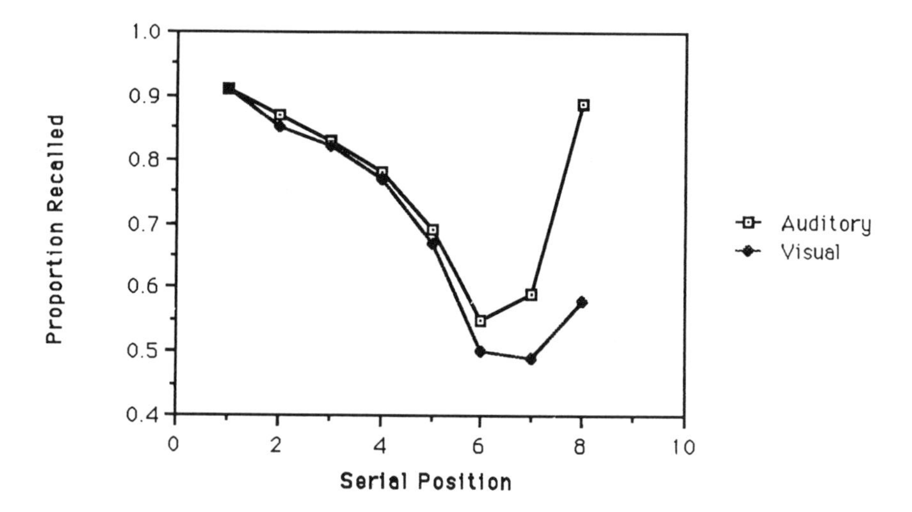

FIG. 2.1. An example of the modality effect.

ity effect. The first modern researcher to note it in this form was apparently Corballis (1966), although similar findings had been known long ago (e.g., Washburn, 1916).

There is another way to demonstrate a modality effect. Assume that all of the items were presented visually. However, on some lists, subjects had to read all of the items aloud as they were shown. On other lists, subjects read them silently (as in the foregoing experiment). When subjects recall the items, you get a pattern basically identical to that shown in Fig. 2.1. That is, at most positions, memory is little influenced by whether subjects read the items aloud or silently. However, for the last item or two, memory will be much better for items read aloud than for items read silently (Conrad & Hull, 1968; Crowder, 1970; Murray, 1966). Thus, it does not matter whether an experimenter reads the items aloud or the subject reads them aloud; as long as subjects can hear the items, they will exhibit exceptional memory for items at the end of the list.

The modality effect is robust across a number of manipulations. An experimenter does not have to use digits as list items; letters, nonsense syllables, and words may be used just as well. One can use a faster or slower presentation rate without eliminating the effect. Modality effects may also be found in free recall of word lists (e.g., Craik, 1969; Murdock & Walker, 1969). Thus, this phenomenon is not limited to a narrow set of circumstances.

THE STIMULUS SUFFIX EFFECT

Assume that you are having subjects hear and recall lists of eight digits, as in the auditory condition in the above experiment. Sometimes, however, you have another sound occurring after the last item but before subjects recall the items. For example, exactly 500 ms after the last digit is presented, the experimenter says the word "END." Subjects know that the word will be said after the list and they know that they will not have to recall it. They are free to ignore it entirely. Presented in Fig. 2.2 are results from such an experiment, again an unpublished one conducted in my laboratory. The lists were followed by silence (the Control condition) or by the word END (the Suffix condition). There is little difference between the two conditions at the early positions. However, at the last position or two, there is a large advantage for the Control condition. In fact, one might say that adding the word END to the list makes recall of auditory items more closely resemble recall of visual items.

The finding that adding on an irrelevant auditory item at the end of an auditory list causes massive interference for the last few items is called a *stimulus suffix effect.* (This refers to the fact that a stimulus is being

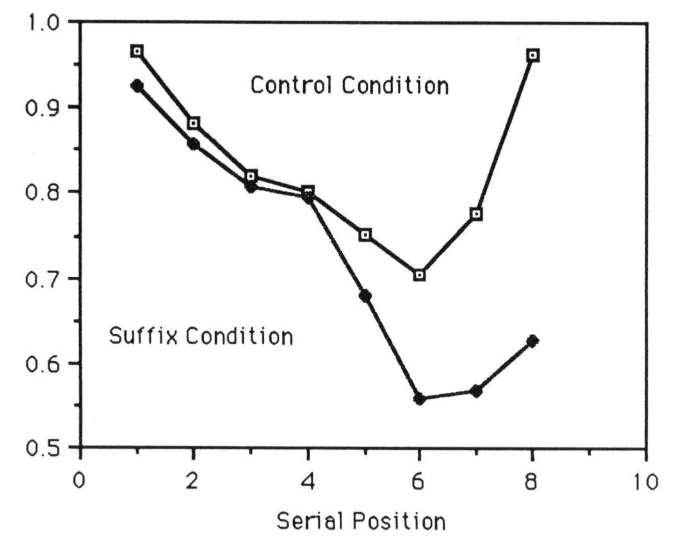

FIG. 2.2. An example of the stimulus suffix effect.

added to the list in the same way that one can add a suffix, like *-ed* or *-ing,* to a word.) Nowadays, people are more likely simply to call it a *suffix effect,* and we'll use that name here. It was evident in the data of Dallett (1965), who examined a large number of ways of presenting irrelevant stimuli. Crowder (1967) was the first to discuss at length the selective interference caused by suffixes on terminal list items. As Crowder pointed out, a surprising aspect of the suffix effect is that adding on a suffix doesn't really increase the memory load placed on a subject at all. Subjects know that the suffix is coming, that they do not have to remember it, and that they should ignore it. Even so, the suffix can have quite a substantial impact on their memory.

The suffix effect is generally a purely auditory phenomenon. When visual lists and suffixes are used, substantial suffix effects are rarely seen. For example, I carried out an experiment where lists composed of a random ordering of the digits 1–9 were shown one at a time on a computer screen. On some trials, the list was followed by a suffix (the digit 0 shown on the screen); on other trials, the screen went blank. Subjects then had to recall the list in order. The suffix had no effect; performance was exactly the same in those two conditions (Greene, 1987). Thus, visual items differ from auditory items not only in exhibiting poorer recall of terminal items but also exhibiting much less, if any, interference from suffixes.

When one is discussing suffix effects here, one must focus particularly on the very last position, the terminal item of a list. Although the suffix may impair recall of earlier items somewhat, there is evidence that suffix effects on preterminal items have a somewhat different basis or cause than suffix effects on terminal items. For example, the suffix effect on preterminal items may be influenced by the amount of practice a subject has had at this task and by the presentation rate; the suffix effect on the terminal item is much more resistant to these manipulations (Balota & Engle, 1981). The suffix effect on preterminal items can be greatly increased by requiring subjects to pay attention to the suffix, whereas the suffix effect on the terminal item is not affected by this (Greenberg & Engle, 1983). Preterminal and terminal suffix effects may be affected in opposite ways by the length of the suffix in syllables (Baddeley & Hull, 1979). Knowing exactly how many items will be on the list may influence the suffix effect on preterminal items but not on terminal items (Penney, 1985). What all of this is meant to point out is that, although a suffix may impair recall of items at several positions on the list, the suffix effect at the very last position is unique. There is a growing consensus that suffix effects at earlier positions reflects the use of particular strategies by the subjects; these preterminal effects can be influenced quite easily by changing the strategy that a subject is following. In contrast, the suffix effect at the last position is not influenced by these strategic manipulations and thus seems to be telling us something about relatively fixed structures in human memory (for discussions of this point, see Baddeley & Hull, 1979; Balota & Engle, 1981; Greenberg & Engle, 1983; Penney, 1985).

PAS: PRECATEGORICAL ACOUSTIC STORAGE

Although there have been a number of theories that have been proposed to explain modality and suffix effects, there is one theory that has been far more influential than other accounts. This is the theory of *precategorical acoustic storage* (PAS) developed by Crowder and Morton (1969). In brief, they see the modality and suffix effects as evidence for the existence of an auditory sensory memory store (which they termed PAS but has also been called echoic memory; see chap. 1) that persists for at least several seconds after the end of a stimulus.

The PAS theory assumes that, after the end of a visual or auditory stimulus, there remains a relatively raw, unanalyzed representation of the stimulus. This representation is precategorical because it has not made contact with any of the categories that a person has learned and stored in memory. In the case of visual stimuli, this precategorical information decays quickly, under most circumstances in less than a second. (This assumption was based on Sperling's, 1960, findings using the partial-report task, reviewed in chap. 1.) This would be too quick to be useful in serial recall. However, Crowder and Morton (1969) assumed that auditory information could persist in echoic memory "at least on the order of a few seconds" (p. 366). This would be long enough for subjects to use in serial recall. Therefore, the modality effect reflects the fact that subjects have an additional source of information for auditory items that they do not have for visual items, namely, the information persisting in echoic memory.

Why is the modality effect restricted to the end of the list? As each auditory item is presented, it interferes with (or *masks*) earlier items in echoic memory. After the whole list is presented, only the last item is still present in a clear, unmasked form. Therefore, it is only at the end of a list that one has a large advantage for auditory over visual presentation.

The suffix effect also reflects masking. When the suffix is presented, it operates as a mask and interferes with the representation of the last item in echoic memory. It makes this sensory information less usable and thus tends to make recall of auditory lists more similar to recall of visual lists. The suffix may also interfere with other items, perhaps by distracting the subject. However, as we have seen, the suffix's effect on the very last item is different than its effect on preterminal items and is believed by Crowder and Morton (1969) to reflect masking in echoic memory.

An important point to keep in mind is that this echoic information is supplementary to other information that the subject has in memory about the list. As the list is presented, subjects categorize each item and try to remember it. Subjects use all of their knowledge and memorizing skills to retain the list, and this is responsible for how they remember most of the items. However, according to Crowder and Morton's (1969) theory, subjects have an additional source of information if the list was presented auditorily: They have the echoic trace of the last item still persisting in auditory sensory memory. This can be used to supplement whatever other information they may be trying to use.

This notion that echoic memory is being used to supplement other memory information has an interesting implication: The size of the modality and suffix effect should depend on how badly subjects need to use echoic memory. On trials where subjects can remember the last item anyway, one would find no evidence for echoic memory. For example, Balota, Cowan, and Engle (1990) asked subjects to recall auditorily presented sentences immediately after each was presented; some of the sentences were followed by a suffix. The presence of a suffix caused a statistically significant impairment of recall of the last word. However, the magnitude of this suffix effect was much smaller than is found in the typical experiment using random digits or letters as stimuli. Why was the effect with sentences so much smaller than with lists of random items? With a sentence, you are able to use the meaning to help you recall the last word; you are not so dependent on the echoic trace as you would be with a random sequence. Thus, the more nonechoic information that a subject has available, the less that the subject will have to rely on echoic memory and therefore the smaller the suffix effect would become. Similarly, particularly large suffix effects may be found in populations that show impairment of their other memory abilities. For example, children may show a larger suffix effect than adults (Engle, Fidler, & Reynolds, 1981), not because they have a larger echoic memory but because their other memory abilities are not as well advanced and so children are more likely to need to use the echoic trace than are adults. Even among children, it seems that those who are cognitively behind their peers in higher mental processes may show a particularly large suffix effect (Sipe & Engle, 1986). All of these findings are consistent with the notion that echoic memory is used to supplement other memory processes.

It should be noted that Crowder and Morton (1969) were not the only researchers who attributed modality and suffix effects to echoic memory. Other theorists have made similar suggestions and have at times argued that echoic memory may have somewhat different properties than those envisioned by Crowder and Morton (see, e.g., Broadbent, Vines, & Broadbent, 1978; Craik, 1969; Watkins & Watkins, 1980). Since Crowder and Morton's theory was the most influential account, it will be used here as representative of the class of theories that explain modality and suffix effects through some form of echoic memory.

Effects of Acoustic Similarity

If Crowder and Morton's (1969) PAS theory is true, under what circumstances would you expect *not* to find a modality or a suffix effect? One class of circumstances would be if the information in echoic memory was useless for some reason. If the persisting echoic trace did not help you to know which item occurred last, you would not expect to find a modality effect or a suffix effect.

Crowder (1978b) devised such a set of circumstances. He used lists composed entirely of homophones, words that sound the same but are spelled differently. For example, a subject may see a list such as BUY–BY–BUY–BYE–BY–BYE–BUY–BYE. The subject would have to read some of the lists aloud and the other lists silently. Normally, one expects to find a modality effect when comparing lists read aloud or silently. However, when the list contains only homophones, whatever echoic information a subject happens to have would not help in deciding which items occurred where. The sound is entirely useless. Therefore, the PAS account would lead to the prediction that there should be no modality effect here. That is indeed what Crowder found: Reading the items aloud gave absolutely no benefit to memory.

Using homophones is a rather extreme manipulation of acoustic similarity. One can use a lesser manipulation, for example, by asking subjects to remember similar (but not identical) stimuli, such as DA–BA–GA–TA–CA–PA–VA. With these kinds of similar stimulus materials used as list items, one typically finds reduced (but not entirely eliminated) modality and suffix effects (Crowder, 1971, 1973). These results are consistent with the notion that the magnitude of modality and suffix effects will depend in part on how useful echoic information is in a particular situation.

Ineffectiveness of Attentional Manipulations

Echoic memory is believed to be a very basic aspect of our cognitive architecture. Admission of a stimulus to echoic memory should not be influenced by the particular strategies or attentional processes that subjects are carrying out. Therefore, according to Crowder and Morton's (1969) PAS account, modality and suffix effects should be relatively unaffected by attentional or strategic manipulations.

The evidence is generally in favor of this prediction. Cantor and Engle (1989) varied the amount of attention that subjects could apply to a list as it was being presented. Subjects had to perform another cognitive task as they were perceiving the items. The difficulty of this secondary task was manipulated. Although overall performance in serial recall was influenced by the difficulty of the competing task, this manipulation had no effect on the magnitude of the modality effect.

Nairne and Crowder (1982; see also Greenberg & Engle, 1983) studied the role of attention in the suffix effect. Would suffix effects be larger if subjects were required to pay attention to the suffix? In one condition, subjects were given the usual instructions to ignore the suffix. In another condition, they were required to write down the suffix before beginning recall of the list. This was done to ensure that subjects were attending to the suffix. This manipulation of attention had no influence at all on the magnitude of the suffix effect.

Another way of manipulating the role of attention in the suffix effect is through practice. As subjects have more and more practice at this task, they should be better able to withhold attention from the suffix. However, in general, the amount of practice at this task does not influence the effect of the suffix on recall of the last item (Balota & Engle, 1981). Watkins and Sechler (1989) were able to find some evidence that people could adapt (or *habituate*) to the suffix and that this habituation could lead to a reduction in the magnitude of the suffix effect. However, this reduction was extremely modest and could be accomplished only by playing the suffix continuously through a long experimental session. In short, the suffix effect is quite difficult to influence through any sort of attentional manipulation, as would be expected on the basis of Crowder and Morton's (1969) PAS account.

Timing of the Suffix

Crowder (1978a) manipulated the amount of time that passed between the presentation of the last list item and the suffix. He found that suffixes generally became ineffective if more than 2 s passed after presentation of the last item. There are two possible interpretations of this finding. The first is that echoic information decays in 2 s. Therefore, if more than 2 s pass before the suffix is presented, there would no longer be any information left in echoic memory, and the suffix would be ineffective. An alternative is that, if there is an extended pause after the last item, subjects will use that time to read out information from echoic memory. They would thus already know perfectly well what the last item was, and it would not matter that a suffix was then presented.

Later evidence supported the second of these possibilities. Perhaps the most striking evidence here was supplied by Watkins and Todres (1980). After a list was presented, they required subjects to engage in a demanding arithmetic task for 20 s. This arithmetic task involved no sound. It was designed to demand the subjects' attention fully and to prevent them from reading out information from echoic memory. On some trials, after this 20-s interval was over, a suffix was presented; on other trials, there was no suffix. Subjects then had to recall the list. Watkins and Todres found that there was still a suffix effect, even after this 20-s interval. This result was later replicated by Balota and Duchek (1986). If interpreted in light of Crowder and Morton's (1969) theory, this suggests that information decays only very slowly, if at all, in echoic memory. Usable information must persist in echoic memory for at least 20 s.

Physical Properties of the Suffix

Crowder and Morton (1969) assumed that modality and suffix effects are the result of precategorical information, information that cannot be called meaningful. If this assumption is true, then it should be the case that these phenomena should not be influenced by variables involving meaning (as long as these variables are not having their effect by influencing recall of other items). However, since echoic memory represents the persistence of echoic stimulation, these phenomena may be influenced by the physical properties of the stimuli.

The data generally are in support of this prediction. Morton, Crowder, and Prussin (1971) conducted a number of experiments on the suffix effect. They found that a suffix that came from the same semantic category as the list items caused no more interference than one that came from a different semantic category. Indeed, as Crowder and Raeburn (1970) showed, meaningless backward speech can be used as an effective suffix. Morton et al. and subsequent investigators showed that the physical properties of a suffix may determine the magnitude of a suffix effect. A suffix played in a different location than the list items is reduced in effectiveness. A suffix read in a different voice than the one that read the list items is only partly effective. Indeed, a nonspeech suffix, such as a tone or a buzzer, is so physically different than the list items that it is not effective at all. Morton, Marcus, and Ottley (1981) later used the fact that nonspeech suffixes are entirely ineffective to study the attributes of a sound that make it seem speech-like to a listener. They manipulated the physical properties of sounds to make them sound either more or less like human speech and were interested to see what changes would eliminate the effectiveness of these sounds as suffixes.

There have been occasional attempts to refute the claim that only the physical and not the semantic properties of a suffix determine its effectiveness. Most of these attempts (e.g., Salter & Colley, 1977) can be easily reconciled with Crowder and Morton's (1969) theory. One finding, however, cannot be easily explained away. Ayres, Jonides, Reitman, Egan, and Howard (1979) used a *wa* sound as a suffix after telling some subjects that the suffix would be the spoken syllable "wa" and others that it would be a note played on a trumpet. The suffix was presented after a list of words. There was a substantial suffix effect in both conditions. However, there was a significantly greater suffix effect when subjects believed that the sound was human speech than when they believed that it was a musical note. This suggests that the meaning that subjects attribute to a suffix may play some role in determining its effectiveness.

Thus, the bulk of the evidence manipulating the physical and semantic properties of the suffix is in agreement with predictions based on Crowder and Morton's (1969) PAS theory. However, the Ayres et al. (1979) study, which suggests that how subjects interpret a suffix may influence the effect, is inconsistent with the PAS approach and suggests that the information underlying the suffix effect may not be as sensory as Crowder and Morton initially believed.

Disinhibition and Suffix Effects

Crowder and Morton (1969) assumed that suffix effects reflected masking in echoic memory. However, they did not try to develop an explanation of exactly how such masking would occur. Crowder (1978a, 1982b) later tried to develop such an explanation.

Perhaps the most straightforward explanation would be that the suffix would somehow cover up (or overwrite) the last list item. This would be analogous to a blanket covering up an object beneath it. Crowder (1978a, 1982b) tested this sort of account by presenting multiple suffixes. In the control condition, subjects would have to recall lists of items followed by silence or by an ineffective tone. In another condition, a suffix would be presented after the last item. In still another condition, the list items would be followed by two or three suffixes, one after another. The overwriting sort of explanation would lead to the prediction that adding suffixes should cause even more interference than presenting a single suffix. Therefore, the more suffixes that are presented, the worse recall of the last item should be. This was not what Crowder found. Instead, presenting multiple suffixes caused *less* interference in recall than presenting a single suffix. Thus, the overwriting approach to explaining how suffixes operate seemed disproven.

Crowder offered an alternative, an ***inhibition account***. In this model, as each item is presented on a list, it interrupts (or inhibits) processing of the preceding stimulus. The suffix can interrupt processing of the last item. However, if a second suffix is presented after the first one, it can interrupt processing of the first suffix. This will eliminate the effect that the first suffix was having on the last list item and would allow resumption of the processing of the last list item. The result is ***disinhibition***: A second suffix can inhibit the inhibitory effect of an earlier suffix. Thus, memory for the last list item can be better after two suffixes are presented than when only one suffix is presented.

Crowder's (1978a, 1982b) model was the only complete model of how suffixes might have their effect in echoic memory. Later research has challenged some of its specific assumptions (e.g., Frankish & Turner, 1984; Kallman & Massaro, 1983). However, theories, such as Crowder's, dealing with exactly how echoic memory produces modality or suffix effects soon came to be seen as beside the point. Unexpected evidence was found that raised questions as to whether there was any relationship between echoic memory and these phenomena. Rather than challenging specific models, this evidence called into question Crowder and Morton's (1969) basic assumption that modality and suffix effects were caused by echoic memory. We will now turn to that evidence.

EVIDENCE AGAINST THE PAS ACCOUNT OF MODALITY AND SUFFIX EFFECTS

Lipreading

Imagine an experiment where subjects hear lists of items read aloud by an experimenter and then have to recall them. After some lists, there is no suffix. Obviously, performance will be quite good at the last position in this condition. After other lists, the experimenter does not say anything but rather silently articulates (or "mouths") a suffix (the word *zero*). Subjects are looking at the experimenter as this suffix is presented and so inevitably lipread the suffix. However, there is no sound. According to Crowder and Morton's (PAS) theory, this lipread suffix should be entirely ineffective at causing interference for the last item on the list. After all, no sound was presented, so it should be impossible for the word *zero* to act as a mask in echoic memory. Spoehr and Corin (1978) carried out this experiment and obtained results that challenged the whole basis for the PAS theory. They found that the lipread *zero* served as a very effective suffix. It caused a significant amount of interference with recall of the last list item although the suffix was not audible.

Just as Spoehr and Corin (1978) showed that a lipread stimulus could create a significant suffix effect, Campbell and Dodd (1980) investigated whether lipreading could lead to a modality effect (that is, whether recall of a lipread list would exhibit the same pattern of excellent recall of the terminal item as recall of an auditory list does). Lists of random digits were made up. The experimenter was filmed reading each list. The camera was arranged so that it showed a close-up of the experimenter's face. However, there was no sound on the tape. Subjects were seated in front of a television and watched the tape of the experimenter reading lists of digits. They had to determine the contents of each list simply by observing the experimenter's mouth movements on tape. (This sort of lipreading is not too difficult when one knows that all the stimuli being read are digits.) After each list was presented, subjects had to recall the items in order. The crucial finding is that subjects did exceptionally well on the last position of these lipread lists. That is, serial recall of lipread lists more closely resembled recall of auditory lists than recall of visual lists. In this sense, Campbell and Dodd showed that one could obtain a modality effect with lipread stimuli without any sound being presented. They disproved the assumption of the PAS theory that auditory presentation is required for high levels of recall of terminal items.

Greene and Crowder (1984b, Experiment 3) designed an experiment that would combine the Spoehr and Corin (1978) finding of a lipread suffix effect and the Campbell and Dodd (1980) finding of a lipread modality effect. The materials for this experiment involved videotapes. A woman was filmed saying lists of nine random digits. For half of the lists, sound was included on the tape: One could hear the woman speaking as well as see her lips move (the audiovisual condition). On the other lists, the sound was turned off so that the subject would have to perceive the lists entirely by lipreading (the visual condition). On some of the lists, there was no suffix: The speaker simply looked down after saying the last list item. On other lists, there was an audiovisual suffix: The speaker would say a word (usually the word "begin") after the last item, and one could both see and hear her speak the suffix. On the remaining lists, there was a visual (i.e., lipread) suffix: The speaker would say the suffix, but the sound was removed from the tape. Thus, in this experiment, there were six conditions: List items could be lipread (the visual condition) or both lipread and heard (the audiovisual condition), and lists could be followed by no suffix, by an audiovisual suffix, or by a lipread visual suffix. On audiovisual lists, there was a substantial rise at the end of the list (i.e., a modality effect). However, there was a roughly equivalent rise on the lipread lists, replicating the findings of Campbell and Dodd (1980) that are troublesome for the PAS account. Both visual lipread suffixes and audiovisual suffixes caused substantial impairment in recall of the last few items, replicating the findings of Spoehr and Corin (1978). Audiovisual lists were affected more by audiovisual suffixes than by purely visual lipread suffixes. However, visual lipread lists were affected more by visual lipread suffixes than by audiovisual suffixes. This is a case where adding sound to a suffix made it less effective, which the PAS theory could not predict.

Silent Mouthing

Earlier, we saw that modality and suffix effects can be found either if subjects hear an experimenter reading stimuli aloud or if they themselves read stimuli aloud. In the last section, we saw that modality and suffix effects can be found if subjects see an experimenter silently articulating stimuli. What if the subject is the one who is silently articulating the stimuli? Would silent mouthing of visually presented stimuli by subjects lead to modality and suffix effects?

This was the reasoning that led Greene and Crowder (1984b) to investigate the effects of silent mouthing on immediate recall. The lists were composed of digits, and all stimuli were printed visually on a computer screen. On half of the lists, subjects were told to read all of the list items aloud. On the other lists, subjects were told to mouth each item silently. That is, they had to articulate each item clearly but were told to avoid making noise. An experimenter sat across from them to monitor the subjects' behavior. On some lists, there was no suffix. On other lists, the word "begin" appeared after the last digit, and subjects were required to read this suffix aloud. On the remaining lists, the word "begin" was shown after the last digit, and subjects had to mouth it silently. In short, there were six conditions: Two presentation modalities (aloud and mouthed) and three suffix conditions (no suffix, aloud suffix, and mouthed suffix). Greene and Crowder found that both the aloud and mouthed conditions exhibited sharp improvements at the end of the list.

Thus, silent mouthing can lead to patterns of recall that resemble those found with auditory stimulation. Aloud and mouthed suffixes caused substantial interference in recall. Aloud lists were more impaired by aloud suffixes than by mouthed suffixes. Mouthed lists were more impaired by mouthed suffixes than by aloud suffixes. As was found by Greene and Crowder in lipreading, the mouthing data present another case where a suffix can become less effective if sound is added to it.

Nairne and Walters (1983) independently studied modality and suffix effects in recall of mouthed stimuli and reported results similar to those found by Greene and Crowder (1984b). These mouthing effects have since been replicated several times (e.g., Crowder, 1986; Greene, 1989a; Greene & Crowder, 1986; Turner et al., 1987), so they represent a real and important challenge to the PAS theory. Perhaps one way to reconcile the PAS theory with these findings would be to deny that the lipreading and mouthing effects reflect the same processes as the standard modality and suffix effects. If one assumes this, then one could keep the PAS account of the standard effects and develop new theories to explain the mouthing and lipreading findings. Such an approach has been taken by some (Turner et al., 1987) but appears quite unlikely. One would have to assume that the striking similarity of recall of mouthed and lipread stimuli to recall of auditory stimuli resulted merely from coincidence. Moreover, there is growing evidence that the mouthing effects are influenced by several variables in the same way as are standard modality and suffix effects. Just as standard modality effects are reduced when the list items are acoustically similar (e.g., Crowder, 1971), so are mouthing effects (Greene & Crowder, 1984b). Also, the standard modality effect may be reduced when list items come from a small vocabulary of possible stimuli (Manning & Robinson, 1989), and the mouthing modality effect is also reduced for small vocabularies (Turner et al., 1987). A concurrent memory load has equivalent effects on recall of auditory and mouthed items (Cantor & Engle, 1989). Therefore, it appears quite unlikely that auditory and mouthing modality effects are entirely unrelated.

Crowder (1986) extended these mouthing results in a clever way. He presented subjects with lists of visually presented items and required them to read the items aloud. However, in one condition, subjects were simultaneously hearing loud white noise (like static from a television tuned to a channel that isn't broadcasting). The white noise was loud enough that subjects could not hear themselves say the items. Although subjects actually were saying the items aloud, they were getting no auditory feedback. Therefore, the PAS account would predict that there should be no echoic representation for the items. However, subjects still exhibited a modality effect, with recall being quite good at the last position. As with the results involving mouthing, these data indicate that modality effects may occur in the absence of sound. Mouth movements may be all that are needed.

There is an important qualification on the claim that mouth movements can substitute for the presence of sound in this area. Engle, Cantor, and Turner (1989) tested memory in deaf subjects. The subjects saw printed stimuli and read them silently or aloud. After each list was shown, subjects had to recall the items. Across experiments, Engle et al. used several different recall tasks. At least in the serial-recall experiments, the data were quite clear: The deaf did *not* exhibit a modality effect. It made no difference whether they had read the items aloud or silently. This suggests that mouth movements are not sufficient to cause modality effects. Perhaps the person must have had years of experience of associating certain mouth movements with particular sounds (which hearing subjects, but not deaf subjects, have had) before mouth movements can lead to modality and suffix effects in the absence of sound.

Other Sources of Modality and Suffix Effects

The work on lipreading and silent mouthing was instrumental in raising widespread doubt as to the adequacy of the PAS account of modality and suffix effects. One result was that investigators began investigating a variety of nonauditory presentation formats to see if modality and suffix effects could be found in still more domains. There have been a variety of claims, counterclaims, and failures to replicate. However, there are at least two other domains that have been repeatedly shown to exhibit modality- and suffix-like phenomena.

One of these is the sense of touch. Tactile stimuli can exhibit both modality and suffix effects. Watkins and Watkins (1974b) designed an experiment to find tactile suffix effects. They used a list of tactile stimuli (tapping each subject's fingers with a pen or a paperclip). Recall of the last few stimuli was impaired more by a tactile suffix than by an auditory suffix. Manning (1980) found similar results. Nairne and McNabb (1985) showed that recall of the last item on a list of tactile stimuli was superior to recall of the last item on a visual list. These results all suggest that tactile stimulation may exhibit patterns of recall similar to those found with auditory stimuli.

One should note that these findings are not necessarily inconsistent with Crowder and Morton's (1969) PAS account. That is, they assumed that auditory sensory memory persisted for a longer period of time than visual sensory memory, and they used this assumption to explain modality and suffix effects. They made no claim as to whether there existed a tactile sensory memory and, if so, whether this store also lasted longer than the visual store. Although Nairne and McNabb (1985) chose to interpret their findings with tactile stimuli as evidence against the PAS theory, one can easily explain these phenomena by attributing them to a "precategorical tactile store" that resembles PAS in its duration. There is a fundamental difference between this work and the findings from lipreading and mouthing stimuli. It had been repeatedly shown that mouthed and lipread suffixes can interfere with recall of auditory items and vice versa (e.g., Greene & Crowder, 1984b; Nairne & Crowder, 1982; Nairne & Walters, 1983; Spoehr & Corin, 1978). Thus, mouthed and lipread stimuli must be gaining access to *the same system* as the one used to store auditory stimuli. This directly contradicts Crowder and Morton's (1969) claim that modality and suffix effects arise in a purely auditory store. In contract, because there is no evidence that tactile and auditory stimuli interfere with each other, there is no reason to believe that these studies using tactile stimuli are telling us anything about how auditory stimuli are stored.

A similar explanation may be given for the other presentation format that has been shown to exhibit modality and suffix effects. When deaf subjects are presented lists of words in American Sign Language, at least small modality and suffix effects may be found (Krakow & Hanson, 1985; Shand & Klima, 1981). Again, since there is no evidence that these ASL stimuli are gaining access to the same memory system that would be used to store acoustic stimuli, these findings could be explained by the PAS account by assuming that the deaf have had to develop alternative coding and storage mechanisms in memory.

In short, not every report of a modality and suffix effect using a presentation format other than sound is necessarily inconsistent with Crowder and Morton's (1969) PAS account. Rather, only those presentation formats (lipreading and silent mouthing) that have been shown to interfere with auditory memory and thus must be stored in the same system as auditory stimuli represent a fundamental challenge to the PAS theory.

Modality Effects in Long-Term Memory

Crowder and Morton (1969) attributed modality differences in recall to a memory store that was easily overwritten by subsequent auditory stimuli. This proposal would suggest that an auditory advantage in memory should be found in only a very constrained set of circumstances, namely, when no other sound occurs between when a stimulus is presented and when it is tested.

There is evidence that, under some circumstances, modality effects may be somewhat more robust than this. One set of circumstances involves studies where auditory and visual items were mixed together on a single list, rather than being presented in separate lists. When mixed-modality lists are used, the advantage for auditory items over visual items becomes much larger and is found at all positions on a list. This increase in the size and breadth of the modality effect is due both to an increase in recall of auditory items on mixed lists relative to pure auditory lists and a decrease in recall of visual items on mixed lists relative to pure visual lists (Greene, 1989a). This enhanced modality effect on mixed-modality lists is found even when subjects are later tested for long-term recognition (Conway & Gathercole, 1987) or frequency judgments (Glenberg & Fernandez, 1988). These effects are still poorly understood but are not easily explained in the PAS framework.

Another set of circumstances where modality effects can be found in long-term memory was discovered by Gardiner and Gregg (1979). In their experiments, they compared recall of lists of auditory words with recall of lists of visual words. Each list item was preceded and followed by a period of distractor activity (e.g., counting backwards). This distractor activity involved spoken activity. This spoken activity, when presented after the last item, should have acted as a suffix and eliminated any echoic memory for the last item. However, when subjects were asked for recall of the list items, they did much better on the last item or two on auditory lists than on visual lists. This finding has since been replicated several times (e.g., Glenberg, 1984; Glenberg & Swanson, 1986; Greene, 1985; Greene & Crowder, 1986). It is as if presenting a period of distractor activity after every item somehow inoculates the last item from suffix interference.

Certainly, an echoic-memory theory, such as Crowder and Morton's (1969), would not predict this. However, an important question is whether one should use results from this sort of experiment to challenge accounts of standard modality and suffix effects. The experiments by Gardiner and Gregg (1979) and by the researchers who have followed up their work have generally involved free recall of word lists. Such a task presumably involves very different memory processes than the tests of immediate serial recall of digits used by Crowder and Morton (1969) to compose and test their theory. When one does study serial recall of digit lists, the Gardiner and Gregg phenomenon is not found: There is no sign of a modality effect in serial recall of digits presented spaced apart. Spaced presentation leads to a long-term modality effect only when lists of words (with each word occurring on only one list for each subject) are used as study materials (Greene, Elliott, & Smith, 1987). (For another dissociation between modality effects in free recall of word lists and serial recall, see Engle et al., 1989.)

Without a doubt, these experiments on modality effects in long-term memory have proven that Crowder and Morton's (1969) PAS theory can not offer a comprehensive account of how auditory and visual stimuli differ in memory. What is much less clear is whether this work should be seen as refuting that theory. It is possible that presentation modality has multiple effects on memory and that one should not expect a single theory to explain all of these effects. On the other hand, it seems unlikely that it is sheer coincidence that auditory presentation leads to such similar patterns in these different tasks. Unfortunately, it is very difficult to know exactly how much any theory should be expected to explain.

THEORETICAL REACTIONS

We have seen that there is evidence that challenges (to varying degrees) Crowder and Morton's (1969) PAS account of modality and suffix effects. This evidence has proven to be liberating for researchers' imaginations, as there has been a variety of theoretical accounts proposed as alternatives.

A Revised PAS Account

One approach that Crowder and I have taken (Greene & Crowder, 1984b; see Morton et al., 1981, for a similar suggestion) is to keep the basic framework developed by Crowder and Morton (1969). That is, we argued that modality and suffix effects really are caused by echoic memory but that a new conception of echoic memory was needed. This approach was specifically designed to explain the effects of mouthing and lipreading that we have discussed.

The function of echoic memory is the determination of the auditory features present in a stimulus. This process ordinarily depends on the acoustic properties of the stimulus. However, Crowder and I suggested that nonauditory information, as well as purely acoustic information, can play a role in this process of auditory feature synthesis. In particular, visual information about speech gestures can influence the auditory features that are synthesized. For example, seeing a person pronounce a vowel with rounded and protruded lips will guide the auditory system to perceiving the sound "OOO." Since information about mouth movements enters the auditory system, a lipread utterance with the mouth in that configuration will lead in some way to perception of the same auditory feature in the complete absence of acoustic information. Crowder and I also assumed that feedback from one's own speech gestures functions the same way as does the sight of another person's speech gestures.

Why should one assume that visual information about speech gestures gains access to the auditory perceptual system? There is some supporting evidence from the field of speech perception. There has been considerable interest in that field in the ways that visual information about speech gestures may influence the sounds that people report hearing. An influential study was reported by MacDonald and McGurk (1978), who devised a situation where gestural and acoustic cues conflicted. In these experiments, subjects heard a series of consonant–vowel syllables while watching a videotape showing a speaker articulate a different list of syllables. MacDonald and McGurk reported that people often reported hearing sounds consistent with the visual gestures they saw. This was *not* a case of subjects trying to perceive a series of soft sounds in a noisy environment and desperately using the visual speech gestures as a way of making a guess as to the sounds that had been heard. When there are no conflicting visual speech gestures, people can perceive the sounds easily. However, seeing conflicting visual gestures leads people to *hear* sounds consistent with the gestures they saw.

If one assumes that visual and motor information about speech gestures can enter the auditory perceptual system and therefore be used in echoic memory, the findings that lipreading and silent mouthing can lead to modality and suffix effects (Campbell & Dodd, 1980; Greene & Crowder, 1984b, 1986; Nairne & Walters, 1983; Spoehr & Corin, 1978) are easily explained. Lipreading and silent mouthing would be sending information into echoic memory in exactly the same way that acoustic stimulation does and should therefore lead to phenomena attributed to echoic memory. This approach has the advantage of being able to explain all of the results formerly accounted for by Crowder and Morton's (1969) PAS theory, as well as the more recent lipreading and mouthing data. It could explain why reading stimuli aloud leads to modality effects even when there is so much background noise that subjects can't hear what they're saying (Crowder, 1986). It would also explain why deaf subjects do *not* exhibit modality and suffix effects when they read stimuli aloud (Engle et al., 1989). Hearing subjects have learned through years of experience to associate certain speech gestures with particular sounds. Since deaf subjects have not had that experience, seeing a speech gesture would not lead to the perception of any one particular auditory feature.

One should also keep in mind some serious limitations on this revision of PAS theory. It would not offer an explanation as to why tactile stimulation (Manning, 1980; Nairne & McNabb, 1985; Watkins & Watkins, 1974) or American Sign Language stimuli presented to deaf subjects (Krakow & Hanson, 1985; Shand & Klima, 1981) may exhibit modality and suffix effects. These data would presumably be due to the utilization of other sensory memory stores that operate separately from, but analogously to, echoic memory. This revised PAS theory would also not address modality effects in long-term memory but would be forced to assume that these effects are unrelated to standard modality and suffix effects. Perhaps due to these limitations, there are a number of theorists who are ready to abandon the PAS approach entirely and develop new theories for this area.

The Changing-State Hypothesis

Campbell and Dodd (1980; see also Campbell, Dodd, & Brasher, 1983) noted one important difference between visual and auditory presentation. Visual stimuli are usually presented so that all of their parts may be perceived at the same time. That is, when a word is shown visually, we are able to see the word as a whole. This is not true for auditory presentation. When we hear a word, the different parts are presented sequentially, not simultaneously. In this sense, auditory stimuli may be said to unfold over time in a way that visual stimuli do not. To perceive an auditory stimulus, we must be able to perceive the changes in auditory stimulation that occur over time. Campbell and Dodd suggest that modality and suffix effects "may reflect a general tendency for changing state information to be processed differently than information (usually visual) which can be resolved simultaneously" (1980, p. 97). Campbell et al. (1983) later suggested more specific mechanisms through which changing-state stimuli might be processed in a way that would lead to the presence of modality and suffix effects.

This changing-state hypothesis would be able to explain the standard findings regarding modality and suffix effects. Moreover, since both lipread and silently mouthed materials change over time, this approach could explain the results with these classes of stimuli. The presentation of items in American Sign Language would also involve changes in state, so this approach could also explain the presence of modality and suffix effects with these stimuli (however, see Shand & Klima, 1981, for arguments against the changing-state hypothesis as an explanation of the ASL data).

There are data that are harder for this approach to explain. It is not clear that tactile stimuli necessarily change over time, so reports that these stimuli exhibit modality and suffix effects are troublesome. Also, this approach offers no clue as to why modality and suffix effects may sometimes be found in long-term memory tasks. The changing-state hypothesis would have to take the same approach that the PAS theory does here, namely, to argue that these long-term effects are not caused by the same processes that bring about modality and suffix effects in immediate serial recall.

Crowder (1986) attempted a direct test of the changing-state hypothesis as an explanation of the modality effect. He used visual stimuli that changed over time. As his stimuli, he used large numerals that appeared gradually on a computer screen. Subjects would watch the screen as each numeral was presented a portion at a time. The timing of these item presentations was designed to approximate the time it would take for spoken digit names to be presented. The central finding here was that there was no sign at all of a modality effect. Presenting digits in this gradual, changing-state fashion did not improve recall at all relative to recall of visually presented stimuli presented in a normal fashion. Similar results were reported by Manning and Gmuer (1985). Although there have been a few reports that a changing-state presentation may have small effects on recall (Campbell et al., 1983; Kallman & Cameron, 1989), the literature as a whole is inconsistent with this account of modality and suffix effects.

The Primary Linguistic Code Hypothesis

Shand and Klima (1981) offered another alternative theory. They based their account on Conrad's (1964) finding that subjects in short-term memory tasks usually rely on some sort of speech code; items, whether presented auditorily or visually, are maintained and rehearsed in a form that resembles speech. Shand and Klima thus claimed that speech is a primary linguistic code; that is, it is a code habitually used in short-term memory. When list items are presented visually, subjects have to recode them to place them in a speech code. No such recoding is necessary for spoken items. Shand and Klima assumed that modality and suffix effects arise when stimuli are presented in a format compatible with an individual's dominant short-term memory code. The exact mechanism through which this would lead to modality and suffix effects was never specified.

Shand and Klima's proposal is able to explain the standard modality and suffix effect findings. If one assumes that lipread and mouthed stimuli function like speech and do not have to be recoded, then this approach could also account for the presence of modality and suffix effects with these presentation formats. This proposal also offers a simple explanation why deaf subjects whose native language is American Sign Language exhibit modality and suffix effects in recall of ASL stimuli. It does not address the presence of modality and suffix effects in long-term memory. It also is unable to explain the presence of modality and suffix effects in the recall of tactile stimuli (Manning, 1980; Nairne & McNabb, 1985; Watkins & Watkins, 1974). Surely, the sense of touch is not a primary linguistic code. This theory is also unable to explain why modality and suffix effects are found in recall of nonspeech auditory stimuli, such as musical notes (Greene & Samuel, 1986; Roberts, 1986). Until specific mechanisms are proposed that explain why presentation in a primary linguistic code leads to modality and suffix effects and that can explain the contrary evidence discussed here, this must be considered an unsatisfactory account.

The Feature-Overwriting Hypothesis

Several authors (e.g., Broadbent & Broadbent, 1981; Campbell et al., 1983; Nairne, 1988, 1990) have offered a featural account. Generally, such an account would see a memory item as consisting of a bundle of features. Features may be overwritten individually by later stimuli. That is, when Stimulus A is followed by Stimulus B, only those features in A that are also present in B will suffer interference. It is assumed that the probability of recall of a stimulus is a function of the number of features in that stimulus that had not been overwritten by subsequent events. Modality effects are usually explained by assuming that auditory stimuli contains more features than visual stimuli. Suffix effects are used as evidence for the overwriting process.

For example, Nairne (1990) assumed that "auditory traces may have a richer collection of physically based features, perhaps because of the inherent coding properties of primary memory" (pp. 256–257). There is some sense in which Nairne seems to be assuming that which must be explained: That is, he explains why auditory items are better remembered than visual items by assuming that auditory traces are richer (i.e., more memorable). While this undoubtedly makes theory building easier, it is unclear how informative the resultant theory becomes. The speculation about coding in primary memory is a reference to Shand and Klima's (1981) primary-linguistic code hypothesis. If this speculation were to be taken seriously as a part of his model, he would have to explain the evidence discussed here that contradicts the usefulness of primary linguistic coding as a construct here.

Nairne (1990) explains suffix effects through the overwriting of traces: "An individual feature of a primary memory trace is assumed to be overwritten, with probability F, if that feature is matched in a subsequently occurring event" (p. 252). The suffix, if it is physically similar to the last item, overwrites its physically based features, thereby making it less likely that it will be recalled. Nairne did not discuss the mechanisms involved in overwriting. However, he did admit that Crowder's (1978a) finding of disinhibition in suffix effects suggests that such mechanisms may have to be quite complex.

There is considerable evidence that overwriting of individual stimulus features cannot be used to explain the suffix effect. Some of this evidence was discussed earlier in the sections on lipreading and silent mouthing. When subjects lipread a list of items, a lipread (visual) suffix was significantly more effective than an audiovisual suffix (Greene & Crowder, 1984b). In other words, *adding* (auditory) features to a suffix made it *less* effective than a suffix that had fewer features. According to a featural overwriting account, such as Nairne's (1988, 1990), it should be impossible to reduce a suffix effect by adding features to the suffix. The same point can be illustrated using mouthed stimuli. When subjects mouthed a list of items, a suffix read aloud was less effective than a mouthed suffix (Greene & Crowder, 1984b). Again, adding features to a suffix can make it less effective. A model such as Nairne's (1988, 1990) assumes that the magnitude of the suffix effect would be determined by the number of physical features contained in the last stimulus that are also found in the suffix. This number could never be decreased by adding features to a suffix.

A study by Routh and Lifschutz (1975) also contradicts the notion of featural overwriting. These experimenters found that the suffix effect was reduced when a tone was played during the presentation of the list but was not included as part of the suffix. The tone was an uninformative feature; that is, even if it was not overwritten by the suffix, it contained no information that would help the subject recall the items. However, adding a tone to the list items presumably reduced the overall, holistic similarity of the list items to the suffix, and this was sufficient to reduce the magnitude of the suffix effect. All of these studies suggest that the global similarity of the suffix to the last list item is a better predictor of the magnitude of the suffix effect than is the number of features from the last item that are contained in the suffix.

Curiously enough, there are times when physical similarity has little or no effect on the magnitude of suffix interference. An example comes from a series of experiments by Morton et al. (1981). These authors showed that a single-pitch pulse from the vowel sound "aah," when run through a high-pass filter so that it no longer sounded like human speech, did not interfere with recall of normally spoken digits. However, if the list items were filtered so that they no longer sounded like human speech, significant suffix effects were found with both the filtered single-pitch pulse suffix and the normal unfiltered suffix. In general, speech-like list items will be affected only by speech-like suffixes, but list items that do not sound like speech will be affected either by acoustically similar suffixes or by speech-like suffixes. Greene and Samuel (1986, Experiments 2 and 3) found further support for this empirical generalization using piano notes as stimuli. These data are very hard for overwriting accounts to explain.

Feature-overwriting accounts do not offer satisfactory explanations of the literature on standard modality and suffix effects. Moreover, they generally avoid attempting any explanation for modality effects in long-term memory. These accounts are thus too limited to be useful.

Temporal-Distinctiveness Accounts

Several authors have suggested that modality effects reflect the greater distinctiveness in memory for the last item on auditory lists than the last item on visual lists. Suffix effects would reflect interference that decreased the distinctiveness of the last item. The most clearly specified such account was developed by Glenberg (1987; Glenberg & Swanson, 1986).

This theory begins with the important observation that laboratory memory tasks typically involve temporal discrimination. That is, a person who is shown a list of words and is then asked to recall them is not being asked to write down every word that he or she knows. Rather, the person is being asked to write down words that were presented at a certain period of time. The fact that people are able to perform such recall tasks means that they must have recorded temporal information about the words; that is, the memory traces that were formed must contain information about the time of occurrence of the events. Also, the fact that people seem capable of restricting their recall primarily to items that actually were presented suggests that subjects are also using temporal information in retrieval. At the time of retrieval, subjects are essentially asking themselves, "what words were shown during this particular period of time?"

In short, temporal information is stored in a memory trace and is used to recall events. Glenberg (1987) assumed that time of presentation is recorded more accurately for auditory stimuli than for visual items. This difference in temporal coding was considered the cause of the modality effect. The modality effect is usually restricted to the end of the list because it is only for recent items that subjects use fine-grained temporal information in retrieval.

Glenberg (1987) presented a detailed temporal-distinctiveness model for the modality effect. He did not dwell at length on the suffix effect. However, Glenberg and his colleagues have suggested that suffix effects might reflect overloading of temporal cues. The effectiveness of any retrieval cue depends on how precisely it can indicate the information in memory that is being sought. A retrieval cue that is associated with a lot of unwanted information, as well as with the desired memory trace, will not be as effective as a more specific cue. Suffixes that share the same approximate time of occurrence as the list items may also be contacted by the temporal retrieval cues and thereby make them less effective.

A unique aspect of the Glenberg (1987) theory is that it is truly a long-term memory theory. Other theories of the modality and suffix effect emphasized the temporary aspect of these phenomena. The fact that these effects were restricted to the end of a list even in immediate recall led people to see them as reflecting some short-lived aspect of human memory (either sensory memory, as in Crowder and Morton's, 1969, theory, or a component of short-term memory, as in most of the alternatives that have been presented). Glenberg's theory, however, sees modality and suffix effects as reflecting permanent aspects of the memory system. In part, this emphasis arises from the particular studies that have been used as evidence for this approach. Glenberg and his colleagues have primarily used experiments on modality effects in long-term memory as support for this theory (see e.g., Glenberg, 1984, 1987; Glenberg & Fernandez, 1988; Glenberg & Swanson, 1986; Glenberg, Mann, Altman, Forman, & Procise, 1989). This long-term memory work, which is usually ignored or explained away by other theories, becomes the primary source of evidence here.

How well does this temporal-distinctiveness theory work in explaining modality and suffix effects? This judgment will depend in part on how one feels about the crucial assertion that time of presentation is more accurately encoded for auditory presentation than for visual presentation. There is some evidence for this claim. When subjects see a list of items and have to make a judgment about the position of particular items on the list, there is usually an auditory advantage that is found both at the beginning and the end of a list (Glenberg & Fernandez, 1988; Greene & Crowder, 1988). The presence of an auditory advantage for *early* items is particularly noteworthy: This suggests that an auditory advantage in temporal coding is more general than the auditory advantage in recall that is restricted to the last few items. This is at least compatible with the claim that auditory superiority in temporal coding underlies the modality effect in recall. Glenberg et al. (1989) found an auditory advantage in the perception and reproduction of temporal rhythms. Rhythms presented in auditory fashion were perceived and remembered better than visual rhythms, and this difference was again not restricted to the end of a sequence.

On the other hand, there are some temporal tasks that do not exhibit a modality effect. Crowder and Greene (1987; see also Schab & Crowder, 1989) used a task where list items are presented at irregular presentation rates. On each list, there would be different amounts of time between adjacent list items. After a list was presented, subjects were asked to make relative judgments about the amount of time that passed between adjacent items. Although subjects were able to perform this task at a better-than-chance level, there was no difference between auditory and visual lists.

In short, there is a genuine auditory advantage when memory tasks involve temporal judgments on an ordinal scale ("In what order were these items shown?", "What position in the ordering did this item occupy?"). When a memory task involves judgments of absolute time (e.g., "How many milliseconds passed between these events?"), there is little, if any, evidence for an advantage of auditory presentation over visual presentation. Glenberg's (1987) theory predicts an auditory advantage for both kinds of temporal information. Still, the fact that temporal-order judgments consistently show a large and general modality difference must be considered as important support for this approach. Moreover, insofar as this theory is the only one that deals at any length with modality effects in long-term memory, it has an important advantage over all of the other theories that have been proposed.

CONCLUSION

We have as yet no satisfactory theory for modality and suffix effects. The classic Crowder and Morton (1969) account, which attributed these phenomena to a purely acoustic echoic memory, has been disproven. It is possible to revise that approach (Greene & Crowder, 1984), and such a revision still offers a satisfactory explanation of the basic findings but only at a cost of excluding many phenomena (e.g., modality differences in long-term memory) that seem on the surface to be relevant. A temporal-distinctiveness approach (Glenberg, 1987) may be the most promising route for future development, although its current formulation is not entirely consistent with the data.

An interesting observation by Glenberg (1987) suggests that there may be common ground between PAS and temporal-distinctiveness approaches. Specifically, he suggests that the longer persistence of auditory than visual sensory information may be precisely the factor that leads to better registration of temporal information for auditory stimuli. Thus, these two approaches need not be seen as mutually exclusive. In any event, any satisfactory theory of modality and suffix effects is likely to be considerably more complex than the PAS account of Crowder and Morton (1969). However much one might prefer simple theories, this preference has a way of conflicting with the complexities of human cognition, where there exists no stable boxes as are found on information-processing flow diagrams. On a positive note, theories such as Glenberg's (1987) suggest that modality and suffix effects may be reflecting important general principles in memory and thus may have more central implications for cognitive psychology than was formerly believed.

CHAPTER THREE

Recency Effects in Free Recall

In 1878, Nipher reported a striking finding. When people memorize a list of items, their retention is affected in a systematic way by the position an item occupies in the list. Items occupying middle positions are not remembered as well as those at the beginning or the end. Nipher thus deserves credit for having discovered *serial-position effects* in memory, presumably the first memory phenomena ever studied experimentally. One would like to be able to claim that Nipher's (1878) report attracted widespread interest and excitement. In reality, however, it was basically forgotten until it was discussed by Stigler (1978) a century later. The journal that published Nipher's report, *Transactions of the Academy of Science of St. Louis,* ceased publication shortly thereafter. In all, this was not an auspicious start for the experimental study of human memory.

However, serial-position effects are so powerful and so obvious that their rediscovery was inevitable. Ebbinghaus (1885/1964, 1902) conducted the first research on memory that had a persisting impact on the field. He tested himself on serial learning, gradual acquisition of a list of ordered items, and he noted that the first items that he was able to master came from the two ends of the list. Subsequent investigators of serial learning followed up on this observation, though no consensus as to the origins of serial-position effects was reached (see Crowder, 1976, for a review of these studies).

Much greater interest in serial-position effects arose when memory researchers began to use the task of *free recall* as their measure of choice. In free recall, subjects receive a list of items, usually one at a time, and then recall them in any order. Murdock (1962) was the first person to generate enthusiasm in the study of serial-position effects in free recall. Shown in Fig. 3.1 is a prototypical example of the accuracy of immediate free recall as a function of serial position. The data come from an unpublished experiment in my laboratory. The term *primacy effect* is used to refer to the advantage for items at the beginning of the list. The term *recency effect* refers to the advantage at the end. Although this would depend in part on how the experiment was done, the recency effect in immediate free recall is usually somewhat larger than the primacy effect.

THE PRIMACY EFFECT

The topic of this chapter is not primacy effects. Rather, this chapter will focus on recency effects. This concentration is consistent with the interests of researchers, who in the last 30 years at least have paid much more attention to the recency effect than to the primacy effect. This relative lack of interest reflects the feeling that psychologists have achieved a satisfactory (and unfortunately somewhat uninteresting) account of primacy effects. This account assumes that early items are remembered better than middle or late items simply because they receive more rehearsal or attention.

Imagine that you are a conscientious subject receiving a list of items one at a time that you are trying to memorize. When the first item occurs, it has your undivided attention. You rehearse it in some way until the next item appears. When the second item appears, you try to rehearse

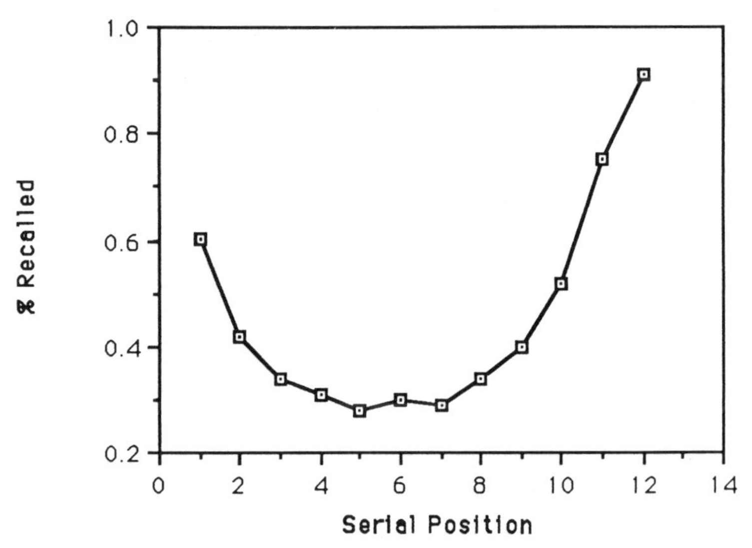

FIG. 3.1. An example of the recency effect in immediate free recall.

it, but you also try to keep the first item accessible by rehearsing it as well. In other words, you would begin sharing rehearsals between the current item and the first item. As more items are presented, this process of sharing rehearsal becomes more difficult. Since there are more and more previous items to try to maintain, you give less rehearsal to the current item as you get further into the list. In other words, since you are always dividing your cognitive effort between the current item and earlier ones, the first few items would end up with a greater cumulative amount of rehearsal or processing than later items. The primacy effect could then reflect the fact that items are easier to remember if they received a lot of rehearsal or processing.

Welch and Burnett (1924) were early proponents of this approach. They hit upon an easy way to test it. They simply instructed subjects to rehearse an item only while it was being presented. In other words, they eliminated sharing of rehearsals between a current item and previous items. The use of this instruction led to the elimination of the primacy effect, a finding that has been replicated by many other investigators (Brodie & Prytulak, 1975; Fischler, Rundus, & Atkinson, 1970; Glanzer & Meinzer, 1967; Gorfein, 1970).

A similar way of testing this rehearsal account of primacy effects is by using *incidental learning*. In an incidental-learning experiment, subjects receive a list of items but are not aware that their memory for the list will be tested subsequently. Since they do not expect a test on the items, subjects should not rehearse any of the items. Since the earlier items are not receiving more rehearsal than other items, there should be no primacy effect when memory for incidentally learned material is tested. This prediction has generally been upheld (Baddelely & Hitch, 1977; Glenberg et al., 1980; Marshall & Werder, 1972; Seamon & Murray, 1976).

A final source of support for the rehearsal account of primacy effects comes from studies where subjects were asked to do all of their rehearsals aloud. The experimenter kept a tally of how often each item was rehearsed. The results showed that early list items received far more rehearsals than did other items (Rundus, 1971; Rundus & Atkinson, 1970).

An additional point should be made here. It is quite possible that early items not only receive more rehearsals than later items but also better rehearsals. Since subjects do not have to divide their attention so much, they are able to concentrate on using fancy mnemonic strategies when rehearsing early items. In other words, the rehearsal that is devoted to early items is likely to be more elaborative than the rehearsal devoted to later items, a fact pointed out by Craik and Lockhart (1972). Also, distributed rehearsals (that is, rehearsal devoted to previous items) may be more effective mnemonically than rehearsal to the current item, perhaps because there is more effort involved in bringing earlier items to mind

(Modigliani & Hedges, 1987). Since early items have more of an opportunity for distributed rehearsals than do later items, this should also work in their favor.

In short, it seems that the primacy effect may be explained quite satisfactorily by assuming that the most (and the best) rehearsal goes to early items. This is a relatively uninteresting explanation, largely because it is so straightforward. Any serious theory of memory would have to propose that items should be remembered better if they receive more rehearsal and elaboration. Therefore, this explanation of primacy effects would be compatible with any serious model of memory that is likely to be proposed. However, recency effects have inspired more controversy. Subjects seem to devote less rehearsal to the last few items than to the others (Rundus, 1971; Rundus & Atkinson, 1970). Why then should these items be remembered so well?

THE TWO-STORE ACCOUNT OF RECENCY EFFECTS

The classical explanation for recency effects is that they reflected the presence of a short-term memory store. This sort of account was first popularized by Waugh and Norman (1965). They proposed a two-store account of free recall. According to their theory, information that is perceived enters a short-term store that they termed *primary memory*. Primary memory has a limited capacity; it can only contain a few items. However, retrieval from primary memory is quite easy. If a piece of information is present in primary memory, the person is almost certain to be able to recall it. While information is in primary memory, it may be rehearsed. Rehearsal has two functions. It tends to maintain information in primary memory, and it can cause transfer of the information to the long-term memory store (which Waugh & Norman called *secondary memory*). If information is not rehearsed, then it is lost (forgotten) from primary memory, perhaps without ever being transferred to secondary memory. Secondary memory differs from primary memory in several ways. It has an unlimited capacity. Waugh and Norman saw no reason not to assume that an essentially infinite amount of information could be stored in secondary memory. Also, there was no evidence that information is ever lost from secondary memory after it has been transferred there. However, retrieval from secondary memory is much more difficult than retrieval from primary memory. Even if a piece of information is present in secondary memory, we might not be able to find it.

How would this sort of explanation account for the serial-position curve shown in Fig. 3.1? The first few items receive more rehearsal than later items. They would therefore be the items that would be most likely to be transferred to secondary memory (and, if one also believed that rehearsal could strengthen secondary-memory traces, they might also be the items easiest to find in secondary memory). The last few items would still be present in primary memory. Therefore, they would have a high probability of being recalled. In contrast, the items in the middle of the list would no longer be in primary memory because they would have been displaced by later items. Also, since the middle items received less rehearsal than early items, they may never have been transferred to secondary memory. Therefore, probability of recall would be lowest for those items.

The Waugh and Norman (1965) model became the standard approach to explaining recency effects. Atkinson and Shiffrin (1968) later proposed a similar model that was considerably more detailed mathematically, and other authors (e.g., Glanzer, 1972) also proposed variations. Not everyone liked the terms "primary memory" and "secondary memory." For example, Atkinson and Shiffrin used the terms "short-term store" and "long-term store," and these terms may have become more popular than Waugh and Norman's. Also, some authors (e.g., Atkinson & Shiffrin, 1968; Smith, Barresi, & Gross, 1971) argued that Waugh and Norman's notion of transfer from primary memory to secondary memory needed modification. However, the basic outline of these approaches followed Waugh and Norman.

Perhaps one reason why two-store theories, such as that of Waugh and Norman (1965), gained widespread popularity was that they reminded people of how memory is organized in computers. Computers often have at least two kinds of memory storage. One kind is a limited-capacity system that contains information that the computer is able to access quickly and easily. There is also a long-term storage memory system (often utilizing disks for storage), which has a much larger capacity but takes much longer to access. Since the idea that the human mind operates as a kind of a computer began to gain widespread acceptance in the 1960s, many people thought that it was natural that human memory should resemble the memory architecture found in computers.

Dissociations Between Prerecency and Recency Recall

Waugh and Norman's (1965) theory provides a straightforward explanation for recency effects in free recall. However, there was still a need for evidence supporting this approach. A considerable amount of such evidence was supplied in the late 1960s and early 1970s. The logic behind this evidence was that Waugh and Norman had argued that different memory stores were used to recall the last few items and earlier items.

If primary and secondary memory truly are separate entities, there would be no reason to expect them to be influenced in exactly the same way by every experimental manipulation. If variables could be found that had different effects on recall of the last few items than they had on recall of earlier items, this would be consistent with the idea that different memory stores are used to recall recency and prerecency items. This would then support the Waugh and Norman theory. The term *dissociation* is often used to refer to demonstrations that a single variable has different effects on two or more measures.

A number of such variables were found. A few of the clearest and most striking cases will be discussed here (for more extensive listings, see Glanzer, 1972, or Greene, 1986b). In general, recall increases as a function of word frequency. That is, more common words (e.g., GIRL, TABLE) are easier to recall than rare words (e.g., SUMP, KIOSK). However, this effect depends on serial position. Common words are easier to recall than rare words at early positions, but there is no difference between them at the last few positions (Raymond, 1969; Sumby, 1963).

Presentation rate typically influences recall. A slower presentation rate allows for more rehearsal and organization of the items, thereby facilitating recall. However, presentation rate influences recall only for prerecency items and not for the last few items on a list (Glanzer & Cunitz, 1966; Murdock, 1962; Raymond, 1969).

Longer lists are usually harder to remember than shorter lists. As list length increases, there is more competition among items for rehearsal and also a greater potential for interference. However, list length has no effect on recall of the last few items of a list (Lewis-Smith, 1975; Murdock, 1962; Postman & Phillips, 1965). This interaction between list length and serial position makes sense from the perspective of Waugh and Norman's (1965) theory. There is a definite limit as to the number of items that could be placed in primary memory. Increasing list length would simply lead to more items being placed in secondary memory but would not affect the number of items in primary memory.

So far, only variables that influence recall of prerecency (but not recency) items have been discussed. It is possible to find a few variables that exhibit the opposite pattern. The clearest case involves inserting a filled retention interval between list presentation and recall. Rather than being able to recall the list immediately after presentation of the last item, subjects would be required to do some other task (e.g., mental arithmetic) for a while before they could begin recall. As long as this distractor interval is 20 s or more, the recency effect is completely eliminated, with recall of the last few items being much lower than would be found in immediate recall. However, recall of early items typically shows essentially no effect from the insertion of this distractor task (Glanzer & Cunitz,

1966; Postman & Phillips, 1965). From the perspective of the Waugh and Norman (1965) theory, the distractor task tends to prevent rehearsal and to displace items from primary memory. If all of the items are displaced from primary memory, then there should be no recency effect. However, earlier items no longer present in primary memory would be unaffected by the use of a distractor task.

Negative Recency Effects

Craik (1970) performed an experiment in which subjects would see a list and then have immediate free recall. This was repeated several times, so that each person had seen several lists. The conventional serial-position function was found. Then, Craik gave subjects an unexpected final-recall test in which they would have to recall all of the words presented during the experiment. There was a normal primacy effect in this final free recall but no recency effect. In fact, subjects recalled the last few items worse than any of the other items, a finding that Craik termed a *negative recency effect.*

The negative recency effect is consistent with a primary-memory account. Terminal items receive less rehearsal than earlier items (Rundus, 1971). This would mean that they would be the items least likely to be transferred to secondary memory. This is not a problem in immediate recall, because subjects can use primary memory to recall the last few items. In fact, the knowledge that the last few items will be easily recallable may lead subjects to rehearse them less than other items. However, on Craik's (1970) final free-recall test, none of the items would still be in primary memory, and subjects would have to rely on secondary memory for recall of all of the items, placing terminal items at a serious disadvantage. If care is taken to ensure that the last few items do not receive less rehearsal than midlist items, the negative recency effect is reduced or eliminated (Watkins & Watkins, 1974a).

Measurement of Primary Memory

How much information is able to be stored in primary memory? Miller (1956) had noted that the average memory span (the number of stimuli that could be recalled in order) was approximately seven items. Some authors have seen this as a good estimate for the capacity of primary memory. However, Waugh and Norman's (1965) theory suggests that this might be inadequate. Their theory makes the point that, on any kind of memory task, subjects might be retrieving information from either primary memory or secondary memory. Thus, performance on any one task is unlikely to yield a pure estimate of the capacity of primary memory. Rather, one must first be able to subtract the contribution of secondary memory to a task before it would be possible to know how much of a contribution primary memory is making. This reasoning suggests that calculation of the capacity of primary memory is likely to be somewhat more complicated (and to yield a number somewhat smaller) than simply finding a person's memory span.

Waugh and Norman (1965) developed a technique that would allow calculation of the capacity of primary memory. They constructed the following equation

$$R_i = PM_i + SM_i - PM_iSM_i$$

where R_i is the probability that item i is recalled. PM_i is the probability that item i can be retrieved from primary memory. SM_i is the probability that it can be retrieved from secondary memory. The probability of recall is not simply a sum of the probability that the item can be retrieved from either primary or secondary memory since it is possible that the item could be retrieved from both stores. The probability that an item could be retrieved from both stores is equal to the product of the probability that the item is available in primary memory times the probability that the item is in secondary memory.

To know the probability that an item is in primary memory, one can rearrange the terms to create this equation:

$$PM_i = [(R_i - SM_i) / (1 - SM_i)]$$

Waugh and Norman (1965) go on to make some simplifying assumptions, notably that the probability that an item can be retrieved from secondary memory is a constant for the final list positions and can be estimated by the asymptotic level of recall for items in the middle of the list. As an example, say that the average level of recall for items in the middle of a 12-word list was .10, and the level of recall for the last word was .90. Then, R_{12} would equal .90, and SM is assumed to equal .10. When one solves the equation, one finds that PM_{12}, the probability that the 12th item can be retrieved from primary memory, equals approximately .89. To calculate the capacity of primary memory in this experiment, one would add together the probabilities that an item can be retrieved from primary memory across all the serial positions.

There is a problem with Waugh and Norman's (1965) method, as was pointed out by Watkins (1974). The method does not take into account the phenomenon of negative recency effects. That is, it assumes that the probability of recall of midlist items can be used to estimate the probability of recalling the last few items from secondary memory. However, Craik's (1970) finding of negative recency effects implies that the last few items have a lower probability of being recalled from secondary memory than do midlist items. Several authors have suggested corrections to account for this (Raaijmakers, 1982; Watkins, 1974, 1979). These corrections are notable chiefly for their complexity and never became widely used.

Some different approaches to measuring primary-memory capacity have been proposed (Murdock, 1967; Raymond, 1969; Tulving & Colotla, 1970). All of the methods tend to give similar estimates for the average capacity of primary memory (usually between two and four items). At one time, it would have been considered worthwhile to spend time trying to decide which method is the most satisfactory way of estimating primary-memory capacity from the serial-position curve. However, more recent findings suggest that the entire two-store approach is an inadequate way to explain serial-position effects.

Immediate-Recall Findings Troublesome for Two-Store Accounts

The two-store approach offers a satisfactory account for most of the research concerning serial-position effects in immediate free recall. However, there have been several findings here that appear inconsistent with this approach.

Effects of Concurrent Distraction. As has been noted, the recency effect can be eliminated if a challenging distractor task is given after presentation of the list (Glanzer & Cunitz, 1966; Postman & Phillips, 1965). This finding makes sense from the two-store account because the distractor task should prevent the subject from maintaining the last few items in primary memory. However, a two-store account would seem to predict that a concurrent distractor activity (a task that subjects perform while receiving the list items) should show the same pattern. This prediction has been falsified (Baddeley & Hitch, 1977; Murdock, 1965; Shiffrin, 1970).

For example, Murdock (1965) required subjects to sort a deck of cards while they were hearing a list of words for immediate free recall. Murdock varied the difficulty of this sorting task. This difficulty manipulation significantly affected recall of early items but had no influence on the magnitude of the recency effect. This finding is challenging to two-store accounts because a more difficult distractor task should occupy more of primary memory than an easy task and should therefore reduce the recency effect. Similarly, Baddeley and Hitch (1977) showed that recall of early items was impaired by requiring subjects to copy digits while they were seeing a list of to-be-recalled words. However, the recency effect was again not influenced by this manipulation, a puzzling finding for two-store theorists.

Recall of Multicategory Lists. Watkins and Peynircioglu (1983) gave subjects a 45-item list that contained three sublists of 15 items each. For example, the three sublists might be riddles, objects, and sounds. The three sublists alternated throughout the list. Subjects were then asked for immediate free recall but were cued to recall particular sublists first, second, or third. Recall for each of the three sublists showed a recency effect that was as large as would have been found if that sublist had been presented alone. Two-store accounts would have trouble explaining this finding without making the strange assumption that the capacity of primary memory somehow becomes enlarged in this situation.

Results from concurrent-distraction studies and multicategory-list studies suggest that the recency effect in immediate free recall might be based on a memory store that was not as clearly limited in capacity as two-store theorists believed primary memory to be. Further support for this idea came from studies of delayed recall, where long-term recency effects were found in situations that could not have involved primary memory at all.

LONG-TERM RECENCY EFFECTS

The Continuous-Distractor Paradigm

As we have mentioned, one variable that selectively influences recall of the last few items on a list is the insertion of a distractor activity after the last item but before the signal to begin recall. The fact that this distractor activity eliminates the recency effect (Glanzer & Cunitz, 1966; Postman & Phillips, 1965) was seen as strong evidence for a two-store account because the distractor activity would presumably occupy primary memory and force the subject to rely entirely on secondary memory for recall of the list items.

However, this interpretation was seriously challenged by surprising and important results reported by Bjork and Whitten (1974; see also Tzeng, 1973). These authors used a procedure (usually known as the *continuous-distractor paradigm*) in which the presentation of each word (or pair of words, in some experiments) was preceded by a short period of distractor activity. The last item was followed by another period of distractor activity, which by itself would have eliminated the recency effect if a conventional method of presentation had been used. When Bjork and Whitten asked their subjects for free recall, a significant positive recency effect was obtained. In short, if a distractor activity occurs only after the last item, the recency effect is eliminated; if a distractor activity occurs throughout the list, as well as after the last item, recency effects are found. This latter finding is inconsistent with primary-memory accounts of recency effects in that the distractor activity after the last item should have occupied primary memory. The advantage of the last item in the continuous-distractor paradigm has often been called the *long-term recency effect.* The finding of recency effects in delayed recall in the continuous-distractor paradigm has been replicated many times. It has been shown using different kinds of to-be-remembered material and different kinds of distractor task. Also, it can be shown to occur when subjects are told to begin recall at a particular place on the list (Whitten, 1978). The replicability of this finding is therefore no longer an empirical question.

The Ratio Rule. Bjork and Whitten (1974), along with subsequent authors (Glenberg et al., 1980; Glenberg, Bradley, Kraus, & Renzaglia, 1983) have noted that the magnitude of recency effects in free recall can be described as resulting from a basic principle, the *ratio rule.* All other things being equal, the magnitude of the recency effect will be a positive function of the ratio of the duration of the interpresentation intervals (the distractor intervals between items) to the duration of the retention interval (the distractor interval after the last item). When this ratio is not much below 1.0, positive recency effects will be found. In immediate recall, where the interpresentation and retention intervals are negligible, recency effects are present. If a long-filled retention interval is inserted after the last item, the ratio drops, and recency effects are eliminated. However, if long interpresentation intervals are inserted (as was done by Bjork & Whitten), the ratio approaches 1.0 again, and recency effects are once again found.

Manipulations of interpresentation and retention intervals have usually been on the order of seconds. Glenberg et al. (1983) extended this principle to much longer time periods. In one experiment, they used a retention interval of 40 min and interpresentation intervals of either 5 or 20 min. The recency effect was significantly greater when the longer interpresentation interval was used. Even more strikingly, Glenberg et al. performed another experiment where the retention interval was either 1 day or 14 days and the interpresentation intervals were either 1 day or 7 days. The recency effect was shown to be a function of the ratio rule; it increased when the longer interpresentation interval was used, and it decreased when the longer retention interval was used. This is striking confirmation of the generalizability of this rule.

Dissociations Between Prerecency and Recency Recall. The main evidence that had been used to argue for a two-store account of serial-position effects in immediate recall was that many variables had different effects on the recency and prerecency parts of the serial-position curve. Could a similar pattern be found in the continuous-distractor paradigm even though it appears doubtful that primary memory could be used here?

One variable that had been shown to affect only prerecency items in immediate free recall was word frequency (Raymond, 1969; Sumby, 1963). Greene (1986a) performed an experiment to see whether word frequency would have a similar effect in the continuous-distractor paradigm. Each subject received 12 lists, with each list having a 20-s filled interpresentation interval before each item and a 20-s retention interval after the last item. Half of the lists contained words commonly used in everyday English. The other lists contained rare words. Word frequency had a large effect at every position until the end of the list. At the last position, there was absolutely no effect of word frequency. Thus, word frequency shows exactly the same pattern in the continuous-distractor paradigm that it shows in immediate recall.

Word frequency is not the only such variable. For example, list length influences recall of prerecency items but not recency items in both immediate free recall (Lewis-Smith, 1975; Murdock, 1962; Postman & Phillips, 1965) and in the continuous-distractor paradigm (Greene, 1986a). Also, the semantic similarity of the list items to each other has no effect on recall of the last few items although it has a big effect on earlier items; this pattern is found in both immediate free recall (Craik & Levy, 1970) and in the continuous-distractor paradigm (Greene & Crowder, 1984a).

There are two important conclusions to be drawn here. The first is that these findings make it seem likely that recency effects in immediate recall and in the continuous-distractor paradigm have a common basis. Since the serial-position curves in these two tasks are influenced similarly by many variables, it is reasonable to conclude that similar processes underlie the serial-position effects found there. The second conclusion is that finding variables that have different effects on prerecency and recency recall does not imply that two different memory stores are used. Rather, it only means that subjects do not use exactly the same processes to recall prerecency and recency items. The different processes involved in recall of prerecency and recency items may be different memory stores. However, they may also be different encoding or retrieval processes.

The Habituation Hypothesis. On the surface, the finding of recency effects in the continuous-distractor paradigm seems inconsistent with the claim that recency effects are due to primary memory. However, proponents of a two-store account have not given up that easily. They have tried to reconcile the two-store approach with the continuous-distractor approach. The most common way to do this has been to argue that primary memory may still make a contribution to recall in the continuous-distractor paradigm because the distractor activity occurring after the last item may not have been sufficient to occupy all of primary memory. The clearest statement of this approach has been made by Koppenaal and Glanzer (1990; for similar viewpoints, see Nakajima & Sato, 1989; Poltrock & MacLeod, 1977). Koppenaal and Glanzer proposed a habituation account for the long-term recency effect. They argued that, when subjects have to perform a distractor activity after every item, they become habituated to it. That is, subjects become so used to doing the task that it does not demand their full attention anymore. Instead, their minds wander to the last few list items. Subjects thus rehearse the list items while they are performing the distractor activity and are able to maintain the last item or two in primary memory during the retention interval. Because this habituation to the distractor task will occur more rapidly if subjects are doing it after every item (as in the continuous-distractor paradigm) than if they are only doing it after the last item, it is possible for a distractor task to eliminate the recency effect completely if it is presented only after the last item but to be much less effective if it is presented throughout the list. Koppenaal and Glanzer report one striking piece in support of this hypothesis: Recency effects are not found in the continuous-distractor paradigm if the experimenter occupies the retention interval with a distractor task that is different than the one used to fill the interpresentation intervals. (A similar finding was reported independently by Nakajima & Sato, 1989).

On balance, however, there is considerable evidence that recency effects in the continuous-distractor paradigm are not due to primary memory. One relevant finding is that the magnitude of the long-term recency effect seems to be about equal for incidentally and intentionally learned lists (Glenberg et al., 1980). When subjects learned the list incidentally, they did not know that they would be tested on the items and thus had no reason to attempt to rehearse or maintain them during the filled retention interval. To explain this finding, Koppenaal and Glanzer (1990) would have to assume that subjects devote about as much covert rehearsal to the last few items when they are not expecting a test as when they do expect to be tested. This would appear unlikely.

A second piece of evidence against the claim that storage of items in primary memory could account for recency effects in the continuous-distractor paradigm comes from manipulations of the difficulty of the distractor task. Glenberg et al. (1980) showed that, as the difficulty of the distractor task used to occupy the interpresentation and retention intervals was increased, recall of early list items was significantly impaired. However, recall of the last few items was not affected. If a habituation account were correct, an easier task should require less capacity in primary memory and should show a larger recency effect. This pattern was not found, which is inconsistent with Koppenaal and Glanzer's (1990) approach.

A third piece of evidence against this approach comes from an experiment by Glenberg et al. (1983). In this experiment, subjects first saw and recalled two lists presented in continuous-distractor format; recall of these lists exhibited a clear recency effect. (According to Koppenaal & Glanzer, 1990, this would mean that subjects had habituated to the distractor task.) Then, Glenberg et al. (1983) presented another list. On this list, there were no filled interpresentation intervals (that is, the words were presented one right after another). There was a retention interval filled with the same distractor task that had been used in the first two lists. However, when subjects recalled the items on the third list, there was no recency effect. This presents a serious problem for the habituation account: If subjects had habituated to the distractor task on the first two lists, one would have thought that this would extend to the third one, leading to a recency effect there as well. To explain the absence of a recency effect on the third list, Koppenaal and Glanzer would be forced to assume that the effects of habituation disappear entirely after each list, a rather unlikely assumption.

In all, there is considerable evidence that recency effects in the continuous-distractor paradigm are not due to storage in primary memory. Since it also appears likely that recency effects in immediate recall and in the continuous-distractor paradigm have a common basis, this suggests that recency effects in immediate recall are not due to primary memory either.

Ordinal/Contextual Theories of the Recency Effect

If the recency effect in the continuous-distractor paradigm is not due to storage in primary memory, how are we to explain it? Bjork and Whitten (1974) assumed that the distinctiveness of a trace in memory determines in part how easily it can be retrieved. Recency effects can then be interpreted as resulting from the differential distinctiveness of the positions on a list. In particular, positions at the end of a list are more distinctive than those in the middle, thus leading to improved recall of the last few items. This differential distinctiveness helps recall only when the items constitute a well-ordered series, that is, when each item is coded in memory in terms of its relative or absolute position. If there is little or no order information remaining in memory, recency effects will not be found.

According to Bjork and Whitten (1974), the probability that the order of memories would be discriminable depends on two factors: The separation in time between the memories and the age of the newer memory. Crowder (1976) suggested an analogy to spatial perspective: When one is riding on a train and passing telephone poles, the distance between the observer and poles will affect how distinct each one seems. When the distance from the observer to the last pole is kept constant, the distinctiveness of the poles will be a function of the distance between them. Bjork and Whitten argued that the continuous-distractor paradigm keeps items separated, thus making their ordering distinct for a longer time and leading to a recency effect. If the retention interval is made very long, relative to the interpresentation intervals, the recency effect is eliminated because the ordering of the items will no longer be distinct in memory.

Bjork and Whitten's (1974) account was very abstract. Glenberg and his associates (Glenberg et al., 1980, 1983; Glenberg & Kraus, 1981) proposed a similar theory that was more concrete. Glenberg assumed that the psychological context in which the list was learned was composed of a number of separate, fluctuating elements. Each item on the list becomes associated with some elements in the context when that item was presented. Contextual elements are always changing, but not all elements change at the same rate. At recall, subjects use the test context to help retrieve the list items. Because contexts in laboratory situations tend to change gradually over time, the more recently an item was presented, the more similar its presentation context would be to the test context. This would make the test context a particularly effective retrieval cue for the last item.

A recency effect is a relative phenomenon; it consists of how well people do on the last item relative to how well they do on the other items. By Glenberg's theory, the magnitude of the recency effect will depend on how effective the test context is as a retrieval cue for the last item relative to how effective it is for other items. How effective the test context will be for the last item is largely a function of the retention interval; the longer the retention interval, the more time there is for contextual change to occur and the less effective the test context will be as a retrieval cue for the last item. How effective the test context will be as a cue for the other items depends in part on the length of the interpresentation intervals. When these intervals are long, each item would have been learned against a very different context, and the advantage at the last item would be much more striking. This increased recency effect as a function of the duration of the interpresentation intervals would be due both to the fact that the test context would be an ineffective retrieval cue for preterminal items and by reduced interference (or cue overload) in using the test context to retrieve the last item.

Glenberg and his associates have emphasized the differences between their contextually guided retrieval hypothesis and the well-ordered series account of Bjork and Whitten (1974). However, these theories are very similar and would be hard to choose between. Both see recency effects as resulting not from storage in primary memory but rather from a retrieval strategy in which the retrieval cues are more effective for the last item than for the earlier ones. They differ in the kind of retrieval information that they believe is used (ordinal or contextual). However, because both context and order necessarily change as a function of time, they are closely related. Moreover, there is evidence that ordinal information is represented in memory in terms of context (Hintzman, Block, & Summers, 1973). Associations are formed between list items and contextual elements, and these associations are then used to "date" the items. If this suggestion is true, then ordinal and contextual approaches would necessarily be indistinguishable.

An important point to keep in mind is that these accounts do not claim that only ordinal or contextual information is used in retrieval. Other sorts of information, such as interitem associations are also used, especially for early items. Ordinal and contextual cues are just one kind of information used during retrieval. These cues are principally used to retrieve the last few items, both because they are more effective there than for earlier items and also because subjects are unlikely to have rehearsed the last few items enough to establish other effective retrieval cues. Thus, these accounts necessarily assume that at least two retrieval processes are employed in recall. They would therefore be able to explain why factors such as word frequency, list length, and semantic similarity affect recall only for early items on a list. These factors presumably do not affect subjects' ability to use ordinal or contextual cues in retrieval. However, they do influence whether subjects are able to use other sorts of retrieval information, such as interitem associations. Since ordinal or contextual cues are used to retrieve the last few items and other information is used to retrieve earlier items, one would expect factors such as word frequency, list length, and semantic similarity to influence recall only for prerecency items.

These ordinal/contextual accounts also have no difficulty explaining why negative recency effects may be found in final free recall (Craik, 1970). The last few items receive less rehearsal and processing time than other items (Rundus, 1971). This would make it difficult to retrieve them using interitem associations and other cues dependent on rehearsal. This would not matter in immediate free recall because subjects would be able to use ordinal or contextual cues to retrieve the last few items. However, in a final free-recall test, which necessarily has a much longer retention interval than the immediate test, these ordinal and contextual cues would no longer be very effective. This could lead to poor recall of the last few items. An additional factor may be that subjects are able to use the same retrieval strategy for prerecency items on immediate and final recall tests. However, since contextual and ordinal cues would be effective on the immediate but not the delayed test, subjects have to change retrieval strategies for recency items (Marmurek, 1983). This might disrupt recall.

Other Recency Effects in Long-Term Recall

If the only time that recency effects were ever found in delayed recall was in the narrow conditions of the continuous-distractor paradigm, then the findings of Bjork and Whitten (1974) might be dismissed as an isolated curiosity. However, recency effects can also be demonstrated in delayed recall in other sorts of experiments.

Baddeley and Hitch (1977) presented subjects with a series of 12 four-letter anagrams. Each subject was allowed up to 30 s to solve each anagram. After 12 anagrams had been presented, the subject was asked to count backwards for either 10 or 30 s. The subject was then instructed to recall the anagram solutions. Because the test was unexpected, subjects had no reason to try to maintain the anagram solutions in primary memory. Moreover, counting backwards should have been an effective distractor task and fully occupied primary memory. Still, large recency effects were found in this experiment.

Rundus (1980) found strong recency effects in an experiment on maintenance rehearsal using the distractor-recall paradigm (Glenberg, Smith, & Green, 1977; Rundus, 1977). In this paradigm, subjects are told that they are in an experiment on short-term recall of numbers. They are shown a multidigit number at the beginning of a trial. Then, a pair of words is shown, and subjects have to rehearse the words aloud for a certain period of time before recalling the number. After many such trials, the experimenter gives an unexpected recall test for the words. Rundus found a clear recency effect in this paradigm, even though retrieval of the words from primary memory could not be responsible.

Baddeley and Hitch (1977) studied recency effects in an everyday setting. They took players from a rugby team and asked them for free recall of the teams that they had played that season. A recency effect was found, with subjects being most likely to recall their most recent opponents. In addition, Baddeley and Hitch found evidence that the number of interpolated games was the crucial factor determining recall; when this was controlled, the amount of elapsed time since a game was played had little effect.

Bjork and Whitten (1974) pointed out another situation in which recency effects occur in delayed recall. When subjects learn and recall a number of different lists and, at the end of the experiment, are given an unexpected final-recall test in which they have to recall items from all of the lists, subjects show a list-recency effect: They recall more words from the most recent list than words from earlier lists.

Studies of long-term recency effects in the continuous-distractor paradigm had found that it was essential that items be separated (through use of long interpresentation intervals) for recency effects to be found. All of the experiments in this section also involved separation of the items. The anagrams in Baddeley and Hitch's (1977) anagram experiment were separated by the long solution times. In Rundus's (1980) experiment, the words were separated by the recall intervals for the digits. The rugby players studied by Baddeley and Hitch (1977) had their games separated by several days. In Bjork and Whitten's (1974) study of list-recency effects, the presentations of the lists were separated by recall intervals. Moreover, because all of these studies involved unexpected recall tests, subjects presumably did not try to engage in cumulative rehearsal, which would also help to keep the items separated. The recency effects discussed in this section could not be explained by primary-memory accounts but are predicted by theories that emphasize the temporal or contextual separation of the items.

CONCLUSIONS

A two-store account of memory strikes most people as very reasonable. Subjectively, we feel that there is a big difference between our ability to deal with information we are currently thinking about and our ability to retrieve information that perhaps we haven't recalled in years. This division of memory was believed to be captured by the serial-position curve in immediate free recall, with recall of early items being dependent on retrieval from permanent long-term storage (secondary memory) and recall of the last few items being easily retrieved from a limited-capacity short-term system (primary memory).

However attractive one may find this two-store approach, we now know that it is not satisfactory as an explanation for the serial-position curve. The recency effect seems to be due not to primary memory but rather to the greater retrievability of the last few items from long-term memory. As Crowder (1982a) has pointed out, this leaves us in a position where there is little or no evidence for separate short-term and long-term memory stores at all.

Two-store theories necessarily imply that recency effects have little relevance to forgetting processes over longer intervals. However, one of the most fundamental aspects of everyday memory is that forgetting accumulates over time, so that people remember more recent events better than older events. If recency effects in laboratory list-recall experiments are indeed due to retrieval processes from long-term storage, one may see the serial-position curve as just one more example of the inevitable deterioration of memory over time.

CHAPTER FOUR

Distraction and Forgetting: The Brown–Peterson Paradigm

All of us have been faced with situations when a momentary distraction caused us to forget information with amazing rapidity. We look up a number in the telephone book but are interrupted before we can dial it; we then find we have to look up the number again. Or we are introduced to a person and, after a little conversation, find that we have forgotten that person's name already. What these two examples have in common is that they show that even a small amount of information may be quickly forgotten if some sort of distraction occurs.

The role of distraction in forgetting was obvious enough to merit study by early researchers interested in memory. For example, W. G. Smith (1895) had subjects begin counting aloud. When the subject was fully engaged in the task, a matrix of 12 letters (4 letters in each of 3 rows) was shown. The subject had to keep on counting while the display was shown and for an additional 2 s after it was removed. Then, the experimenter requested recall of the letters. Recall was quite poor. A similar study was performed by T. L. Smith (1896), who found substantial forgetting of lists of 10 syllables when subjects were engaged in a counting task. In both of these experiments, the poor recall was presumably due to both the overloading of memory by a long list and by the distracting effect of the counting task.

Daniels (1895) made two important contributions to the study of forgetting. The first was the use of a very small set of to-be-remembered items: On each trial, subjects were required to retain three digits, an amount of information that would be recalled perfectly in the absence of distraction. Daniels also studied the time course of forgetting: Recall was requested either 0, 5, 10, 15, or 20 s after presentation of the digits. In this study, subjects were required to read an interesting story aloud. At some point, the experimenter would say three digits while the subject continued to read aloud. When the subject recalled the digits immediately after they were presented, 76% of the digits were correctly recalled. The fact that performance was not perfect suggests that subjects had trouble correctly hearing the digits as they were reading the story aloud. Much more important, however, were the effects of delay. As recall was delayed 5, 10, 15, or 20 s performance dropped to 38%, 15%, 6%, and 4%. Even very small amounts of information may be forgotten quickly if a subject is involved in a distracting task.

THE WORK OF BROWN AND OF PETERSON AND PETERSON

The work of Daniels (1895), W. G. Smith (1895), and T. L. Smith (1896) was unfortunately forgotten as the experimental study of memory grew. However, the effects of distraction were rediscovered by Brown (1958) in England and by Peterson and Peterson (1959) in the United States. These investigators developed a technique that became quite common in memory research. This technique is sometimes called the *distractor paradigm.* More commonly, however, it is referred to as the *Brown–Peterson paradigm,* in honor of its rediscoverers.

Brown (1958) showed subjects a set of one to four consonants that they were required to read aloud. Immediately after presentation of the consonants, a set of five pairs of digits was shown, and subjects had to read these aloud as well. Then, the experimenter requested recall of the consonants. Subjects' memory for the consonants was quite poor, especially when more than one or two consonants had to be remembered. Brown went on to show that recall could be improved by inserting an unfilled delay between the presentation of the to-be-remembered consonants and the distractor digits. Thus, allowing subjects to rehearse the consonants before the beginning of the distractor task reduces the vulnerability of the stimuli to forgetting.

Peterson and Peterson (1959) explored the time course of forgetting under conditions of distraction. In their study, the experimental session began when the subject was informed "You will not be shocked during this experiment" (p. 194) (which serves as a pretty good indication of what other kinds of research were being conducted at the time!). Each subject was seated in front of a black box with a green light. The experimenter read three consonants and a three-digit number, and the subject was required to begin counting backward by threes from that number until a red light appeared on the black box. The subject then attempted to recall the consonants. In all, each subject went through two practice trials and then 48 test trials. On equal numbers of test trials, subjects had to count backward for 3, 6, 9, 12, 15, or 18 s before recall of the consonants. The results are shown in Fig. 4.1. The major finding is the rapid drop in performance as a function of retention interval; even small amounts of information could be forgotten rapidly when subjects are engaged in a distracting activity. Like Brown (1958), Peterson and Peterson also inserted a rehearsal interval between presentation of the to-be-remembered letters and the beginning of the distractor task. Peterson and Peterson, like Brown, found that adding this rehearsal interval improved performance. However, since Peterson and Peterson also manipulated the length of the retention interval, they were able to show that allowing rehearsal did not affect the *rate* of forgetting. That is, rehearsal did not affect the slope of the forgetting function shown in Fig. 4.1. Rather, it affected only the asymptote, the point at which the curve finally flattens out. Similar findings were later reported by Hellyer (1962) and Fuchs and Melton (1974).

Are there any variables that do affect the slope of the forgetting function? Murdock (1961) showed that one such variable is the amount of information that subjects have to remember. When subjects were required to remember only one item, the rate of forgetting was less and the eventual asymptote higher than when recall of three items was required. Interestingly, there was no difference between recall of three consonants

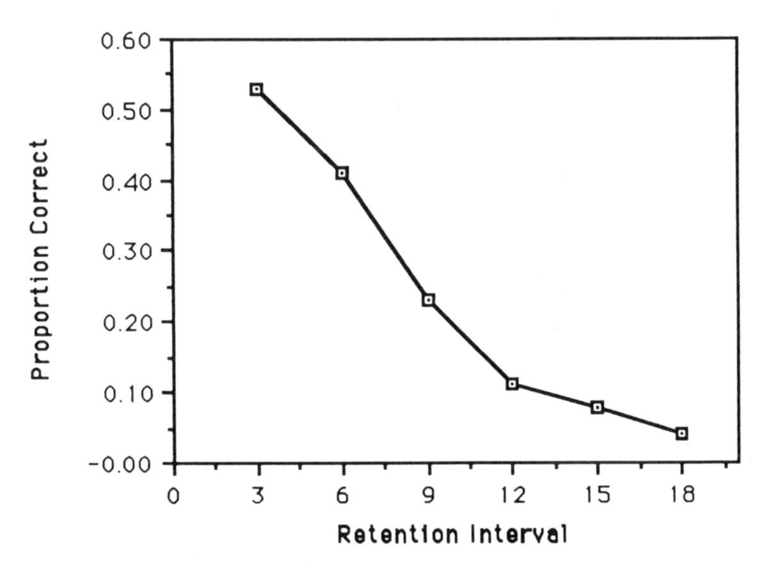

FIG. 4.1. Proportion recalled after a filled retention interval. From Peterson and Peterson, 1959. Reprinted by permission.

and recall of three words. The critical factor influencing memory is the number of units or chunks that are formed by the subject.

Decay Theory

How should one interpret these data? Brown (1958) and Peterson and Peterson (1959) agreed that their experiments represented evidence for a *decay* process in human memory. By "decay," we are referring to a forgetting process that happens simply as a result of the passage of time. According to Brown and Peterson and Peterson, the occurrence of a list of items leads to the creation of a memory trace. This memory trace then begins to fade away as soon as it is formed. However, it is possible to postpone the onset of this decay process by rehearsing the items. If rehearsal is prevented by requiring subjects to perform a demanding distractor task, the memory trace decays. The rate of this decay process is equivalent to the slope of the forgetting function, such as the one in Fig. 4.1. When recall drops to asymptote, the decay process is apparently complete.

Another complication has to be added, however. Even after a very long distractor task, it is rare that the asymptote of the forgetting function bottoms out at exactly zero. Rather, subjects usually have a small but nonzero probability of recalling the items. Thus, there must be two possible sources of information in memory for the items. The first source is very accurate but decays quickly in the absence of rehearsal. The second source is more permanent but allows for a lesser probability of recall. One could identify the first source as Waugh and Norman's (1965) *primary memory* (or short-term memory store) and the second source as *secondary memory* (or long-term memory store). According to this conception, as long as information is in primary memory, probability of recall is quite high. However, information would be forgotten from primary memory quickly unless it is rehearsed. Even after the information has been lost from primary memory, there is always a possibility that it had already been transferred into secondary memory. However, retrieval from secondary memory is much more difficult than retrieval from primary memory, so the level of recall is much lower. It is often assumed that rehearsal of information in primary memory increases the probability that it will be stored in secondary memory. This would explain why Peterson and Peterson (1959) and others found that allowing rehearsal of the items before the distracting activity leads to an increase in the asymptotic level of recall. This rehearsal would have increased the likelihood that the stimuli would have been transferred from primary to secondary memory and thus improved the probability that the items would be retrievable from secondary memory. Asymptotic level of recall would be a pure measure of the contribution of secondary memory to this task.

NATURE OF THE DISTRACTOR TASK

The primary purpose of the distractor task is to prevent rehearsal. Therefore, one of the most important properties of the distractor is its difficulty. A more challenging task should be more effective at eliminating rehearsal than a less challenging one. Indeed, it has been shown that more difficult distractor tasks lead to more rapid loss than easier ones (e.g., Kroll & Kellicutt, 1972; Nakajima & Sato, 1989).

Another aspect of the distractor task that has been examined is its similarity to the to-be-remembered items. Brown (1958) was the first researcher to manipulate this factor. He required subjects to recall a list of consonants and had a reading-aloud task as his distractor. He found that it made little difference whether the distractor materials were consonants (like the to-be-remembered material) or digits. However, later investigators have generally not reached the same conclusion but have instead found that a distractor task leads to more forgetting if it involves processing of stimuli that are similar to the to-be-remembered items (Corman & Wickens, 1968; Wickelgren, 1965).

Similarity is particularly important when sensory modality is manipulated. A distractor task is much more effective if it presented in the same modality (visual or auditory) as the list items (Elliott & Strawhorn, 1976; Proctor & Fagnani, 1978). One possible explanation for these data is that a distractor task is more effective at eliminating rehearsal if it is in the same modality as the list items. This can be illustrated by a study by Pellegrino, Siegel, and Dhawan (1976). Subjects received either triads of words or triads of pictures as to-be-remembered material. When an auditory verbal distractor task was used, recall of pictures was much higher than recall of words. When the distractor task involved visual processing, this advantage for pictures was eliminated. Presumably, when subjects are trying to remember words, they rely on verbal rehearsal, and this process is particularly impaired by having to perform an auditory task. When subjects are trying to retain pictures, they may rely on visual, pictorial rehearsal (Watkins, Peynircioglu, & Brems, 1984), and this form of rehearsal may be impaired by processing visual distractor stimuli. At least in the case where similarity of the distractor task and to-be-remembered material is manipulated using presentation modality, the effects may be explained in terms of how effective the task is in disrupting rehearsal.

Since the rate of forgetting in this task is partly a function of the similarity of the distractor task to the to-be-remembered items, some researchers have tried to discover what happens when the two are as dissimilar as possible. Reitman (1971) had subjects remember a list of three words and used a nonverbal tone detection task as a distractor. She found that word recall was still perfect after a 15-s distractor interval, suggesting that there is little memory loss when a nonverbal distractor task is used. However, Reitman (1974) later showed that there was a significant amount of forgetting after 15 s of nonverbal distraction when a five-word list was presented on each trial.

CHALLENGES TO THE DECAY ACCOUNT

Brown (1958) and Peterson and Peterson (1959) saw their task as a measure of a gradual decay process in which information is forgotten over the course of 15–20 s. However, there are several challenges to this interpretation. One challenge is to their estimation of how quickly information is forgotten here: The forgetting process may be much more rapid than Brown and the Petersons believed. A second challenge is to the cause of this forgetting. Decay may not be occurring in this task at all.

Very Rapid Forgetting in the Brown–Peterson Task

Muter (1980) argued that there had been no satisfactory estimate for the rate of forgetting in the Brown–Peterson task. Subjects know that they will have to remember the list of items. Therefore, they would be motivated to try to engage in covert rehearsal while performing the distractor task. Also, they may try to employ a mnemonic strategy to form a more lasting memory trace for the items as they are being presented. Muter argued that, if one wanted to derive a pure estimate for the forgetting rate in this task, one would have to arrange the experiment so that subjects were not expecting a test.

Muter (1980) devised an experiment where subjects knew that it was unlikely that they would have to recall the items. On each trial, subjects would see a set of three letters and then a set of three digits. Subjects were required to count backward by threes aloud from that three-digit number. On 98% of the trials, subjects were *not* required to recall the letters after the period of counting backward was completed. However, on 2% of the trials, recall of the letters was required. Since recall of the letters happened so infrequently after the counting task, subjects presumably had little reason to engage in covert rehearsal or fancy mnemonic strategies. On those rare occasions where recall of the letters was tested, performance was surprisingly poor. After as little as 2 s of counting backward, the proportion of letters recalled was already below 10%. Muter concluded that, in a situation where subjects did not anticipate a test, forgetting happened far more rapidly in this task than theorists had previously believed.

Sebrechts, Marsh, and Seamon (1989) replicated these results and extended them by manipulating the type of processing that subjects had to perform on the list items. Sebrechts et al. used a set of three words as their to-be-remembered stimuli on each trial. In one condition, subjects had to perform a semantic orienting task on each trial; they had to indicate whether each word was animate or inanimate. In a second condition, subjects had to perform an acoustic orienting task, namely, to indicate whether there was a long "e" sound present in each word. In a third condition, subjects merely had to read each word aloud. After completion of this orienting task, a three-digit number appeared, and subjects had to count backward by threes for a period of varying length. Usually, the trial ended after the period of counting backward was completed. However, on a few trials, recall of the words was requested. Recall was affected by the task that subjects had had to perform on the words; memory was best for the words only read aloud, followed by the semantic orienting task, and then the acoustic orienting task. (This ordering possibly reflects the difficulty of the tasks; an easy task, such as reading the words aloud, may allow subjects to allocate more resources to forming a complete representation of the words in memory.) More importantly, there was tremendous forgetting of the three words in as few as 2 or 4 s. When performance was scored on the basis of whether the three words on a trial were recalled in the right order, performance was zero in all three conditions after 4 s of distraction. Thus, very rapid forgetting of stimuli in this task occurs for stimuli processed in a variety of ways.

The significance of the Muter (1980) and Sebrechts et al. (1989) findings lies in their challenging of the rate of forgetting. Whereas Brown (1958) and Peterson and Peterson (1959) assumed that forgetting was occurring over 15–20 s, Muter and Sebrechts et al. showed that, when subjects were placed in a situation that minimized the possibility of their performing covert rehearsal or mnemonic strategies, massive forgetting occurred in the first few seconds after stimulus presentation. These studies only challenged assumptions about the rate of forgetting. They did not call into question the cause of forgetting here, which Brown and the Petersons believed to be decay. However, there are other studies that challenge whether decay is occurring here at all.

Proactive Interference in the Brown-Peterson Paradigm

Before Brown (1958) and Peterson and Peterson (1959) reported their findings, memory theorists had hesitated to give decay a role in forgetting. Instead, the mechanism most often used to explain forgetting was *interference:* Memories that are similar to each other somehow interfere with each other and thereby lead to forgetting. The exact processes through which interference operates in forgetting were controversial. (Some of these controversies are reviewed in chap. 8.) However, the fact that interference plays an important role in forgetting has been documented empirically since the late-19th century.

There are two classes of interference. The first is *retroactive interference* (also called *retroactive inhibition*). Here, memory for an event may be impaired by similar, later events. The second is *proactive interference* (or *proactive inhibition*), where memory for an event is forgotten as a function of interference from similar, earlier memories. Brown (1958) and the Petersons (1959) had designed their experiments so that retroactive interference was unlikely to play a major role there. They made sure that only the distractor task intervened between presentation of the list and recall and that the distractor task involved stimuli so dissimilar from the list items that they were unlikely to interfere with each other. Could proactive interference be happening? This could occur if memory for early trials is somehow interfering with memory on later trials. One way to determine if proactive interference is occurring is to see whether performance becomes worse as subjects go through more trials. The Petersons checked for this and found little evidence that proactive interference was occurring. However, they had always included several unscored practice trials at the start of their experiments. If proactive interference developed rapidly, its effects might be obvious only if the very first few trials are included.

In a classic experiment, Keppel and Underwood (1962) showed that proactive interference was indeed occurring in the Brown-Peterson task. They tested subjects on only six trials and (unlike the Petersons), they scored performance on all trials, including the first few. On each trial, subjects had to recall a set of three consonants after a distractor interval filled with counting backward by threes. The distractor interval could be 3, 9, or 18 s long. The results are shown in Fig. 4.2. First note that there is clear evidence for proactive interference. If one took the average of the retention intervals at each trial, one would see that performance dropped as a function of trial number. Also note that, on the first trial, it made no difference whether the distractor interval was 3, 9, or 18 s; performance was almost perfect no matter how long the retention

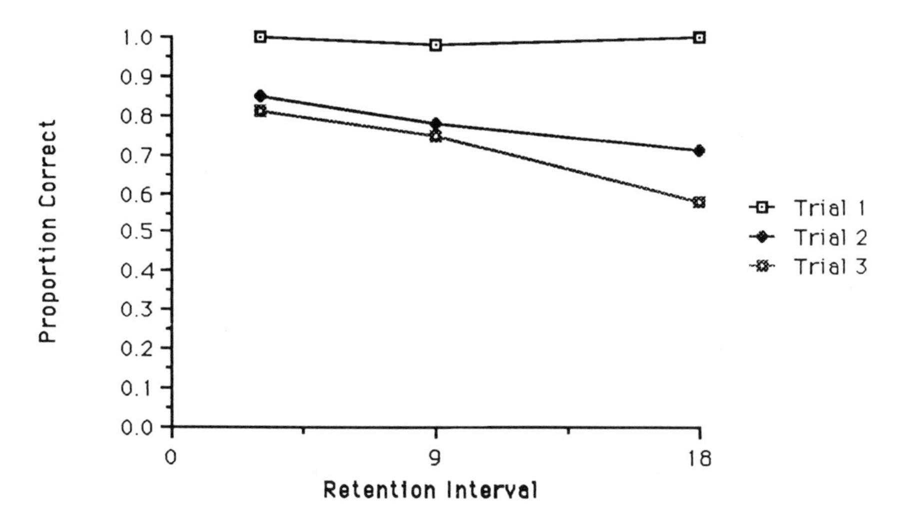

FIG. 4.2. Proportion recalled as a function of retention interval and trial number. From Keppel and Underwood, 1962. Reprinted by permission.

interval was. It was only on later trials that there began to be an advantage for the condition with the briefer distractor intervals. On the very first trial, there seemed to be no forgetting of the items during the distractor interval.

Forgetting on the First Trial. The first trial of a Brown-Peterson experiment is the only one in which it is likely that proactive interference cannot be happening. Therefore, if one wants to determine whether forgetting in this task occurs in the absence of proactive interference, one must pay particular attention to this trial.

Because this issue is so theoretically important, several authors have made a point of attempting to replicate Keppel and Underwood's (1962) results. Let us be clear about what is needed here. One must use lists that are short enough that performance on them is essentially perfect when there is no distraction; in practice, this means that lists of no more than three items must be used. Then, one must show that performance stays at this near-perfect level no matter how long a period of distractor activity is inserted before recall. There are one or more conditions in several experiments that show this pattern (Baddeley & Scott, 1971; Cofer & Davidson, 1968; Fuchs & Melton, 1974; Gorfein, 1987; Loess, 1964; Turvey, Brick, & Osborn, 1970; Wright, 1967). There are no reports of experiments where performance is near-perfect in immediate recall but drops when a period of distractor activity is inserted before recall on the first trial. Thus, one can say that there is no forgetting on the first trial in a Brown–Peterson experiment.

Some authors have tried to extend this claim by using slightly longer lists, long enough so that immediate recall would not be perfect. Although the data here are not as clear as those that have been reviewed, there is still no *consistent* finding of a drop in recall as a function of the length of retention interval (Baddeley & Scott, 1971; Fuchs & Melton, 1974; Loess, 1964). After reviewing these data, Crowder (1989, p. 279) concluded that "first-trial forgetting is the exception rather than the rule."

A particularly interesting experiment was reported by Sebrechts et al. (1989). They used the Muter (1980) procedure where subjects do not anticipate recall of the list items and are therefore unlikely to engage in memorization or rehearsal of them. Sebrechts et al. only varied the distractor interval from 2 to 4 s. Although this is not a very wide manipulation, it is certainly possible to find significant differences between these intervals using the Muter procedure. However, the data reported by Sebrechts et al. do not suggest any differences between these two intervals when the very first list is given an unanticipated test. Thus, even when the Muter procedure is used, a technique that typically leads to very rapid forgetting, there is no evidence for forgetting on the first trial of the experiment.

What are the implications of all of these experiments? If forgetting in this paradigm is due to decay (as proposed by Brown, 1958, and Peterson & Peterson, 1959), then one should see as much forgetting on the 1st trial as on the 50th. There is no reason to believe that a decay process would only operate on later trials. However, this prediction has clearly been falsified. Thus, it is clear that proactive interference is responsible for forgetting in this paradigm. Each trial is being interfered with by earlier trials. Since these earlier lists are not being maintained by the person in short-term (or primary) memory, they must only be represented in long-term memory. Thus, the locus of interference in this paradigm must also be in long-term memory. Although many researchers saw the Brown–Peterson paradigm as being a measurement of a short-term memory store, it really appears to be measuring proactive interference in long-term memory.

Between-Subject Manipulation of Distractor Intervals. Peterson and Peterson (1959) set a precedent that has been followed by almost all of their successors. When they studied the effects of the duration of the distractor interval, they manipulated it in a within-subject fashion. That is, all subjects were exposed to trials of all interval lengths, with the different interval conditions being mixed together randomly. When this is done, one replicates the Petersons' finding of rapidly declining recall as the interval is lengthened. However, it is important to determine whether this finding is found only when the Petersons' design is used. One could use a between-subjects design, where each subject experiences trials of only one distractor length and different groups of subjects are tested at different intervals.

Turvey et al. (1970) performed an experiment in which, for the first four trials, a subject received only trials containing one duration for the distractor interval. Different groups underwent 5, 10, 15, 20, or 25 s of distraction on each trial. Turvey et al. found no significant effect of distractor duration on these four trials. For example, if one looks only at the two extreme intervals, the proportions of items recalled on the first trial were .87 for the 5-s distractor group and .95 for the 25-s distractor group. On the second trial, these proportions were .33 and .55. On the third trial, they were .30 and .30. On the fourth trial, the proportions were .28 and .33. Obviously, not only was there no significant effect of distractor duration but the differences tended to go in the unexpected direction, with longer distractor intervals leading to slightly better performance. If forgetting in this paradigm is defined as the loss of information as a function of the duration of distraction then forgetting can be said to occur only when distractor duration is manipulated in a within-subject fashion.

One should note that the finding described here of no forgetting on the first trial (Keppel & Underwood, 1962) can be considered a special case of the finding that distractor duration has no effect if is manipulated between subjects. On the very first trial, subjects would have experienced only one distractor duration and so an experiment cannot truly involve a within-subject manipulation until more than one trial has occurred. Moreover, both of these findings are clearly inconsistent with the claim that performance on this task reflects the operation of trace decay.

Similarity and Proactive Interference. Not all memories interfere with each other equally. Rather, two memories that are similar to each other will interfere with each other more than will two memories that are not as similar. If forgetting in the Brown-Peterson paradigm is really due entirely to proactive interference, one should be able to eliminate it entirely by presenting very dissimilar materials on different trials.

This was the logic used by Wickens, Born, and Allen (1963). One group of subjects received four trials where the to-be-remembered items were lists of three consonants. Performance dropped on each trial. Another group also received four trials. However, on the first three trials, the to-be-remembered list consisted of digits. On the fourth trial, these subjects had to remember a list of three consonants. On this fourth trial, performance was as good for this group as it had been on the first trial. This is commonly called *release from proactive interference* (or *release from*

PI) because changing the nature of the list results in an elimination of proactive interference.

Wickens and his collaborators carried out an extensive research program on release from proactive interference. Wickens conceived this as a way of determining how subjects encoded the materials. For example, if shifting from one class of stimuli to another (as in the Wickens et al., 1963, experiment) resulted in release from proactive interference, this would suggest that subjects had been using meaning to encode the stimuli. In general, Wickens (1972) found that changes in the meaning of the list items (such as from digits to letters or vice versa) resulted in the most complete release. Even more subtle changes in meaning (such as changing from words with a pleasant connotation to words with an unpleasant connotation) could result in partial release. In general, the amount of release from proactive interference that one finds when shifting semantic categories depends on how similar those categories are; more release is found when one switches from one category to a very dissimilar one than if the change is not as extreme. Syntactical changes (such as switching from verbs to nouns) or physical changes (such as changing the number of syllables) had only smaller effects. This suggests that subjects did not rely on syntactical or physical aspects as much as semantic properties when encoding stimuli. Bird and Campbell (1982) showed that they could manipulate the amount of release of proactive interference by directly manipulating how subjects encoded the items.

Release from Proactive Interference in Recall of More Realistic Materials. The Brown–Peterson paradigm in general (and release from proactive interference specifically) have generally been studied using artificial laboratory materials. However, it is possible to use materials in these experiments that more closely resemble the sorts of stimuli that people deal with in everyday life. For example, Gunter, Berry, and Clifford (1981) suggested that proactive interference may occur as viewers watch a television news show, which typically consists of a series of short items of news that may or may not be related. They devised an experiment where each trial consisted of the presentation of three news items by a newscaster, followed by a minute of a distractor activity (working on a crossword puzzle). After this distractor interval was completed, subjects tried to recall the news items. In all, each subject went through four trials. News items had been classified as either domestic stories or international (foreign) stories. On the first three trials, each subject received only domestic stories or international stories. Recall dropped as a function of trial number: It was best on the first trial, lower on the second trial, and lower still on the third. Some subjects received news items from the same category (domestic or international) on the fourth trial, and recall dropped again for these subjects. However, other subjects received news items from the other category on the fourth trial; that is, subjects who had received domestic news on the first three trials were given international news on the fourth trial, and vice versa. These subjects who had a shift in the category of the news items exhibited release from proactive interference: Their recall of the items on the fourth trial was almost as high as their recall of the items on the first trial had been.

A particularly interesting study was reported by Dempster (1985). On each trial in his study, subjects heard a sentence and were then required to count backward aloud by threes from a particular number for 15 s before attempting recall of the sentences. Each subject went through four trials. On the first three trials, recall dropped when the sentences on the trials dealt with identical or related topics. On the fourth trial, the topic was changed, and recall improved greatly. This is an example of release from proactive interference in sentence recall. Dempster went on to calculate correlations between the magnitude of the proactive interference exhibited by each subject on the first three trials with that subject's scores on the American College Test (ACT). Dempster found significant negative correlations: Those subjects with the best ACT scores tended to be least susceptible to proactive interference. The meaning of this provocative finding is not clear, but it does suggest that this paradigm might be a fruitful way to study individual differences in verbal ability.

THEORETICAL ACCOUNTS OF PROACTIVE INTERFERENCE IN THE BROWN-PETERSON TASK

Brown (1958) and Peterson and Peterson (1959) interpreted their findings as evidence for decay processes in human memory. Time has not been kind to this interpretation. The finding that there is little or no evidence for forgetting on the very first trial of a Brown-Peterson experiment is directly inconsistent with the decay theory, as is Turvey et al.'s (1970) finding that the duration of the distractor interval affects recall only if it is manipulated in a within-subject fashion. That performance drops as a function of the number of previous trials (proactive interference) and that this drop may be eliminated by manipulations of the similarity of the to-be-remembered material on a series of trials (release from proactive interference) suggest that there is no need to involve decay processes at all in our theoretical accounts. Instead, theories of forgetting in the Brown-Peterson paradigm must offer ways of explaining how proactive interference operates here. There have been several approaches that have been taken by theorists.

Unlearning and Spontaneous Recovery

Keppel and Underwood (1962), the first authors to demonstrate the role of proactive interference in the Brown-Peterson paradigm, were also the first to offer an explanation for it. They particularly relied on the concept of *unlearning*—that is, as people try to learn new things and form new associations, they are actively trying to eliminate old learning that is no longer needed. This unlearning process was first hypothesized by Melton and Irwin (1940) in relation to other memory tasks. Keppel and Underwood applied this notion to the Brown-Peterson task. Crucial to this application of the unlearning hypothesis is the concept of *spontaneous recovery*. That is, it is assumed that the unlearning process is not permanent but instead weakens over time. Thus, old associations that had been unlearned will gradually recover some of their strength. As they become stronger, they will cause more and more interference with the new associations that people have formed.

The concept of "unlearning" was intended to be analogous to the concept of "extinction" that is prominent in accounts of animal learning. Extinction in animal learning occurs when a behavior is no longer reinforced and thus becomes weaker. Since the time of Pavlov, extinction was believed to reflect an active suppression of the old, unneeded learning by the animal. However, the effects of extinction may dissipate over time, leading to spontaneous recovery of the formerly extinguished behavior. Keppel and Underwood (1962) assumed that unlearning operated similarly to extinction and that spontaneous recovery would also occur.

How does this sort of account explain the major data found in this task? Keppel and Underwood (1962) saw interference as being the sole cause of forgetting here. Therefore, on the very first trial, when there are no old lists that can interfere with one's memory for the most recent list, there is no forgetting. As a subject completes one trial, the list learned then is no longer needed and is therefore unlearned or extinguished. This unlearning process is not complete, however, and subjects exhibit proactive interference as they learn more and more lists. Moreover, this proactive interference becomes worse when subjects have a trial with a long distractor interval. A long distractor interval allows more time for the spontaneous recovery of the lists from previous trials. Thus, as a result of spontaneous recovery, there is more interference on trials with long distractor intervals than on trials with short distractor intervals, and this explains why recall becomes more difficult as a function of the length of the distractor interval. Since interference is generally assumed to occur only between stimuli that are similar to each other, this account would also be able to explain why release from proactive interference occurs when there is a change made in the nature of the stimulus materials.

One implication of this approach is particularly striking. According to this account, spontaneous recovery increases as more time has passed since the unlearning of old lists. Thus, lengthening the distractor interval on a particular trial only has its effect on forgetting by increasing the amount of time that passed since unlearning of previous trials. Any way of lengthening the time between the unlearning of old lists and the recall of a new list should increase forgetting of the new list.

Loess (1964) had subjects go through some trials in a Brown-Peterson experiment and had them return the following week for more trials. According to the unlearning hypothesis, spontaneous recovery should be occurring during that week. Therefore, when subjects return to the laboratory after a week's absence, they should face massive interference as they try to learn new lists. In fact, the opposite happened: After the week's break, the subjects' performance on the first Brown-Peterson trial was exactly the same as it had been on the first trial the week before. When a week passes between trials, interference does not increase but rather disappears entirely. This finding was later explored by Loess and Waugh (1967), who manipulated the amount of time that passed between trials in a single session. When the intertrial interval exceeded 2 min, there was no sign of proactive interference. The finding that proactive interference decreases as a function of the intertrial interval has been replicated several times (e.g., Lorsbach, 1990; Kincaid & Wickens, 1970; Wickens & Cammarata, 1986) and directly contradicts the idea that spontaneous recovery is happening over time in this task. Therefore, the unlearning hypothesis of Keppel and Underwood (1962) can be dismissed.

Encoding Accounts

One account of proactive interference involves encoding. The claim is that later trials are not remembered as well as earlier trials because they were not encoded as thoroughly. Perhaps subjects simply do not pay as much attention to the list items on later trials as they did earlier in the experiment. Perhaps subjects employ less effective or less efficient encoding strategies as the experiment goes on. Several variations of this account have been stated by theorists (e.g., Posner, 1967; Wickens, 1970). Dillon (1973) may have been most specific when he called proactive interference in the Brown-Peterson paradigm "a dramatic manifestation of insufficient learning" (p. 81). Release from proactive interference would be explained by assuming that a shift in the nature of the to-be-remembered stimuli leads to a return to more complete or effective encoding.

Item-Specific Release. There have been several attempts to influence the amount of attention that subjects pay on particular Brown-Peterson trials. For example, Russ-Eft (1979) used sets of three words as her to-be-remembered stimuli. For several trials, subjects would receive words all coming from a single semantic category. Then, she would shift categories for one of the words in the triad: Subjects would receive three words, two from the old category and one from a new category. Russ-Eft found that release from proactive inhibition could occur for an individual item. The one item from the new category exhibited release from proactive interference, but the two items from the old category did not. If one assumes that a change in one item would increase attention to the whole triad, Russ-Eft's findings are consistent with a simple attentional account.

Direct Manipulation of Attention. MacLeod (1975) tried to control attention by presenting a bright red warning light before some trials. Subjects were told that trials accompanied by the light were particularly crucial ones. However, the presence of the light had no effect and did not lead to release from proactive interference. In contrast, changing the category of the to-be-remembered items had its usual effect of greatly facilitating recall.

Final Free Recall. Several authors have tested encoding accounts by asking for a final free recall of items from all of the trials. If proactive interference is due to the fact that items on later trials were not encoded as thoroughly as earlier items, then later items should be harder to recall at the end of the session than should earlier items. This can be tested by asking subjects at the end of the experimental session to recall all of the items. The consistent finding here is that there is no sign of proactive interference: Items from the first trial are not remembered better than items from subsequent trials (Loftus & Patterson, 1975; Lorsbach, 1990; Watkins & Watkins, 1975). Such a finding is inconsistent with the claim that proactive interference reflects a failure to encode later items thoroughly.

Release from Proactive Interference as a Retrieval Mechanism. The most decisive study in this area was reported by Gardiner, Craik, and Birtwistle (1972). They tested the assertion that release from proactive interference reflects an enhancement of encoding processes. All subjects in this study went through four trials. The first three trials involved recall of words from a single semantic category. On the fourth trial, there was a shift in the nature of the materials but one so subtle that subjects would be unlikely to realize it on their own. For example, on the first three trials, subjects may be recalling names of garden flowers (e.g., CARNATION, ORCHID, ROSE, TULIP), and the fourth trial would require recall of wild flowers (e.g., DAISY, DANDELION, POPPY). One group of subjects went through these four trials and exhibited clear proactive interference on the second, third, and fourth trials. The switch in flower types was so subtle that uninstructed subjects presumably did not realize that there had been a switch at all and so did not exhibit release.

A second group went through the first three trials. At the beginning of the fourth trial, they were told that there would be a shift in the nature of the material (garden flowers to wild flowers). When asked for recall on the fourth trial, these subjects exhibited release from proactive interference. This result is compatible with an encoding account. These subjects knew what the switch would be at the beginning of the trial, and this knowledge could have influenced how well they encoded the items.

The crucial group was actually a third group. These subjects were not told that there would be a switch in the materials at the beginning of the fourth trial. However, after the to-be-remembered items had been presented and subjects had completed the period of distractor activity, the experimenter explained the change in stimulus materials and asked for recall. These subjects exhibited as much release from proactive interference as did the group that had been told about the switch at the beginning of the trial. This finding is completely incompatible with encoding accounts. Subjects who were informed of the change in materials only at the time of test could not have used this information to change their encoding processes. Rather, only their retrieval processes could have changed. This is a decisive experiment and has since been replicated (O'Neill, Sutcliffe, & Tulving, 1976). In combination with the other evidence that tends to rule out encoding accounts, these findings suggest that proactive interference in the Brown–Peterson paradigm should be explained by examining processes occurring at the time of retrieval.

The Gardiner et al. (1972) study illustrates a general point about testing accounts of memory phenomena. Theorists often want to determine whether a particular finding reflects encoding processes or retrieval processes. It is quite difficult to demonstrate that a phenomenon reflects encoding processes. This is because any manipulation that the experimenter introduces to study this effect at the encoding stage may end up also influencing the retrieval stage as well. Since retrieval always occurs after encoding, it is impossible to manipulate encoding without possibly changing retrieval processes as well. However, it is quite possible to manipulate retrieval processes without influencing encoding. The Gardiner et al. (1972) study, where one group was not informed of the change in materials until well after the encoding stage was over, is an example. By making sure that two groups encode the information the same way and by introducing the experimental manipulation only at the time of retrieval, an experimenter is able to be sure that any effect of the manipulation must be due to retrieval processes.

A Temporal Discriminability Account

There is one particular kind of retrieval theory that has been particularly popular. According to this account (first emphasized by Bennett, 1975), the major difficulty in the Brown-Peterson task is being able to discriminate between the most recent list and earlier lists. Let us use the Peterson and Peterson (1959) study as an example of how this approach works. Each subject had to go through 2 practice trials and 48 test trials. On each trial, subjects are being asked to recall the set of three consonants that had been presented on that trial; in other words, the most recent set must be recalled. However, over the course of the experiment, subjects would have seen many consonant sets and may have trouble determining which is the set that must be recalled. To make this determination, subjects would have to decide when a particular set had been shown and choose the set that had been presented most recently. Thus, the Brown–Peterson task is seen as reducing to a test on temporal judgment: Subjects are remembering consonant sets, trying to decide the time of presentation for each, and then choosing the set that had been presented most recently.

There are several factors that had been shown on other tasks to affect memory for time of occurrence. One such factor is the age of the event: We are better able to estimate time of occurrence for recent events than for older events. Another factor is the time between competing events. If we are asked to determine which of two memories is older, we will be able to do that more accurately if there is a bigger difference between the two times of occurrence than if the two times were very close to each other.

Such an account is able to explain the major findings in this area. First, this account predicts that, over the course of the experiment, recall should decline as a function of the distractor interval. As the distractor interval becomes longer, the list that subjects are trying to recall becomes older. As the presentation of the list recedes further into the past, it would become harder for subjects to determine the list's time of occurrence. It would therefore become more difficult for subjects to know which list is the one that has to be recalled on that trial.

Subjects' ability to discriminate between the times of occurrence of the various lists and to decide which is the more recent would also be affected by the amount of time that passes between trials. The more time that passes between trials, the easier this discrimination would be. Thus, this account is consistent with Loess and Waugh's (1967) finding that recall improves when the interval between trials is lengthened. Also, as has been pointed out by Baddeley (1990), a temporal-discriminability account may be able to explain Turvey et al.'s (1970) finding that the duration of the distractor interval had no effect on recall when it was manipulated between subjects. To do this, one must assume that temporal discrimination depends on the ratio of the age of the newest list to the age of other lists. As long as the distractor interval is held constant for any subject, this ratio will also be approximately constant. The newest list will be roughly half as old as the list immediately before it and one-third as long as the list before that. (For example, if the recall time and intertrial interval are negligible, when the distractor interval is 5 s long, the most recent list will be 5 s old when it must be recalled, the preceding list roughly 10 s old, and the list before that 15 s old; when the distractor interval is 25 s long, the most recent list will be 25 s old when it must be recalled, the preceding list roughly 50 s old, and the list before that 75 s old.)

There are situations where temporal discriminability would not be a problem for subjects. On the very first trial, subjects would not have to determine which list was the most recent one because only one list had been presented. Since temporal discrimination would not be an issue here, the level of recall should be high and should not drop as a function of the duration of the distractor interval. Of course, as Keppel and Underwood (1962) showed, this is indeed the pattern that is found. Also, when the stimuli used on one trial differ markedly from stimuli on the previous trials, temporal discrimination may be greatly facilitated. For example, when subjects go through numerous trials using letters as to-be-remembered stimuli and then experience a trial where digits were the to-be-remembered stimuli, they need only remember that digits had been used on the most recent list to know which stimuli should be recalled. Thus, changing the nature of the to-be-recalled stimuli should greatly facilitate temporal discrimination, a fact that could explain the phenomenon of release from proactive interference (Wickens et al., 1963). The temporal-discrimination account sees the phenomena of proactive interference and release from proactive interference as arising only at the stage of retrieval, a claim that is also generally consistent with the evidence (Gardiner et al., 1972; Loftus & Patterson, 1975; Watkins & Watkins, 1975).

Recognition Experiments. Additional evidence testing temporal-discriminability accounts comes from experiments where subjects were not tested for recall of the to-be-remembered lists but were instead tested for recognition (Bennett, 1975; Elliott, Geiselman, & Thomas, 1981; Gorfein & Jacobson, 1973). These experiments required forced-choice recognition. Subjects would be shown the most recent list and a list from a prior trial (called a "foil") and would be asked to indicate which one had been presented on that trial. As the temporal-discriminability account would predict, performance depended greatly on the age of the foil that had been presented on a prior trial. The more recent the foil was, the more difficult recognition became, measured either by accuracy or by response time. Even more strikingly, when the foil did not come from a prior trial but was instead entirely new, recognition performance was quite high and was little affected by the duration of the distractor interval. When new items are used as distractors, subjects do not have to rely on temporal discriminability but are instead able to reject the distractor on the basis of familiarity. When temporal discrimination is not required on a Brown-Peterson task, there is no effect of distractor interval, as would be predicted by a temporal-discriminability account.

CONCLUSION

The Brown-Peterson task was devised as a way to illustrate decay processes in human memory. That concept has now been shown to be false. Instead, this paradigm depends on the subject's ability to discriminate between the ages of competing memories. While such a skill is undoubtedly useful, there are probably more direct ways of measuring it. Perhaps because of this, the popularity of this paradigm has declined in recent years. Baddeley (1990, p. 50) has noted that "it is no longer clear whether or not the technique reflects anything of basic importance." However, the basic phenomena found in this paradigm still have intrinsic interest. We now know why we may rapidly forget a name or a telephone number if we are momentarily distracted. Such forgetting is a result of interference from the many similar pieces of information we have stored in our memories. This interference arises as a result of our inability to distinguish between the information we want to remember and that which we do not need. We may well have a satisfactory solution to the question of how distraction brings about forgetting, a question raised so long ago by W. G. Smith (1895), Daniels (1895), and T. L. Smith (1896).

For much of the last 30 years, the Brown-Peterson paradigm and the recency effect in immediate free recall were jointly used as evidence for the distinction between a short-term store and a long-term store (or, to use the terms of Waugh & Norman, 1965, primary memory and secondary memory). It was widely assumed that the Brown-Peterson task and the recency effect were reflecting a common cause, namely, the short-term store and its susceptibility to rapid forgetting. It has since become clear that the short-term/long-term distinction is entirely irrelevant to both these tasks. As a consequence, there is very little empirical evidence supporting a division of memory into short-term and long-term components (Crowder, 1982a). Curiously, however, the notion that the Brown-Peterson task and the recency effect in free recall reflect similar processes might well be correct. In this chapter, I have argued that a temporal-discriminability account offers the best explanation for forgetting in the Brown-Peterson task. In chap. 3, we saw evidence that the recency effect in free recall reflected the superior discriminability of terminal items in a series. (According to Glenberg, 1987, even the modality and suffix effects discussed in chap. 2 can be seen as arising from differences in temporal discriminability.) Thus, we seem to be arriving at similar accounts for several different paradigms. This illustrates the point that temporal discriminability might well be an essential aspect of many memory experiments. A central problem for subjects in an episodic-memory experiment is to discriminate between the episodes being tested and the rest of the events stored in memory. This would require that subjects be able to date their memory traces accurately. Thus, temporal information must be crucial for success in an episodic memory task. The ways in which this temporal information is affected by particular experimental manipulations seem to underlie some of our most striking findings in memory research.

CHAPTER FIVE

Memory Scanning: The Sternberg Paradigm

In the 1960s, Saul Sternberg developed a memory paradigm that ranks among the most influential and the most controversial. To give a flavor of this paradigm, I will describe an unpublished replication of Sternberg's classic work.

Ten subjects were tested one at a time. Each sat in front of a computer screen keeping a finger on the M key and on the Z key of the computer keyboard. A set of letters appeared in one corner of the screen. There could be either 2, 3, or 4 letters in the set. The set was shown for 1 s. Then, it went off. The screen was blank for half a second. Then, a single letter (which may be called a probe) appeared. The probe may or may not have been a member of the set that the subjects had just seen. Subjects were to press the M key if the probe was a member of the set or press the Z key if it was not a member. This is a trivially easy task. After all, almost everybody would be able to remember 2, 3, or 4 letters perfectly. However, subjects were asked to respond as rapidly as possible. Since the task is so easy and subjects rarely made errors, the chief interest is in how quickly subjects were able to respond. After subjects made a response, the screen went blank again. After an interval of 2 s, another set of letters would appear, and the whole process would begin again until subjects went through 120 trials.

The results for the 10 subjects are shown in Fig. 5.1. Reaction time (that is, the time it took subjects to make a response) is shown as a function of two independent variables. The first is the number of letters in the set: 2, 3, or 4. The second independent variable is whether the trial was positive (that is, the probe was a member of the set, and subjects

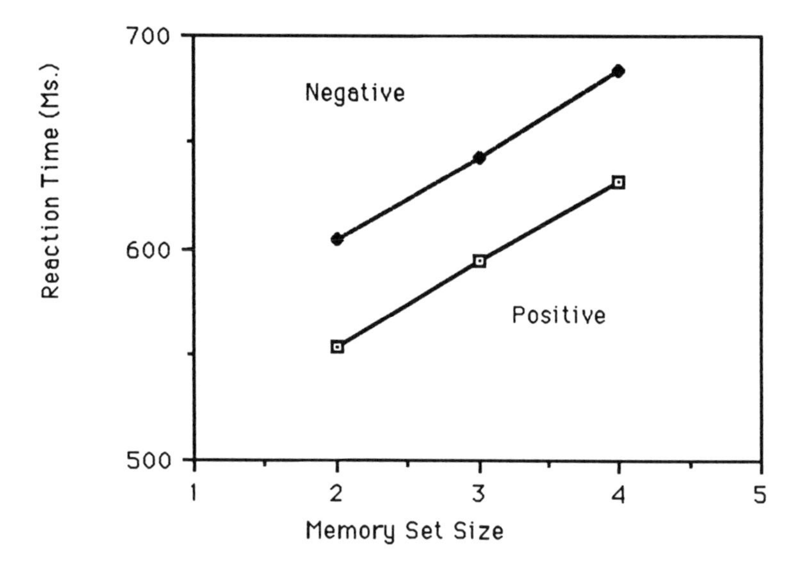

FIG. 5.1. An example of results in the memory-scanning paradigm.

had to respond "yes" by pressing M) or negative (the probe was not a member of the set, and subjects had to respond "no" by pressing Z). As the figure shows, reaction time increases as a function of the number of items in the set. This effect was clearly present for both positive and negative trials to about equal degrees.

THE WORK OF SAUL STERNBERG

The experiment just described was an unpublished one that I conducted in my laboratory. However, it was closely patterned after a series of experiments carried out by Saul Sternberg in the 1960s. At the time that Sternberg was working, there were few workers interested in measuring the time it took people to do cognitive tasks. Rather, psychologists were focusing on the accuracy with which subjects performed tasks. Sternberg's paradigm changed that: Nowadays, cognitive psychologists are as likely as not to be using subjects' response times as the measure of chief interest.

In addition to the development of the task itself, Sternberg made several other contributions to psychology through his development of this task. The first was development of a technique for discovering the stages that are used in a task; this technique is called the *additive-factors method.* The second was the development of a specific theory about how subjects perform this task; this theory has become known as the *serial exhaustive-scanning theory.*

Sternberg's Additive-Factors Method

The Subtraction Method. To appreciate Sternberg's contribution with his additive-factors method, it is helpful to have a look at an earlier method of analyzing reaction times. F. C. Donders (1868/1969), in a paper entitled "On the Speed of Mental Processes," developed the technique that has become known as the *subtraction method.* This method involves comparing tasks that are believed to differ only through the presence of one mental process or stage. For example, Task A may be a simple reaction-time task. In such a task, subjects may see a certain stimulus and will have to respond as soon as they see it. Only one kind of stimulus is ever shown, and only one kind of response is ever required by the subject. In contrast, in Task B, subjects may see either one of two stimuli. They have to make one kind of response to the first stimulus and a different response to the other stimulus. Task B may be seen as involving not only simple reaction time but also the time needed for stimulus categorization (which one of the stimuli am I seeing now?) and the time needed for response selection (which of the two responses do I have to make?). Task C may involve the presence of two stimuli but only one response. Subjects have to make one response to one stimulus and no response to another. Task C may be seen as involving simple reaction time and stimulus categorization time (since subjects have to decide whether the stimulus being shown is the one they have to respond to). However, response selection is not required in Task C (since only one kind of response is ever demanded).

If experimenters using these tasks wanted to know how much time was required for stimulus categorization, they would only have to take the difference between the time needed for Task C and the time needed for Task A. Tasks A and C differ only in that C involves stimulus categorization, and A does not. If these experimenters wanted to know how much time it takes subjects to engage in response selection, they would only have to take the difference between Task B and Task C, since the former requires response selection and the latter does not. Task A would give a pure measure of simple reaction time. Thus, by using subtraction, one can get estimates for the duration of the three mental processes or stages used in these three tasks.

The subtraction method is still used at times in cognitive psychology. For example, Robert J. Sternberg (no relation to Saul Sternberg) has used the subtraction method to study intelligence. He has been interested in how people perform tasks of the sort that might be used on intelligence tests. One such task is analogical reasoning, where subjects have to respond to items such as LAWYER: CLIENT :: DOCTOR: (a. PATIENT, b. MEDICINE). Subjects have to pick the term in parentheses that would best complete the analogy (in this case, PATIENT) and must respond as rapidly as possible. R. J. Sternberg believed that analogical reasoning involved several processes, such as *encoding* each of the terms, *inference* (determining the relationship between the first two terms LAWYER and CLIENT), *mapping* (taking the relationship between the first two terms and relating it to the third term, DOCTOR), and *application* (determining what the ideal completion would be to make the analogy). R. J. Sternberg (1977) determined the time it would take individual subjects to perform these mental processes through a method of precuing, presenting one or more terms before the problem as a whole is presented. For example, he might present the first term and let subjects encode it before presenting the problem. Subjects would be able to do the problem faster now than if no terms had been precued. The difference in response time between the original task and the version with the first term precued would allow you to estimate how long it takes the subject to encode the first term. If the first two terms are precued before the problem is presented, subjects would be able to encode both terms and also engage in the inference process as well. By precuing various terms and using the subtraction method, one could eventually derive estimates of the duration for each of the mental processes listed above.

The subtraction method has been subjected to a number of criticisms over the course of decades. One criticism is particularly worth mentioning. To use the subtraction method, one must be willing to make the *assumption of pure insertion,* namely, that inserting a new stage into a task would have no effect on how much time it takes to do other stages in the task (S. Sternberg, 1969b). To go back to our original example, the comparison of tasks A, B, and C, the subtraction method only makes sense if one can assume that simple reaction time or stimulus categorization time is uninfluenced by having to also engage in response selection. However, this assumption of pure insertion may be false. Perhaps subjects perform the stimulus categorization process differently if they know that they will have to select responses on the basis of this categorization. Alternatively, perhaps subjects devote less mental effort or capacity to one process if they are going to perform other processes on the same task. For any particular experiment, the assumption of pure insertion may hold. However, knowing whether or not it holds is quite difficult (Pachella, 1974), which accounted for a decline in popularity of the subtraction method.

Additive-Factors Method. Saul Sternberg (1969a) proposed a different method for analyzing reaction times. This method was called the additive-factors method. This method assumes that a task is composed of independent stages or processes. Each process receives an input from the preceding stage and performs a particular transformation on it. Each stage is unaffected by the durations of earlier stages. This conception suggests that total reaction time is simply the sum of the durations of the independent stages. If two manipulations affect different stages, their effects will be independent (i.e., additive). That is, the effect of one manipulation will be the same at all levels of the other manipulation. Statistically, this means that the two manipulations will not have a significant interaction in an analysis of variance. If two variables do interact, this means that they must be influencing the same stage.

An example of how to apply this method comes from research by Meyer, Schvaneveldt, and Ruddy (1975). They were interested in studying visual word recognition. In one of their experiments, they manipulated two factors. One factor is whether a test word (e.g., BUTTER) had been preceded by a related word (e.g., BREAD) or by an unrelated word (e.g., NURSE); this manipulation is known as priming. The second factor was whether the word was presented intact or in a degraded form (partially covered so that it was difficult to see). Subjects were able to recognize words faster when they had been preceded by a similar word and when they were presented in intact form. Also, these two manipulations interacted: The effect of one manipulation depended on the level of the other manipulation. In the intact condition, subjects responded to primed words 38 ms faster than to unprimed words. In the degraded condition, subjects responded to primed words 71 ms faster than to unprimed words. In other words, the priming effect is almost twice as great in the degraded condition as in the intact condition. On the basis of the additive-factors method, one must assume that priming and stimulus degradation must influence a common stage.

Several comparisons between the additive-factors method and the subtraction method are worth pointing out. Unlike the subtraction method, the additive-factors method does not make the assumption of pure insertion, the assumption that one can insert or delete particular stages without influencing the other stages. The additive-factors method makes the somewhat weaker *assumption of selective influence,* which assumes that a manipulation can influence the duration of one stage without altering others. Also, unlike the subtraction method, the additive-factors method never gives the experimenter estimates regarding the precise duration of each stage. The subtraction method was meant to tell exactly how long each stage takes. The additive-factors method does not attempt to tell you this. Rather, it was intended to be useful chiefly in developing and testing theories as to what stages constitute a certain process. This goal is somewhat less ambitious than giving precise durations for each stage, but it may be more realistic as well.

Criticisms of the Additive-Factors Method. The additive-factors method has not escaped unscathed from the comments of critics. One observation that strikes many observers and has been noted by several researchers (e.g., Broadbent, 1984; Pachella, 1974) is that the concept of "stages" here appears somewhat artificial. Stages are defined so that variables influencing a common stage must interact and variables influencing separate stages must have additive effects. However, this may not lead to the most useful or enlightening way of conceptualizing stages in any one task. If one defines stages on the basis of other evidence, one may or may not come up with a theory that holds up under additive-factors logic.

A second concern deals with the plausibility of finding tasks neatly divisible into independent stages. McClelland (1979) has pointed out that it may be more reasonable to imagine stages overlapping in time. This could happen if it is possible for one stage to begin before a logically prior stage has completely finished. A later stage may be able to begin processing on the basis of partial information from an earlier stage. For example, when you are reading a word aloud, you must identify the word before saying it aloud. However, this does not mean that the vocalization process must necessarily wait until the word-identification process is done. Perhaps when enough information is available from the word-identification process to narrow the range of possible words, the vocalization process is already preparing the vocal tract to say the stimulus aloud. McClelland termed this kind of arrangement a *cascade,* where there is partial overlap between the stages. When stages are cascaded, the assumptions of the additive-factors method are violated, so one should not apply the method. However, it is difficult, if not impossible to know whether or not the stages in a certain task are cascaded.

This suggests that there are times when the additive-factors method is inappropriate and should not be applied. Some empirical research suggests that the additive-factors method has been misapplied in the past. For example, it has been found several times that pairs of variables that have additive effects may nevertheless both interact with a third variable (Broadbent, 1984; Stanovich & Pachella, 1977). This kind of pattern should be impossible if the assumptions of the additive factors held. If two variables have additive effects, they must influence different stages. However, if they both interact with a third variable, they must all affect the same stage. This contradiction suggests that the assumptions of the additive-factors method do not always hold.

Even so, however, the assumptions of the additive-factors method presumably hold in some cases, and this method continues to be used sometimes. The logic underlying this method formed the basis for Sternberg's explanation of the results from experiments like the one described at the beginning of this chapter. It is to those results and Sternberg's account of them that we now turn.

Sternberg's Serial Exhaustive-Scanning Model

Sternberg (1966, 1969b) was interested in determining how subjects go about performing the task that he devised. On each trial, subjects see a probe and have to indicate whether it matches any of the items in the memory set presented earlier. One can either use one memory set for a block of trials (the fixed-set procedure) or a different memory set for each trial (the varied-set procedure). Both procedures yield similar results, although the fixed-set procedure is perhaps more susceptible to unwanted experimental artifacts (Stadler & Logan, 1989).

To perform this memory task, it seemed to Sternberg that subjects would have to compare the probe with the items in the memory set. How would this comparison be done? It is possible that subjects could carry out a number of comparisons at the same time. For example, subjects may be able to compare the probe with each item in the memory set at the same time. Such a process would be termed a *parallel search,* because all the comparisons are happening at the same time without conflict (in the same way that parallel lines can go in the same direction without colliding). On the other hand, subjects may be able to perform only one comparison at a time. If this were true, then subjects would have to compare the probe with each item individually, one after another. Such a process may be termed a *serial search* because all of the comparisons are happening consecutively, as in a series.

The evidence that led Sternberg to make his choice between these accounts was similar to that depicted in Fig. 5.1. Notice in that figure that, as set size increases, reaction times increase steadily. There is approximately a linear relationship between memory-set size and reaction time; in other words, each item in the memory set seems to add about a constant amount to average reaction times. Sternberg found that each item added about 38 ms to the mean reaction times (Fig. 5.1 shows roughly this same slope). This would be exactly what a serial model would predict. Since each comparison has to follow in a series, each should add a constant amount of time. In contrast, the parallel-search model would not necessarily predict this. Since each comparison happens at the same time as the others, you would not necessarily predict that reaction time would increase at all. Even if one allowed the parallel-search model to predict an increase in time as a function of set size (for example, by assuming that the comparisons are done more slowly as more comparisons are being done simultaneously), the fact that each item adds a constant amount could only be explained by adding on extra assumptions that Sternberg considered unlikely. Therefore, a serial-search model was seen as being the more elegant of the two approaches.

Given that a serial-search process was being carried out, one can try to determine more specifically the nature of this process. Sternberg was particularly interested in the question of whether the serial scan was carried out in a self-terminating or exhaustive fashion. A *self-terminating* search would be one where subjects could stop the process as soon as they find a match. For example, if the probe matches the first item it is compared with, then the subject would not carry out any of the other comparisons. In contrast, in an *exhaustive* search process, all of the comparisons must always be carried out. Even if the first comparison is a match, subjects will carry out the rest of the comparisons.

How should one choose between these two approaches? Again, the crucial evidence is in Fig. 5.1. Note that the slopes for positive and negative trials were about equal. This was what Sternberg found in his experiments: Both positive and negative trials increased about 38 ms for each item added to the memory set. This is inconsistent with the self-terminating account but is consistent with the exhaustive account.

Why is this inconsistent with the self-terminating account? If a self-terminating account were true, then the average number of comparisons would be different for positive and negative trials. On negative trials, the subject would have to compare the probe with all of the list items before knowing to make a negative response. This is not true for positive trials. On some trials, the very first comparison would yield a match, and subjects would be able to stop the process there. The result of this would be that, if the self-terminating account were being carried out, subjects would have to carry out fewer comparisons on average for positive than for negative trials.

There turns out to be a clear relation between set size and number of comparisons needed for positive and negative trials predicted by the self-terminating account. When there is only one item in the memory set, subjects would always have to carry out one comparison for both negative and positive trials. When there are two items in the memory set, subjects would always have to carry out two comparisons on negative trials. On positive trials, the probe would occupy the first position half of the time (thus requiring the subject to perform only one comparison) and the second position half of the time (requiring the subject to perform two comparisons). Therefore, on the average, 1.5 comparisons would have to be performed on positive trials. Similarly, when there are three items in the memory set, subjects would always have to carry out all three comparisons on negative trials. On positive trials, subjects would be equally likely to have to carry out one comparison (when the probe occupies the first position), two comparisons (when the probe occupies the second position), and three comparisons (when the probe occupies the third position). Subjects would therefore have to carry out an average of two comparisons on positive trials. As memory set size increases from one to two to three, subjects would have to increase the number of comparisons they have to carry out on average from one to two to three on negative trials but from one to 1.5 to two on positive trials. In other words, the number of comparisons carried out increases twice as much for negative as for positive trials. Therefore, the slope of reaction time as a function of set size should be approximately twice as large for negative trials as for positive trials.

However, this is not the pattern that is found. Although the mean times are often different for positive and negative trials (as is shown in Fig. 5.1), the slopes are about equal. This is inconsistent with the self-terminating account but is exactly what the exhaustive account would predict. Why would the exhaustive account predict this? Since subjects always have to perform all of the comparisons, the number of comparisons carried out on positive and negative trials would be equal, and therefore the slopes would be equal. On the basis of this evidence, Sternberg concluded that subjects performed his task by using a serial, exhaustive scan of the memory set.

Sternberg (1969b, 1975) has commented on the fact that many people express doubt as to the plausibility of the serial, exhaustive-scan account. Why would subjects keep on making comparisons if the first one yielded a match? One clue may be suggested by the speed of the process. Each comparison would only take 38 ms. We would be able to make comparisons with 26 items in a second. In contrast, people are usually able to recite in their heads at a rate of six characters per second (Landauer, 1962). This scanning process is happening much faster than our rate of inner speech. This speed may prevent us from stopping the scan because the scanning process could be over before we would have a chance to decide each comparison consciously.

The serial, exhaustive nature of memory search in Sternberg's model is what captured people's imaginations in this area. It should be added, however, that Sternberg's theory was somewhat more complex than this. After all, more must be involved in making a correct response than just scanning one's memory. Sternberg actually proposed a four-stage theory. The first stage is a *stimulus-encoding* stage, in which an internal representation of the probe stimulus is formed. The second stage is the *serial comparison* stage. It is in this stage that the serial, exhaustive-scanning process is carried out. The third stage is the *binary decision* stage. It is in this third stage that the person determines whether or not a match has been made during the serial comparison stage. The fourth stage is the *translation and response organization* stage, in which the proper response is determined and executed.

Sternberg (1969b) validated this four-stage model using his additive-factors logic. According to this logic, a variable influencing only one of these stages should not interact with a variable that influences other stages. Sternberg argued that stimulus legibility is a variable that should logically influence the first stage, encoding. After all, it should be easier to encode a stimulus if one can see it easily. The serial-comparison stage should be influenced by the size of the positive set. The binary decision stage should be influenced by response type (positive or negative). Subjects may find it easier to choose one of these responses than the other; for example, many people seem to have a bias to respond positively, which tends to give positive responses an advantage over negative responses (Ratcliff, 1985). The relative frequency of the response type should influence the translation and response organization stage. If one has had a lot of practice giving a certain response, one should be able to execute it faster. Sternberg (1969b) manipulated these variables and found that they had only additive effects with each other. This supported the notion that these variables each influenced different stages.

It should be noted here that Sternberg saw these four stages as representing a minimal model. It may be possible to break up each of these stages further or to find other stages that should fit somewhere in this scheme. However, Sternberg was convinced that at least these four stages were involved in performing this task.

EXTENSIONS OF SAUL STERNBERG'S WORK

Generality of the Empirical Phenomena

Across Stimuli. Sternberg's empirical contribution lies in the discovery that set size influences recognition in this task and that set-size effects are equivalent for positive and negative trials. These empirical phenomena hold up across a wide variety of stimuli and subjects. Sternberg (1969b) reported an experiment by Treisman and himself in which the memory set and probe items could be either digits, photographs of faces, or nonsense forms. Although both the intercepts and slopes of the functions relating reaction time to stimulus class differed for the various kinds of stimuli, equivalent set-size effects for positive and negative trials were found. Sternberg interpreted these results as evidence that a serial, exhaustive scan is carried out on these different stimulus classes, although the rate of scanning may differ somewhat as a function of stimulus class. Exactly how long it would take subjects to scan through a particular kind of stimulus seems almost perfectly predictable from the average memory span that subjects exhibit in recalling those stimuli; stimuli that lead to larger spans (that is, those that are easier to recall) also lead to faster estimates of scanning rate (Cavanaugh, 1972; Puckett & Kausler, 1984).

Sternberg's empirical phenomena seem to hold up even when subjects are not thinking of the memory set. Wickens, Moody, and Dow (1981; see also Wickens, Moody, & Yidulich, 1985) sometimes required subjects to perform a distractor task in between presentation of the memory set and presentation of the probe. For example, subjects might have to count backwards from a particular number for 12 s before the probe appears. Such a task should drive the memory set from conscious awareness, as people become distracted by performing the task. Indeed, performing this task did affect the intercepts of the reaction-time functions. However, this task had no effect on the slopes. Wickens and his colleagues explained their results in terms of Sternberg's model. They argued that subjects in their experiments first retrieved the set as a whole from long-term memory before beginning the serial, exhaustive scan. In other words, introduction of a distractor task introduced a new stage into this process (a *set-retrieval* stage) but did not otherwise change performance on this task. This is a very straightforward account of this task, although not all investigators have found it plausible (see Brannelly, Tehan, & Humphreys, 1989, for a critique).

There are some circumstances under which no set-size effects at all may be found. For example, Seamon (1972) showed that set-size effects were eliminated if subjects had an opportunity to form an image containing all of the items. Similarly, DeRosa and Tkacz (1976) showed that set-size effects were eliminated if the items formed a coherent story. In both of these cases, it is as if subjects were able to unitize the items into a single whole, thereby eliminating the need to compare each one separately with the probe. Another circumstance in which set-size effects may be eliminated is if there is no delay between presentation of the memory set and presentation of the probe (Diener, 1988). It is as if subjects need a little time to organize the list if the conventional effects are to be found.

Across Subjects. Sternberg's empirical discovery holds up impressively between subjects. Although there have been a few isolated findings that subjects high in verbal ability may scan faster than other subjects (Chiang & Atkinson, 1976; Hunt, Frost, & Lunneborg, 1973), the most typical finding is that there is relatively little variation among young, healthy adults in their rate of scanning (Hunt, 1978). In fact, even children as young as 8 may not only show evidence for a memory-scanning process but may actually have set-size slopes roughly equivalent to those of adults (Harris & Fleer, 1974; Hoving, Morin, & Konick, 1970). Aging and mental retardation may increase the slopes but do not change the rough equality of positive and negative slopes (Anders, Fozard, & Lillyquist, 1972; Eriksen, Hamlin, & Daye, 1973; Harris & Fleer, 1974). In fact, only a few populations, such as aphasics (Swinney & Taylor, 1971), seem to exhibit a completely different pattern.

It has been noted that there is a very strong relationship across stimuli between scanning rates and memory spans. In fact, when correlations are calculated across stimuli, this correlation is approximately 1.0. It turns out, however, that this relationship is somewhat weaker when the correlations are calculated across subjects (Brown & Kirsner, 1980). This finding is reasonable, given the evidence discussed here that scanning rates don't differ much from person to person. When there is little variance among people in scanning rate, it is difficult to get very high correlations between scanning rate and another variable, such as memory span. (To take this argument to its extreme, if everybody had exactly the same scanning rate, then it would be impossible for differences in scanning rate to be related to differences in memory span.)

Effects of Interference

One of the most potent sources of forgetting is interference. Does interference play a role in this task? This has been most often investigated by looking at the effects of proactive interference, interference caused by previous stimuli. As subjects go through this task, does their memory for earlier sets interfere with their memory for the set being currently tested? Unfortunately, the evidence here is rather ambiguous. Hanley and Scheirer (1975) found a clear interference effect, but this finding was not replicated by Wickens et al. (1981, 1985). Halford, Mayberry, and Bain (1988) found interference effects at some list lengths but not at others. In short, the search for proactive interference effects in this paradigm has yielded a very inconsistent and inconclusive pattern.

Rather than studying interference from previous lists, Corballis, Murray, and Connolly (1989) studied interference from concurrent lists. Subjects were given two separate memory sets. One set was always fixed in advance of a block of trials, while the other varied from trial to trial. Although some interference was found, with it taking somewhat more time to scan one set as the number of items in the other set was increased, this interference effect was rather small. Subjects seemed generally capable of scanning through the two lists separately and concurrently.

Effects of Practice

Depending on how one does the experiment, it may be possible to either see minimal or startlingly dramatic changes in performance as a function of practice. Let us say that subjects go through a series of trials. On each trial, stimuli are randomly assigned to the positive memory set and to the role of probe. Such an arrangement can be called a *varied-mapping* arrangement because the mapping of stimulus with response (positive or negative) may vary from trial to trial: One time a stimulus appears, it might require a positive response and the next time it appears, a negative response may be required. Under these circumstances, performance in the Sternberg paradigm changes relatively little with practice (e.g., Kristofferson, 1972a). When one looks at the graph-plotting reaction time as a function of memory set size, the intercept may become slightly lower after extended practice (indicating perhaps that subjects are becoming more skilled at encoding the probe and executing the response) but the slope of the function hardly changes at all.

A very different pattern happens when subjects undergo practice under conditions of *consistent mapping:* Here, each stimulus in an experiment is consistently associated with a particular response. Every time a certain stimulus is used as a probe, the same response is always required. This does not necessarily mean that the same positive set is always used. It does mean, however, that an item used as a member of the positive set on some trials would never be used as a negative probe on the other trials. When such a consistent-mapping arrangement is used and subjects are given many days of practice on this task, set-size effects are either greatly reduced (Kristofferson, 1972b) or eliminated (Schneider & Shiffrin, 1977; Shiffrin & Schneider, 1977).

One way to think about this pattern of results is to say that substantial set-size effects are found only when positive and negative items are defined arbitrarily. When positive and negative items come from different categories, subjects do not need to carry out a search of the memory set. Instead, they need only categorize the probe to know the correct response. For example, if the members of the memory set were all digits and the probe was a letter, the subject could know to make a negative response without ever making a search. Indeed, when probes come from categories other than the one containing the memory set items, set-size effects are dramatically reduced (e.g., Jones & Anderson, 1982). Similarly, when the memory set consists of the names of people in your family, you do not need to carry out a search when a name is presented as a probe: It is quicker for you to simply categorize the probe as a family member or not (Clifton, 1973). What consistent-mapping practice may do is to allow the subject to construct new categories. In a situation where B,

F, N, R, and W are always used as positive items, it may be quicker eventually for subjects to learn to categorize a letter as one of those items than to carry out a search in memory.

EVIDENCE AGAINST THE SERIAL, EXHAUSTIVE-SCAN HYPOTHESIS

There are very few theories that have caught the imagination of psychologists the way that Sternberg's (1966, 1969b) serial, exhaustive-scan hypothesis did. To this day, it is recounted in detail in many introductory textbooks. However, there is evidence that this account is wrong.

Repetition Effects

Imagine what happens when subjects are given a memory set such as: 2 7 5 7. How do subjects handle sets that contain repeated elements? There are two ways that the serial, exhaustive-scan theory could handle this. The first is that subjects might treat it as a normal, four-element string. In that case, reaction time to all probes for list would be the same as for four-element lists that did not contain a repetition. Alternatively, the subject might realize that there was a repetition and recode the list to eliminate the repetition: 2 7 5. In that case, reaction times on trials for that list would be the same as for three-item lists that did not contain a repetition. There is one prediction that the serial exhaustive-scan theory must make: Scanning should happen no faster when the repeated element is the probe than when nonrepeated elements are used as a probe.

Baddeley and Ecob (1973) performed an experiment where items in a memory set could be repeated. They found that repeated items were responded to faster than nonrepeated items. They interpreted this as evidence against the serial, exhaustive-scan theory on the ground that the model predicts that the whole set has to be searched regardless of whether a repeated or nonrepeated item was being sought.

However, this need not be seen as conclusive evidence against Sternberg's theory. Remember that memory scanning takes place in only one of the four stages imagined in this theory. What if the advantage for repeated over nonrepeated items were due not to the serial comparison stage (as Baddeley & Ecob, 1973, assumed) but rather to one of the other stages? To pick the most intuitively plausible possibility, what if subjects were able to encode the stimulus faster if it had been repeated on the list than if it had been shown only once? This would result in exactly the pattern that Baddeley and Ecob found, with repeated items being responded to faster than nonrepeated items.

There is a way to choose between Baddeley and Ecob's (1973) interpretation and the encoding explanation of the repetition effect. This would take advantage of the additive-factors logic. If repetition affected the serial-comparison stage, then the additive-factors logic would lead one to predict that that variable should interact statistically with memory set size. Repetition would not interact with variables (such as stimulus legibility) that have been shown to affect the encoding stage. On the other hand, an account that attributes the repetition effect to the encoding stage would predict that repetition and set size would have additive effects but that repetition would interact with stimulus legibility.

Unfortunately, Baddeley and Ecob (1973) did not test the statistical significance of the interaction between set size and repetition. However, an examination of their data suggests that these variables do interact: For example, there is an advantage of repeated over nonrepeated items of 60 ms when set size equaled two, but this effect dwindled away to approximately zero ms when set size was increased to five. This suggests that repetition and set size affect the same stage, which is inconsistent with Sternberg's serial, exhaustive-scan hypothesis.

Stimulus Frequency and Probability Effects

When set size increases, the probability of any particular member of the positive set occurring as a probe decreases (assuming that the overall proportion of positive trials is kept constant). In other words, there is a confound between set size and probability for any specific positive item. Some researchers have wondered what would happen if this confound were removed by varying the probability that a particular item would occur as a probe. There are several ways of doing this: For example, one could simply vary the frequency of occurrence of particular stimuli as probes. Subjects would not be told these probabilities but would presumably discover them after spending time in the experiment. In this case, probability would go along with overall stimulus frequency in the experiment. On the other hand, one could simply tell the subject before each trial that a particular stimulus had a certain probability of occurring. This probability could vary from trial to trial.

Researchers have used both of these methods. The simplest finding is the same in both cases: Response time was decreased for more probable stimuli. If this effect could be attributed to the stage of comparison, then it would be inconsistent with Sternberg's serial, exhaustive-scan model. However, as we have seen, defenders of the serial exhaustive-scan approach might attribute this probability effect to other stages, such as the encoding stage. The way to settle this conflict is to see whether probability interacts with set size.

The answer to that question seems to depend on how probability is manipulated. Studies that have manipulated probability by instructing subjects about the probabilities on a certain trial have found no interaction between set size and probability (Biederman & Stacy, 1974; Klatzky & Smith, 1972), and further evidence suggests that this probability manipulation chiefly affects stimulus encoding (e.g., Miller & Hardzinski, 1981; Miller & Pachella, 1973). However, when probability is manipulated by varying the frequency with which stimuli occur during the course of the experiment, there is a clear interaction between stimulus frequency and set size (Theios & Walter, 1974). This finding is inconsistent with the serial, exhaustive-scan approach: Subjects respond to more frequent stimuli faster than less frequent stimuli, and this effect must be localized in the same stage as where set size has its effect.

Serial Position

Serial-position effects have been among the most heavily studied phenomena in memory research, so it is not surprising that researchers should be interested in whether such effects are found in the Sternberg paradigm. In general, small primacy effects and substantial recency effects are often found (e.g., Aube & Murdock, 1974; Clifton & Birenbaum, 1970; Forrin & Cunningham, 1973; Monsell, 1978; Raeburn, 1974; Seamon & Wright, 1976; Wingfield, 1973). Such effects tend to be particularly large when delays of 2 s or less occur between presentation of the list and presentation of the probe (Forrin & Cunningham, 1973).

These serial-position effects are inconsistent with the serial, exhaustive-scan hypothesis if they interact with set size. Raeburn (1974) showed that this was indeed the case. In her study, increasing set size by one item increased reaction time by 37 ms when nonterminal items were tested. When the very last item was tested, however, the slope was only 8 ms (which did not differ from zero by a test of statistical significance).

Why serial-position effects should be particularly pronounced for short probe delays is not clear. One possibility is that, as delays before the probe lengthen, subjects have more of an opportunity to rehearse the items. The probe may appear when the subject is rehearsing some item other than the last one. Therefore, with longer delays, the most recent item in the subject's mind is less and less likely to be the most recent item on the list. With a sufficiently long delay, all the items should be equally likely to be the most recently rehearsed when the probe appears. This would lead to an elimination of the advantage for items presented at the end of the list. Indeed, Seamon and Wright (1976) had subjects rehearse aloud and found that subjects were much quicker when the probe was the most recently rehearsed item.

Sternberg's (1966, 1969b) serial, exhaustive-scan hypothesis basically predicted that subjects should be equally fast in responding to all members of the positive set because subjects must always go all the way through the set before deciding on a response. We have now seen three kinds of evidence (repetition effects, frequency effects, serial-position effects) that disprove this prediction. Moreover, in all three cases, there is at least some evidence that these effects influence the same stage as memory set size.

Negative Probe Effects

Just as Sternberg's (1966, 1969b) serial, exhaustive-scan theory predicts that all positive items should be responded to equally quickly, it also predicts that all negative probes should be responded to equally quickly. This prediction has been disproven. Negative probes that have occurred more frequently in the experiment are responded to faster than less frequent negative probes (e.g., Marcel, 1976; Theios, Smith, Haviland, Traupmann, & Moy, 1973). Moreover, this negative-probe frequency effect interacts with memory set size (Marcel, 1976), showing again that frequency effects and set size influence a common stage. Monsell (1978) reported that the recency of a negative probe (that is, the number of trials since the last time it was used as a probe) affected reaction time and accuracy. This effect also interacted with the size of the positive memory set.

Marcel (1976) found further evidence that not all negative probes are equally difficult. When the memory set consisted of consecutive digits (not necessarily in order), the reaction times to negative probes were a function of the distance between the probe and the positive items: The greater the distance, the faster subjects responded. This distance effect also interacted significantly with set size, increasing as set size increased.

Response-Signal Procedure

In the typical reaction-time experiment, subjects choose when they want to respond. What if the experimenter took this choice out of the subjects' hands? Reed (1976) used the response-signal procedure, in which a signal occurs during the trial instructing the subject when to respond. Essentially, the subject must stop processing and make a response as soon as the signal is presented. By presenting the signal at various intervals on different trials, the experimenter can track the development of information processing as a function of time.

There are several variations on Sternberg's (1966, 1969b) theory that could be developed for this task. Reed (1976) showed that none of them fit his data well. When it is possible to study the time course of item recognition, the results do not appear consistent with Sternberg's theory.

ALTERNATIVE THEORIES

Sternberg's (1966, 1969b) serial, exhaustive-scan theory has been the account most often discussed and most widely accepted. However, as we have seen above, it has been rather solidly disproven on the basis of several lines of evidence. In general, contradicting the theory, not all positive probes and not all negative probes are responded to with equal speed. Moreover, the time course of information growth does not follow any path predicted by this model. We should therefore turn to some of the alternative theories that have been proposed in this area. In this review of alternative theories, I will be selective, concentrating on the most representative or the most promising accounts.

Strength Theories

One class of theories has tried to eliminate the whole concept of search. These theories have assumed that recognition can be performed without any need for a search through memory or through a search set. Rather, access to a memory trace is an automatic consequence of the presentation of a probe. Memory traces are seen as varying in strength, and recognition judgments are based on the strength of that particular memory trace. If the trace is sufficiently strong, the subject responds positively. If not, the subject responds negatively.

Several such strength theories have been proposed for this task (e.g., Baddeley & Ecob, 1973; Corballis, Kirby, & Miller, 1972; Nickerson, 1972). We shall focus on the one that has gotten the most attention, the model of Baddeley and Ecob (1973). This model assumed that a fixed amount (A) of trace strength is divided among the positive items. Therefore, as memory set size increases, the amount of strength present in each of the traces of the positive items decreases. It is assumed that negative items have a trace strength of zero. As the number of items in the memory set increases, the difference between the average strength of positive items (A divided by set size) and the average strength of negative items (zero) becomes smaller and smaller. In other words, it becomes ever more difficult for subjects to discriminate between the strengths of positive and negative items. This difficulty in discriminability is responsible for the increases in reaction times found for both positive and negative probes as memory set size is increased. This model is capable of explaining much of the evidence that is contrary to Sternberg's serial, exhaustive-scan model. For example, it can be assumed that not all positive items share equally in trace strength. Perhaps those items that are repeated, more frequent, or occurred most recently on the list receive a greater share of trace strength than other items. This could result in faster reaction times to those items than to other items.

Could this model explain the negative probe effects discussed earlier? On the surface, it would appear that it could. One could assume that a certain amount of trace strength "seeps" away to negative stimuli, so that not all negative stimuli would have a trace strength of absolutely zero. This would make it possible for some negative stimuli to be easier than others. For example, perhaps a negative stimulus that is similar to the positive items or that occurred on a recent trial would receive some amount of trace strength. This would make it harder for subjects to discriminate between those negative stimuli and positive items.

However, we then encounter a serious problem: If more frequent negative stimuli have a nonzero trace strength, they should be particularly hard to discriminate from positive items. In other words, it should take a long time for subjects to answer "no" to those items. However, as we have seen, subjects respond *faster* to frequent negative probes than to other negative probes (Krueger, 1970; Marcel, 1976; Theios et al., 1973). This doesn't make any sense from the perspective of a strength theory.

This highlights a problem that strength theories have in explaining all recognition tasks, not only in the Sternberg paradigm. It is a fact that not all items are equally easy to recognize. Strength theories assume that those variables (e.g., concreteness, rarity) that make an item easy to recognize do so by increasing its strength. That should mean that, when those items are used as negative distractors, they should be difficult to respond negatively to (since they have unusually high strength). However, in fact, items easy to recognize when used as positive items, are easy to reject when used as negative items (Glanzer & Adams, 1985). This is impossible to explain if one believes that recognition judgments are based on some simple unidimensional quality, such as "trace strength." On the other hand, this pattern makes sense if one believes that there is a search (or retrieval) process in recognition: The easier it is to find the relevant traces, the easier it is to answer either "yes" or "no." This fact is consistent with other findings that argue for the presence of search processes in recognition (Tulving, 1976). Therefore, when considering theories of the Sternberg paradigm (which is a kind of recognition task), we should give more consideration to those models that include a search process. It is to those theories that we turn now.

Serial, Self-Terminating Search

Theios et al. (1973) suggested a model that differed from Sternberg's (1966, 1969b) serial, exhaustive-scan model in one way. In the Theios et al. model, the search process is carried out in a self-terminating fashion: Subjects stop the process as soon as they find the probe.

To appreciate this model, it helps to think back to why Sternberg (1966, 1969b) favored an exhaustive scan in the first place. He did so because the slope of reaction time as a function of memory set size was equivalent for positive and negative items. This slope could not be equal if subjects searched the positive set and stopped as soon as they found the probe on positive trials.

Theios et al. asked the question: What if subjects searched through a set of positive and negative items and stopped when they found the probe (whether it was positive or negative)? Surely, this would allow positive and negative slopes to be equal. Theios et al. assumed that subjects have a buffer that contains all of the stimuli that are likely to occur in the experiment. Each stimulus is associated with a certain response (positive or negative), and positive and negative items are placed in this buffer. When a probe is presented, subjects search through the buffer and keep going until they find a duplicate of the probe. Subjects then determine what response is associated with that stimulus and make that response. The items are not necessarily searched randomly. Positive items tend to be searched before most negative items (which explains why reaction times to both positive and negative items increase as a function of positive memory set size). Subjects may also order the items in the buffer on the basis of their probability, frequency, or recency, which could explain why these variables influence reaction time. Since negative items are being searched as well as positive items, it is understandable that reaction times on negative trials would be influenced by properties of the probe.

In general, this model is quite successful in accounting for the general findings of the Sternberg paradigm, both those that Sternberg's serial exhaustive model can account for and those it cannot explain. In addition, Reed's (1976) results using the response-signal procedure were fit better by the Theios et al. model than by any of the other models that Reed considered. However, there is one finding that is very troublesome for the Theios et al. account. This model predicts that the fastest reaction times for different set sizes should be constant. This prediction stems from the fact that there is always a certain probability that the probe item will match the very first stimulus examined in the buffer. This probability decreases as a function of the number of items in the memory set; however, even for very big sets, there is always a certain probability that the probe will be the first item found in the buffer. Therefore, if one plotted the distribution of reaction times, the fastest that subjects ever responded on trials with a positive set size of 1 should be no faster than the fastest times with set sizes of 2, 3, 4, and so on. Sternberg (1975) noted that this prediction was false: Data from Lively (1972) and Lively and Sanford (1972) show that the fastest correction reaction time to positive and negative probes increased as a function of the memory set size. These data seem to disconfirm the Theios et al. (1973) model. There is a more general conclusion that should be drawn from those data: The time needed to scan through even one item must be a function of the number of items in the memory set. This is needed to explain why the minimum reaction time increases as a function of set size. The models that will be discussed all make this assumption.

Parallel-Search Models

Parallel-search models are those that allow subjects to compare the probe simultaneously with a number of different traces in memory. Such models have always been attractive to psychologists because they seemed to hold much greater potential for generality than serial-search models. After all, when we attempt to recognize a stimulus in everyday life, it must be compared with the millions (possibly billions) of different stimuli we have stored in our memories. If this comparison process must occur one at a time in a serial fashion, it would seem that recognition would take an implausibly long time to ever occur. Sternberg (1966, 1969a) dismissed parallel models for his task by pointing to the linear increases in reaction time as a function of set size. Sternberg pointed out that such linear functions would be naturally predicted by serial models. No matter how plausible parallel models are for recognition in general, Sternberg felt that a serial model best fit the data for his particular task. He felt that there was no need for a parallel model to even predict any set size effects at all (much less linear effects) since all the comparisons take place simultaneously.

However, it was soon pointed out (by Townsend, 1971, among others) that a parallel model could explain Sternberg's data perfectly well. Specifically, if a parallel model assumed that the time needed to compare the probe with any one stimulus in memory is a function of the number of comparisons being made simultaneously, then a parallel model could predict set-size effects. For example, assume that people have only a limited amount of mental capacity to apply to this task. When the probe appears, subjects compare it with a number of different memory traces. However, the speed of each comparison process depends on how much mental capacity is allotted to it: The more capacity that is allotted to a particular comparison, the faster it will be carried out. Reaction time increases as a function of set size because each comparison takes more time since mental capacity has to be shared among more and more comparisons. In general, parallel models could do a very good job of mimicking the predictions of serial models. Distinguishing between parallel and serial models is not impossible, but it takes far more data and sophistication than originally believed (see Townsend, 1990).

There are a number of variations on this theme of parallel processes competing for mental capacity. For example, Jones and Anderson (1987) created a model in which set-size effects resulted from mental activation spreading out among all of the nodes representing positive items in memory. Glass (1984) assumed that the probe is compared with a processor representing each memory set item. The comparison of the probe with the different processors occurs in parallel, and the amount of time it takes for a processor to emit a positive or negative response depends on the number of comparisons being performed. There are a number of other parallel models, each offering its own terminology but sharing the same essential properties as those that have been discussed. I will focus now on one particular parallel model, the diffusion model of Ratcliff (1978). This model is notable for its mathematical sophistication and the range of data that it has been applied to, both in the Sternberg paradigm and in other paradigms.

Ratcliff's Diffusion Model. This model assumes that the positive set items are stored in memory as separate traces, each trace being composed of a large number of features. When the probe is presented, it contacts traces similar to it. The probe is then compared in parallel with the traces that have been contacted. A positive response is made when subjects find one trace that matches the probe. A negative response is made when all of the comparison processes finish with none of them indicating a match between a trace and the probe.

Ratcliff (1978) uses a resonance metaphor when describing memory retrieval. The probe is compared with a tuning fork. When a tuning fork of a particular frequency is struck and begins vibrating, other tuning forks with similar frequencies also begin vibrating. The magnitude of these sympathetic vibrations depends on how similar the frequency of a certain tuning fork is to the frequency of the original fork that was struck: The higher the similarity, the more sympathetic vibrations will result. Ratcliff envisaged the retrieval process as happening in a similar fashion. When a probe is presented, it leads to resonance from traces similar to the probe. The stronger the resonance, the greater the match between the probe and the trace in memory.

Information about how well the probe matches a certain trace does not arrive instantaneously but rather accumulates over time. Imagine that each feature of the probe must be compared with the features in the memory trace. A count is kept of the combined sum of feature matches and mismatches. Every time features match, the counter is increased, and every time a nonmatch is found, the counter is decreased. This feature process is a "noisy" process: That is, it is not free of error. Subjects may not always encode the probe or the memory set items completely, so even two stimuli that are nominally identical may not match perfectly. There is a certain positive value that serves as the match boundary: When the counter reaches that value, subjects decide a match has been made. There is also a negative value (that is, a value lower than the original starting point of the counter) that serves as a nonmatch boundary. When the counter reaches this nonmatch boundary, the subject determines that the probe does not match that trace. A negative response is made when all of the comparison processes happening in parallel end in a nonmatch. (Ratcliff actually derives the mathematics of his model by assuming that information is accumulated continuously, rather than by using discrete counts as in the foregoing description; however, the logic of the theory is not violated by using a discrete version.)

What factors would influence the speed of any one comparison process? One factor clearly is how quickly information can be accumulated (that is, how quickly can each comparison process be made). A second factor is the degree of match between the probe and the trace. If the probe and the trace are essentially a perfect match, then all of the feature comparisons will be positive, and the counter will reach the positive boundary quickly. When the probe and the trace are very dissimilar, most of the feature comparisons will be negative, and the counter will reach the negative boundary quickly. On the other hand, it will take much longer for the counter to reach a boundary when the similarity falls between these two extremes. The final factor that would influence the speed of any one comparison process is the position of the match and nonmatch boundaries. The more cautious a person wants to be, the farther he or she will place the boundaries from the starting point, and the longer it will take the counter to reach one of the boundaries.

Keep in mind that more than one comparison process is happening at the same time. Exactly how many comparisons are being performed on each trial in the Sternberg paradigm? Ratcliff assumes that the probe always contacts the members of the memory set. It is as if one feature in the probe is that it is occurring on a certain trial, and this feature causes a high enough similarity with all of the memory set items used on that trial to ensure that they would be contacted by the probe. Traces of stimuli not used on that trial may also be contacted, but these will generally have a high degree of dissimilarity to the probe. As a result, these comparisons will finish quickly and will have little effect on reaction times. (Remember that a positive response will be made when one counter reaches the positive boundary. A negative response will be made when all of the comparisons reach the negative boundary. Therefore, reaction time on negative trials will be determined by the slowest counter.)

What factors in this model are responsible for the linear increases in reaction time as a function of set size? On negative trials, as set size is increased, there are more traces that are contacted by the probe and more comparisons that must be completed before the subject can give a negative response. As there are more comparison processes, there is more of a chance that one or more of these comparisons will end up taking a relatively long time, which would lead to longer reaction times. On positive trials, set-size effects are due to poorer matches between the probe and the memory-set items. Imagine that, as set size increases, subjects encode each item less thoroughly. Therefore, each of these traces will be noisier. When these traces are compared with a probe, the comparison process is more likely to make errors when matching features, and therefore it will take longer for any process to reach the positive boundary.

Ratcliff (1978) has handled phenomena troublesome for the serial, exhaustive-scan model. Serial-position effects are believed (like set size) to reflect the degree of discriminability of the traces: Items from intermediate positions may not have been thoroughly encoded and therefore may take longer time to match than items from the beginning or end of the positive test. Stimulus probability may influence the boundaries that are set for a certain comparison process. If subjects know that a certain stimulus is particularly likely, they may move the boundaries closer to the starting point for comparisons between the probe and that stimulus. Repetition of a stimulus in a memory set may lead subjects to form two traces of that item and therefore perform two comparisons of that item with the probe. Subjects will respond positively as soon as the faster of these comparisons reaches the positive boundary, which should lead to an advantage in reaction time over trials where there is only one comparison that could result in a positive response.

Ratcliff's model is therefore able to capture all of the results that we have discussed in regard to the Sternberg paradigm. Admittedly, it can do so only by using a model that seems far more complicated than the other models we have been describing. However, Ratcliff's model is also far more ambitious than the other models. Whereas the other theories have mostly only tried to account for the changes in reaction time as a function of set size, Ratcliff has used his model to make predictions about a number of other characteristics of performance on this task, such as the variance of the reaction-time distributions for positive and negative responses and the precise shape of these distributions. Also, Ratcliff has applied his model to many other paradigms of recognition memory and cognitive decision processes. This is important, because we want our theories to have as much generality as possible. Therefore, although Ratcliff's model is sophisticated, it is no more complex than the tasks that Ratcliff has set out for it.

Ratcliff's model is just one example (albeit the most developed one) of the class of parallel-search theories. These theories have the benefit of having far more surface plausibility than previous accounts, such as Sternberg's. Moreover, they also seem to be more consistent with the empirical facts. Although Sternberg's serial, exhaustive-scan theory still tends to be given blindly by numerous textbooks as the explanation for performance in this task, there is strong evidence against that theory and in favor of models (such as Ratcliff's) that attribute performance to retrieval processes that become less effective as set size is increased.

CHAPTER SIX

Encoding Paradigms

Human memory is not an objective record of the events that have happened to us. Rather, it is influenced by the operations and processing that we perform on the events that we have experienced. (Some theorists would prefer to say that memory is nothing but a record of those operations and processes that we performed; see, e.g., Kolers & Roediger, 1984.) Thus, if we are to be able to say anything about how information is represented in the mind, we must know how it was initially encoded.

In this chapter, we will review three separate paradigms that have been developed to study how the nature of encoding influences later memory. No one of these paradigms has received as thorough an investigation as some of the others discussed in this book; thus, it is more practical to consider all three of them in a single chapter than to write three separate, short chapters. Moreover, these three paradigms grew out of similar concerns and have eventually led to similar conclusions. Thus, it is convenient to consider them in a single chapter from a thematic viewpoint as well.

THE LEVELS-OF-PROCESSING PARADIGM

A particular experimental procedure has been especially popular as a technique for studying encoding effects in human memory. In this procedure, subjects are required to perform some kind of operation on each item on a list. Later, memory is tested for the items. Often, this memory test was unexpected in that subjects had not been warned that they would be tested on the items while they were processing them; this kind of situation is known as *incidental learning.* Although there are many earlier variations on this procedure (see Eysenck, 1984, for a review), a particularly popular form of it was developed by Craik and Tulving (1975; see also Hyde & Jenkins, 1969, for earlier research along similar lines).

Craik and Tulving's (1975) experiments were intended as tests of the *levels-of-processing framework* proposed by Craik and Lockhart (1972). This framework stated that memory for information would depend on the depth to which that information had been processed; stimuli processed only shallowly (that is, only on a physical or perceptual basis) would not be remembered as well as information processed deeply (that is, meaningfully or semantically). In Craik and Tulving's experiments, subjects were told that they were in an experiment on the time it took people to answer various types of question. Before each trial a question would appear on a screen. The question might deal with physical aspects of a stimulus (e.g., "Is the word in capital letters?"), the sound of a stimulus (e.g., "Does the word rhyme with LOG?"), or its meaning (e.g., "Is the word a member of the category ANIMALS?" or "Would it fit in the sentence 'The boy had a pet——'?"). Then, a word would appear, and subjects would have to respond as rapidly as possible to the question. (For example, if the word "DOG" appeared, the person would have answered "yes" to each of the foregoing questions; if the word had been "house," the person would have answered "no.") Then, the word and question go off, followed by another question and another word. Thus, the subject has to answer one question for each word, and each question would demand a different kind of information about the word. After the subject went through a large number of these trials, an unexpected recognition test was given on the words. Some of the results from one of their experiments is shown in Table 6.1. That table presents the proportion of items recognized as a function of the type of question asked in the first phase about a word and whether the response to that question had been "yes" or "no." The most crucial finding was that memory for the words depended on the kind of question that had been answered about it in the first phase of the experiment. If the question had only inquired

TABLE 6.1
Recognition Performance as a Function of Orienting Question and Correct Response to Orienting Question

	Encoding Question			
Response	*Case*	*Rhyme*	*Category*	*Sentence*
Yes	.18	.78	.93	.96
No	.14	.36	.63	.83

From Craik & Tulving (1975).

about the word's appearance, recognition was quite poor. Performance was better for words processed with questions dealing with sound. Recognition was best for words processed with a question involving meaning. Thus, the deeper the processing, the better memory became. This has become a very popular memory technique. Although there is no one generally accepted name, the *levels-of-processing paradigm* seems an appropriate acknowledgment of the source of this experimental task.

One additional finding of the Craik and Tulving (1975) studies should be mentioned. They examined memory not only as a function of the type of question asked in the first phase but also as a function of the type of response in the first phase. Some questions in the first phase were meant to be responded to positively (e.g., the word DOG following the question "Does it rhyme with the word LOG?"). Other questions were intended to yield negative responses (e.g., the word HOUSE following the question "Does it fit into the sentence 'The boy had a pet——'?"). As is evident in Table 6.1, Craik and Tulving found that memory was better for words that had led to positive responses (e.g., DOG in the example given) than words that had led to negative responses (e.g., HOUSE in the example given). Bryant (1990) has replicated and extended this finding. One possible explanation is that subjects who forget a particular word may nevertheless remember being asked a particular question. If there is a strong relationship between the word and the question asked about it, subjects might be able to use the question as a retrieval cue to find the word they are trying to remember. For example, even if a person does not immediately remember having seen the word DOG, he or she might remember being asked about something rhyming with LOG. This could help them recognize positive stimuli such as DOG but would not help them on negative stimuli where there is no relationship between the question and the word.

The levels-of-processing framework had an enormous impact. One author commented that the Craik and Lockhart (1972) paper "undoubtedly has had the greatest influence of any single contribution published in the 1970's" (White, 1983, p. 426). This framework has inspired a lot of research and a considerable amount of heated criticism (e.g., Baddeley, 1978; Nelson, 1977). Time has forced many changes on Craik and Lockhart's framework as it was originally envisioned. Craik and Lockhart believed that only the meaningful aspects of a stimulus were likely to persist for a long time in memory. Certainly, there is evidence (dating back at least to Bartlett's, 1932, classic studies) that the exact wording of a text is usually quickly lost; this evidence would thus be in general agreement with Craik and Lockhart's prediction. However, it is possible to demonstrate memory for either exact wording or for the physical appearance of the stimuli when these aspects are particularly crucial or complex (Kolers, 1979).

One example of memory for physical appearance comes from the work of Kolers and Ostry (1974). These investigators had subjects read 60 sentences, each printed on a card. Half of these sentences were printed normally; the others were printed in an inverted (i.e., upside-down) typography that made then difficult to read. Later, subjects were given an additional set of cards containing sentences. Again, these sentences could be in either a normal or inverted typography. Thus, there were four possible conditions: Normal–Normal (presented in a normal format both times), Inverted–Inverted (presented in an inverted format both times), Normal–Inverted (presented normally in the first set but inverted in the second set), and Inverted–Normal (presented inverted in the first set but normally in the second). Subjects had to classify each of the sentences in the second set as either New (that is, that sentence had not been included in the first set), Same Form (the sentence had been shown in the first set in the same type format that it was shown in the second set) or Different Form (the sentence had been shown in the first set, but the type format had been changed). The results are shown in Table 6.2. The table shows the proportion of times that subjects used each of these three responses as a function of condition.

There are many important aspects to these results. The first to notice is that subjects were pretty accurate in remembering the physical form of the sentences that had been shown in the first set. Subjects were more likely to answer Same Form than Different Form when the Same Form was correct and were more likely to answer Different Form than Same Form when that was correct. This memory for physical form tended to be particularly accurate for sentences that had been originally encoded in an inverted format. Also note that recognition performance (that is, the likelihood of answering either Same Form or Different Form to a sentence that was not new) was higher for sentences that had been presented initially in an inverted form. This finding has been replicated many times and at least partly reflects the extensive processing that subjects had to do to read the inverted sentences (Tardif & Craik, 1989). This ex-

TABLE 6.2
Distribution of Responses as a Function of Condition

	Condition			
Response	*Normal–Normal*	*Inverted–Inverted*	*Normal–Inverted*	*Inverted–Normal*
Same form	.40	.57	.17	.27
Different form	.23	.20	.24	.47
New	.37	.23	.59	.26

From Kolers & Ostry (1974).

tensive processing (which is both perceptual and semantic) leads to better memory performance. Finally, note in Table 6.2 that recognition is better for sentences presented in the same way at encoding and test than for sentences presented in different ways at the two times.

We know now that semantic processing is not always better than physical or phonological processing. For example, when subjects are later given a test that emphasizes the sounds of the items, rather than their identities or meanings, performance is best for words that had been processed for sound. Fisher and Craik (1977; Experiment 1) showed this by testing subjects for cued recall. In their experiments, subjects saw a list of words and had to answer a question about each one. One-third of the questions involved sound, asking whether the word rhymed with another stimulus. One-third of the questions asked whether the word belonged to a particular semantic category. The remaining questions required subjects to indicate whether each word would fit into a particular sentence. Subjects were subsequently given a test where they were given a rhyming word, a category label, or a sentence to use as a cue for each word. The results for positive items are shown in Table 6.3. There are two striking aspects to these results. First, note that there is a levels-of-processing effect. That is, if you were to average the three numbers in each row, you would see that the encoding conditions that involve semantic processing (the category and sentence encoding conditions) lead to much better memory than the one that only requires processing of sound (the rhyme condition). The second striking aspect of the table, however, is the way in which encoding condition interacts with retrieval cue. The highest number in each row falls along the main diagonal where there is a match between encoding and retrieval conditions. Thus, if you are going to be given a rhyme cue at test, you are actually better off if you had processed the word for sound initially. There is no benefit for semantic encoding if the retrieval conditions do not utilize that kind of information. This result is reminiscent of Kolers and Ostry's (1974) finding that recognition performance was best when the typographical form was

TABLE 6.3
Probability of Recall as a Function of Orienting Question and Retrieval Cue

	Retrieval Cue		
Orienting Question	*Rhyme*	*Category*	*Sentence*
Rhyme	.40	.15	.10
Category	.43	.81	.50
Sentence	.29	.46	.78

From Fisher & Craik (1977).

the same at encoding and test. This suggests the generality of the principle that memory performance is best when the encoding and test situations are as similar as possible.

A similar point was made in a study by Morris, Bransford, and Franks (1977). These investigators employed a memory test where subjects had to indicate whether a test item sounded the same as any of the list items. When this kind of sound-based test was given, subjects performed best when they had been given an acoustic-processing question about the word during list presentation, rather than a semantic-processing question. Studies such as those by Fisher and Craik (1977) and Morris et al. (1977) led to the realization that the sort of processing that is best for a stimulus depends on the nature of the test to be given (a principle that has been called either the *encoding-specificity principle* or the *transfer-appropriate processing principle,* depending on the situation and the preferences of the writer). Memory performance is a function of the degree of match between the processing carried out at encoding and the retrieval information that is available at the time of test. The fact that semantic-processing questions generally lead to better recall and recognition suggests that subjects usually rely on meaning in these tasks.

The sort of processing that is optimal may also depend on the nature of the stimuli to be learned. For example, Intraub and Nicklos (1985) have shown that, when the stimuli are visually rich, distinctive pictures, memory is better for pictures processed physically than for pictures processed semantically. (In a 1990 review paper, Lockhart & Craik admit that this study is particularly problematical for their original conception of levels of processing.) It is possible that, when the experimenter does not supply any explicit cues, subjects tend to rely on whichever dimension of the stimulus seems richer or more complex. For most word lists, meaning is richer and more distinctive than structural aspects, like sound or visual appearance. After all, words are all formed from a very constrained set of letters and sounds. However, meaning is much less constrained and may allow for far greater richness of experience. On the other hand, when the stimuli are created to be particularly distinctive in terms of their visual appearance (as was the case with the Intraub & Nicklos stimuli), physical processing might be more effective.

THE GENERATION EFFECT

Slamecka and Graf (1978) initiated systematic work in the area of the memorial consequences of stimulus generation. They had taken note of the common claim that learning by doing is an effective way of acquiring knowledge. Many authors had urged learners to take active roles in the creation and organization of the information they want to acquire. However, Slamecka and Graf noted that there was little experimental research that really documented this claim. This had not been the sort of thing that memory researchers using standard laboratory tasks had heavily studied. What little research had been done in this area was marred either by questionable procedures or inconsistent results.

Slamecka and Graf (1978) designed a laboratory procedure to study the effects of self-creation or generation of to-be-remembered material. They compared two conditions. The first is a *read* condition, where the stimuli are created by the experimenter and shown to the subject who has to read them aloud. The second condition is a *generate* condition in which the subject has to create the stimuli. There is a potential pitfall here. If the generation process is completely unconstrained, the subject might generate items that are not at all comparable with those used in the read condition. The items a subject generates might end up differing on important dimensions such as familiarity, concreteness, or meaningfulness from the items used in the read condition. Therefore, the experiment has to be designed so that the experimenter knows beforehand which words will be generated.

Slamecka and Graf (1978) accomplished this by giving subjects a *generation rule* in the generate condition. Then, subjects are given a stimulus word and the first letter of the word they have to generate. For example, subjects might be told "opposite" as the rule. Then, they would be shown "long—s," and subjects would have to say the response "short" (i.e., the opposite of the word "long"). The other generation rules that were used were associate (e.g., subjects would see "lamp—l" and would give the response "light"), same-category membership (e.g., "ruby—d" for the response "diamond"), synonym (e.g., "sea—o" for the response "ocean"), and rhyme (e.g., "save—c" for the response "cave"). Subjects would go through 100 stimulus–response pairs, with equal numbers of pairs utilizing each of the five rules. In the read condition, both the stimulus and the response terms would be printed out entirely, and subjects had to read them aloud. In the read condition, there were the same five relationships (opposite, associate, category, synonym, and rhyme) between the stimulus and response terms. After subjects had gone through 100 pairs of words, they were given a test on their memory for the response terms; for different groups of subjects, the test could be either recognition or recall. Memory depended in part on the rule determining the relationship between the words. Memory was poorer for the words that rhymed than for the word pairs related by the semantic rules. However, the central comparison here was between the read and generate conditions. The generate condition led to better recall and recognition, and the magnitude of this difference was roughly equal for all of the rules used by Slamecka and Graf (1978). They termed this advantage for subject-generated responses the *generation effect.* (At about the same time, Jacoby, 1978, independently reported similar findings.)

One of the most striking aspects of the generation effect is its broad generality. For example, a number of generation rules could lead to large enhancements over memory. As already mentioned, Slamecka and Graf (1978) used five different generation rules and found roughly comparable generation effects for all of them. Even amazingly simple rules can lead to enhanced recall. One such simple rule is a letter-switching rule. Subjects see items such as "ehAVEN." They are told to copy the word that results from switching the order of the first two letters (in this case, HEAVEN). To make the task even easier, the first two letters are often printed in a different case than the other letters to allow subjects to focus immediately on the letters that must be switched. This sort of task demands no semantic processing at all, and subjects can generally do this error-free. Nevertheless, this letter-switching generation rule leads to much better memory than is found for words presented normally that are read by the subject (Greene, 1988, 1989c; Nairne, Pusen, & Widner, 1985; Nairne & Widner, 1987). Thus, a generation rule need not be difficult to lead to a robust generation effect.

Slamecka and Graf (1978), and most of the researchers following them, were careful to arrange their experiments so that the subjects would almost always be able to generate the response that the experimenter had in mind. The generation task was made quite simple. Although this simplifies the interpretation of this research, it does not correspond to how generation often occurs in everyday life, where we may often try (and fail) to find the response that we are trying to generate. Slamecka and Fevreiski (1983) examined the situation where generation fails. In one of their conditions, they used a very challenging generation task. The list consisted of word pairs that were relatively unfamiliar opposites. In the generate condition, subjects saw each stimulus term and the first letter of each of the response terms (e.g., "trivial—v," and the subject should respond "vital"). These unfamiliar opposites were rather difficult to generate, so there was a significant number of generate pairs where the subject was not able to supply the necessary response. In those cases, the experimenter supplied the response, and the subject merely read it. When a free-recall test was given, performance was equivalent on the responses that had been generated or that subjects had failed to generate. In each case, performance was much higher than for the read words. Thus, the subject does not have to generate an item to bring about a generation effect. Rather, this effect is found as long as the subject *tries* to generate the item.

Most researchers in this area have used verbal stimuli, but it is easy to demonstrate the generation effect with numbers as well. Gardiner and Rowley (1984) performed an experiment in which subjects saw 20 cards presented one at a time at a 4-s rate. Half of the cards presented an equation (e.g., $9 \times 4 = 36$), and subjects had to read the equation aloud. On the other half of the cards, the answer to the problem was missing (e.g., $8 \times 5 = ?$), and subjects had to read the equation aloud, including the multiplication product that they had to generate. Later, subjects were given either a recognition or a free-recall test on the products. Memory was much better for those products that the subject had to generate than for those that the subject only read aloud. Crutcher and Healy (1989) showed that the way that subjects generated a solution was important. The generation effect for numbers was found only when subjects had to find the answers using their own knowledge. On the other hand, when subjects were given calculators and were allowed to use these devices to generate the arithmetical answers, memory performance for these products on a later test was much poorer. In fact, there was no significant difference between the products that had been determined using a calculator and those that had been merely read. This demonstrates that the magnitude of the generation effect depends on the amount of mental work that goes into the generation process. Of course, this finding also has practical implications as well. If a person wants to remember the answer to a calculation, it is better if that person did the arithmetic work, rather than relying on a calculator. This might be particularly important for young children as they are first mastering multiplication. Working out a problem for themselves without a calculator might help them to memorize the products that they have to learn eventually.

Theoretical Accounts of the Generation Effect

There have been a number of theoretical accounts that have been proposed. Ideally, one would like to be able to say that, as these accounts evolved, they became sharper and more refined. Unfortunately, it is more accurate to say only that they have become more complicated. However, although we would always prefer our theories to be parsimonious, one should not resist complex theories when the data demand them.

Effort. The first thing that strikes people as they consider the difference between read and generated material is that the learner must direct considerably more effort on the latter than on the former. Perhaps this is the whole basis for the effect. It is certainly true that those memorization strategies that are most effective require effort on the part of a learner. The generation effect could then be seen as part of a general relationship between effort and memorability. Presumably, this kind of explanation could be extended to the levels-of-processing findings as well. Perhaps the reason why semantic orienting questions lead to better retention than questions concerning physical appearance or sound (Craik & Tulving, 1975) is just because semantic questions are more difficult to answer.

It should be noted that such an effort account would not be truly an explanation. After all, even if one accepts the claim that generation effects merely reflect the effort that is expended in generation, it would be necessary to go on and offer an explanation for why effort influences memory. Still, if the evidence did point to an effort account of this phenomenon, that would be a valuable contribution in that it would point in the direction that theories of the generation effect must go, namely, in the direction of processes broader than generation itself. Presumably any experimental manipulation that influenced the effort expended by subjects would thus have an influence on memory.

This effort account would predict that the nature of the stimuli should be irrelevant here. Any stimulus that is more difficult to generate than to read should exhibit generation effect. Let us specifically consider the case of *nonwords,* that is, letter strings that do not make up words. It is surely possible to have subjects generate a nonword. For example, given a rhyming generation rule, subjects could be given "samp w" and would respond with "wamp." This does not seem any less effortful than when such a rhyming rule is applied to words. In fact, one might even argue that the use of nonwords could make the task slightly more effort demanding, insofar as the subject would not be able to retrieve the correct response from memory. Thus, an effort account might lead to the prediction that generation effects would be larger for nonwords than for words.

McElroy and Slamecka (1982) were the first investigators to examine the effects of generation on nonwords. Subjects received a list composed of word pairs and nonword pairs. The word pairs were opposites (e.g., hot–cold). In the read condition, both words in a pair were shown; in the generate condition, subjects had to generate the second term from the first one. An example of a nonword pair used was "dand–snad." Some nonword pairs were merely read by the subject. Other nonword pairs had to be generated through a letter-transposition rule. Subjects would be shown "dand—s" and would be required to put the first three letters of the stimulus in backward order after the consonant provided as first letter of the response. Although this task certainly seemed to require some effort, McElroy and Slamecka found no effect of generation on nonwords in either recall or recognition. In contrast, the standard generation effect was found on the word responses. When McElroy and Slamecka switched the nonword generation rule to one involving rhyme, they again found that there was no difference between read and generated nonwords. This suggests that effort alone cannot be responsible for the generation effect since generation of nonwords would appear to be at least as effortful as generation of words. Later investigators have replicated this null effect on nonwords (e.g., Greene, 1988; Nairne et al., 1985).

One might notice that, in the McElroy and Slamecka (1982) experiments, either both the stimulus term and the response term were words or they were both nonwords. Technically, one cannot be sure how the use of nonwords limits the generation effect. To obtain a null effect of generation, must both the stimulus and response be nonwords or would having only one of them be a nonword suffice? Payne, Neely, and Burns (1986) addressed this question. Using a rhyming generation rule, they factorially separated the effects of the lexical status of the stimulus and response terms. Possible pairs included "chop–shop," "chop–thop," "phop–shop," and "phop–thop." In other words, there were word–word pairs, word–nonword pairs, nonword–word pairs, and nonword–nonword pairs. Equal numbers of pairs were read or generated by the subject. Payne et al. found that only the lexical status of the response terms mattered. No generation effect was found when the response term was a nonword, whether or not the stimulus term was also a nonword.

Nonwords are not the only stimuli that fail to exhibit generation effects when used as to-be-remembered material. Nairne et al. (1985) found that the magnitude of the generation effect depended on the frequency with which words occurred in everyday English. No generation effect was found when low-frequency words were used as stimuli. Subsequent research established that word frequency per se was not as important as the familiarity of the words to the subject (Gardiner, Gregg, & Hampton, 1988; Nairne & Widner, 1988).

Familiarity plays a role here even when it applies to compound stimuli. For example, Gardiner and Hampton (1985) found that there was no generation effect when subjects had to generate noun compounds that were unfamiliar (e.g., *cheese ketchup*). In contrast, the typical generation effect was found when subjects had to generate familiar noun compounds (e.g., *tomato ketchup*). Similarly, generation effects were found when subjects generated familiar letter compounds (e.g., *ET,* a popular movie of the time) but not when unfamiliar letter compounds were generated (e.g., *EC*).

The reason why familiarity is crucial here is not clear. One possibility discussed by Nairne and Widner (1987) is that subjects tend not to encode unfamiliar stimuli holistically. Rather, they focus only on that part of the stimulus that they themselves have to generate. When subjects are later tested for their memory for the whole unit, they do rather poorly. Nairne and Widner go on to report some evidence in support of this conjecture. For our present purposes, it is sufficient to note that the fact that generation effects depend on the nature of the stimuli used and not just on the effort expended by the subject is very damaging for simple effort accounts of this phenomenon.

Moreover, an effort account of the generation effect is plausible only if there is convincing evidence that effort inevitably influences memory performance. Such evidence is lacking. After a review of the relevant empirical studies, Mitchell and Hunt (1989) concluded that "the literature provides ample evidence that changes in cognitive effort are not sufficient to produce changes in memory" (p. 343). Thus, other explanations must be sought for the generation effect.

Rehearsal. A rehearsal account would be a more specific version of the effort account. That is, rather than saying that increases in any sort of effort expenditure are sufficient to improve memory, some theorists (most explicitly, Slamecka & Katsaiti, 1987) have argued that one particular kind of expenditure, namely, rehearsal, is implicated here. Since many other memory phenomena have been attributed to the role of rehearsal, this account would have the advantage of seeing generation effects as just one more manifestation of a broad phenomenon.

The impetus for this account came from experiments that employed a different design than most previous generation-effect studies. Typically, early investigators had presented a list that contained both to-be-read items and to-be-generated items. In other words, generation was generally manipulated as a *within-subjects variable.* However, several investigators carried out a line of research where generation was manipulated as a *between-subjects variable:* That is, some subjects received a list containing items that they read, and other subjects received a list composed entirely of items that had to be generated. The surprising result was that there was no generation effect. Generated lists were remembered no better (and sometimes slightly worse) than read lists (Begg & Snider, 1987; Schmidt & Cherry, 1989; Slamecka & Katsaiti, 1987).

This surprising result led Slamecka and Katsaiti (1987) to argue that rehearsal strategies were responsible for earlier reports of generation effects. These authors argued that, when subjects received a list containing both read and generated items, they adopt a strategy of devoting little rehearsal to the items they had to read. Instead, subjects devote most of their time to the rehearsal of generated items. When subjects receive a list containing only read items or only generated items, they are not able to follow this sort of strategy, and therefore generated items would not be at an advantage any more.

There are several unsatisfactory aspects to this account immediately. It is not at all clear why subjects would follow a strategy of rehearsing generated items more than read items. Moreover, there is no straightforward answer as to why nonwords and other unfamiliar stimuli do not exhibit generation effects even when generation is manipulated within lists. Slamecka and Katsaiti (1987) simply suggested that subjects follow a different rehearsal strategy when memorizing nonwords. Reasons why this should be true and empirical evidence supporting this suggestion are both lacking.

However, it was a straightforward experiment that eliminated rehearsal accounts of generation effects. Watkins and Sechler (1988) examined incidental memory for read and generated items. Subjects were shown a list containing both to-be-read and to-be-generated items. However, they were given the impression that their memory for the items would not be tested. Thus, these subjects would have no reason to adopt any sort of a rehearsal strategy. Nevertheless, a substantial generation effect was found. (In fact, the magnitude of the generation effect was significantly larger for incidental-learning subjects than for a group of intentional-learning subjects who had been warned beforehand that their memory for the list would be tested.) The presence of a generation effect in subjects who were not employing deliberate rehearsal strategies is inconsistent with Slamecka and Katsaiti's (1987) rehearsal account of this phenomenon.

Multiprocess Theories. Several theorists have noted that generation effects may be found for many kinds of stimuli on many different kinds of memory task. Moreover, a large number of different generation rules may be successfully employed. For the sake of parsimony, early researchers assumed that a single theory would be sufficient to account for all of the manifestations of the generation effect. However, beginning in the 1980s, this parsimonious approach has been abandoned. Increasingly, researchers have become aware that the precise explanation that must be given for the finding of a generation effect may depend on the stimuli, generation rule, and memory task that were employed. (Additional factors, such as the nature of the subject population used, may also be important, but there is currently little evidence on this.) Thus, complicated *multiprocess theories* have increasingly become popular in this area (see particularly Burns, 1990; Hirshman & Bjork, 1988; McDaniel, Waddill, & Einstein, 1988).

McDaniel et al. (1988) have argued for a three-process theory. They suggested that three kinds of processing are enhanced by generation. First, subjects perform increased processing of the stimulus that they generate. Second, they strengthen the association between the generated stimulus and the cue that was given. Third, subjects might strengthen the associations among the generated stimuli on the list. For example, when subjects saw "long—s" and are told to use an "opposite" generation rule, the processing required to generate the word "short" leads to the placing of more *item information* about the word "short" in memory. Also, since generation depends upon the relationship between the word "long" and the word "short," subjects store more *relational information* about the connection between those two words. In addition, subjects will continue to ponder the word "short" while other words on the list are being generated. This will lead to an increase in *whole-list information,* that is, to increased associations between one generated stimulus and another. McDaniel et al. see even this three-process account as being an oversimplification, stating that "generation will enhance processing of whatever information subjects are able to utilize to accomplish the generation task, and generation effects will occur to the extent that the memory test requires that information" (pp. 534–535).

A large number of empirical findings can be explained by this approach (see McDaniel et al., 1988, for an extended defense of this proposal). The most troubling aspects of this account are its complexity and vagueness. Saying that generation may enhance any kind of information means that it becomes very hard to know how to disprove this kind of account. However, this may have been inevitable. In retrospect, it appears unlikely that one would have expected generation of any kind of stimulus according to any kind of rule to have effects that could be captured by a simple theory. More precise theories will have to be developed for specific situations.

MAINTENANCE REHEARSAL

The two paradigms discussed earlier in this chapter both illustrated a basic point, namely, that the way in which a stimulus is processed will influence later memory for that stimulus. A related question is how memory is affected when subjects devote as little processing as possible to a stimulus. Given that there are some kinds of processing that are better than others in benefitting memory, is there a kind of processing that is completely ineffective?

This question is addressed in the literature dealing with *maintenance rehearsal.* This literature was truly begun by Craik and Lockhart's (1972) landmark paper on the levels-of-processing approach. They made a distinction between Type 1 and Type 2 processing. According to Craik and Lockhart, Type 1 processing is "repetition of processes which have already been carried out" (p. 676). This sort or processing "merely prolongs an item's high accessibility without leading to formation of a more permanent memory trace" (p. 676). On the other hand, Type 2 processing is "deeper analysis of the stimulus" (p. 676) and leads to the creation of a long-lasting trace. When discussing Type 1 rehearsal, Craik and

Lockhart had in mind the sort of mnemonic activity you might do when looking up a telephone number. You would look up the number and then perhaps say it over and over in your head while you walk to the phone and begin dialing. This sort of rote repetition would help you to maintain the phone number until you are finished dialing. However, if asked for the number later, it is unlikely that you would exhibit any memory for it. It is as if the rote repetition of the number simply maintained the phone number while having little impact on your long-term retention. On the other hand, when Craik and Lockhart described Type 2 processing, they had in mind the sorts of creative analysis of a stimulus that could lead to good long-term memory.

The distinction between two different kinds of processing became popular. The Type 1–Type 2 terminology fell out of fashion and eventually the terms *maintenance rehearsal* and *elaborative rehearsal* became more widely used. Maintenance rehearsal usually refers to the continuous repetition and maintenance of information using minimal cognitive resources. Elaborative rehearsal is usually used to refer to all other mnemonic processes, such as chunking, forming images, organizing items, and so on. There is no question that elaborative rehearsal can benefit memory and that memory generally improves when subjects are allowed to devote more time to the elaborative rehearsal of a stimulus. However, considerable effort was expended beginning in the 1970s to determining how maintenance rehearsal affected memory for a stimulus.

Maintenance-Rehearsal Procedures

Directed-Forgetting Experiments on Maintenance Rehearsal. Some of the first work studying maintenance rehearsal was performed using a directed-forgetting manipulation. A study by Woodward, Bjork, and Jongeward (1973) has served as the prototype here. In this study, items were presented individually and were each followed by an unfilled rehearsal interval of 0, 4, or 12 s. Then, the subjects were required to recall the item. After this recall, subjects were told either to try to remember the item for a later test or to forget it. After going through 36 trials, subjects were asked to recall the words they had been told to remember. Then subjects went through 36 more trials. The experiment continued until subjects had gone through four lists, each composed of 36 trials. Then, subjects were given an unexpected request to recall all of the items on the list, including the ones that they had been told would not be tested. Recall was above chance even for words that subjects had not expected to be tested. However, recall was uninfluenced by retention interval; subjects were no more likely to recall words that they had initially rehearsed for 12 s than words that they had not been allowed to rehearse at all. After this recall test was completed, subjects were given a recognition test on the items. Recognition performance did improve slightly but significantly as a function of initial rehearsal interval.

What is the logic behind this study? Woodward et al. (1973) assumed that subjects would only be maintaining the item during the rehearsal interval. Because there was no way of knowing whether the item would have to be remembered, it would be reasonable not to engage in effortful elaborative processing during the rehearsal interval but rather to engage in the less demanding process of maintenance rehearsal. If one assumes that subjects engaged in pure maintenance rehearsal here, then this study suggests that engaging in such rehearsal can lead to above-chance performance on both recall and recognition tests but that the duration of maintenance rehearsal affects only recognition but not recall. There are some serious methodological problems with this technique. Perhaps the most worrisome is the possibility that subjects engaged in elaborative rehearsal during the rehearsal interval for each item. Other paradigms have thus been developed to address the question of how maintenance rehearsal influences memory.

Rehearsal-Interval Experiments. In a number of experiments, researchers have examined the effects of maintenance rehearsal by comparing retention of items that had been accompanied by either unfilled rehearsal intervals or intervals filled with a rehearsal-preventing distractor task. Perhaps the most compelling of these studies was reported by Dark and Loftus (1976). The Brown-Peterson paradigm was employed here. Subjects were given short lists (three to five words). These lists had to be retained through an interval during which the subjects were either allowed to rehearse aloud or were required to perform a distracting task. After this interval, subjects were sometimes asked to recall the list; other times, they were given another task to do until presentation of the next list. After going through a large number of lists, subjects were given an unanticipated final free-recall test for all of the words that had been presented in the experiment. Final recall increased as a function of retention interval when that interval involved rehearsal. However, when subjects were not allowed to rehearse during the retention interval, the duration of this interval had no effect on this final recall test. Thus, results from this sort of task generally suggest that recall is affected by the amount of maintenance rehearsal devoted to a stimulus.

Scanning Experiments. In these experiments, subjects are given a long series of words. They are told that they will have to report the last word in the series of a certain type (e.g., the last word that begins with the letter C). Then, subjects are given an unexpected recall test on the words of that type. The rationale here is that, when subjects see a word of the appropriate type (e.g., COW), they will use maintenance rehearsal to keep that word easily accessible until they see a later word of that type. Then, they stop rehearsing the older word and begin rehearsing the new word while they continue scanning the list. The amount of maintenance rehearsal that each item receives would be a function of the distance between words of the target type. Thus, one can see how the duration of maintenance rehearsal influences recall by seeing how recall is influenced by the amount of time for which a word was the last one encountered of that type. Although the results have not been totally consistent, in general, increased rehearsal time does seem to lead to small but significant improvements in later recall (Maki & Schuler, 1980).

Distractor Experiments. The most popular approach to studying the effects of maintenance rehearsal was developed independently by Glenberg et al. (1977) and Rundus (1977). Subjects are told that they are in an experiment on short-term memory for digits. They are shown a short string of digits. Then, one word (or a small set of words) appears, and subjects have to rehearse it aloud over and over for a period of time. Then, subjects are asked for recall of the digits. This goes on until subjects have gone through dozens of trials. Throughout the experiment, subjects are given the impression that only recall of the digits matters and that repeating the words aloud is just a nuisance task. Thus, subjects are motivated to minimize the attention that they devote to the words so that they can better retain the digits. At the end of the experiment, subjects are given one or more unexpected memory tests on the words, and experimenters examine how retention of the words is affected by the length of time for which each had been rehearsed. The general finding is that the duration of rehearsal consistently has significant effects on recognition of the words. When a free-recall test was given instead, the effects of duration rehearsal are much smaller and sometimes nonsignificant (Glenberg et al., 1977; Rundus, 1977, 1980). The results from this task seem particularly convincing because it appears to be the most methodologically sound way of studying maintenance rehearsal.

How Does Maintenance Rehearsal Affect Memory?

Results from all four of the procedures that have been discussed converge on the conclusion that memory is affected by the duration of maintenance rehearsal. The more rehearsal that is devoted to an item (no matter how easy and mindless the rehearsal is), the better later memory for that item will be. The effects are often small and are more consistently found when recognition is used as the memory task than when recall is tested. Still, there is little doubt that maintenance rehearsal does affect the accessibility of items in memory.

The mechanisms through which maintenance rehearsal has this effect have been illuminated by an experiment reported by Glenberg and Adams (1978). Words were maintained for a rehearsal interval that could vary between 1.33 s and 13.33 s. Subjects were led to believe that they would not be tested on the words; thus, it is reasonable to believe that they simply maintained the words with as little effort as possible. At the end of the experiment, subjects were given an unanticipated five-alternative, forced-choice recognition test on the words. One of the alternatives was a word that had been presented in the experiment. Another alternative was a word that sounded like a word that had been presented in the experiment. A third alternative was a word that had a meaning similar to the one that had been presented earlier. The two other alternatives were just filler words. Subjects were required to pick the word out of each set of five alternatives that had been shown on the list. In agreement with the findings reviewed here, accuracy at this task increased as a function of the duration of rehearsal that had been devoted to that word. However, the errors that subjects made were particularly interesting. When a subject had rehearsed a particular word for a long time, they were more likely to choose the alternative that sounded like the right response, rather than one of the other incorrect alternatives. The probability of choosing the alternative with a meaning similar to the correct choice did not significantly vary as a function of rehearsal time. In short, it appears from this study that, as maintenance rehearsal progresses, subjects are storing more and more information about how an item sounds. Thus, they become more likely to choose the correct word or an alternative that sounds like the correct word as a function of the duration of maintenance rehearsal.

Why is it that it has been easier to find effects of maintenance rehearsal when testing recognition rather than recall? It is generally accepted that recall and recognition tasks are differentially influenced by particular kinds of information stored in a memory trace (e.g., Anderson & Bower, 1973; Gillund & Shiffrin, 1984). In recognition, subjects are shown the list items again. The probability of recognizing an item will largely depend on the amount of *item information* that had been stored for that word. In contrast, in free recall, the difficult part of the task arises from trying to locate the possible responses in memory. Free recall tends to be particularly influenced by *whole-list information,* that is, associations between items. There is considerable evidence that maintenance rehearsal is a very inefficient way of strengthening associations between words on a list (Bradley & Glenberg, 1983; Glenberg & Bradley, 1983; Nairne, 1983). Thus, maintenance rehearsal tends to have weaker and more inconsistent effects on free recall than it has on recognition.

CONCLUSION

Three different memory paradigms have been examined in this chapter. Each one addresses the question of how retention for an event is influenced by the initial encoding of that event. Results from the levels-of-processing paradigm have demonstrated that memory for an event is influenced by the exhaustiveness with which it had been processed. The literature on the generation effect shows that memory for stimuli is particularly good when subjects have to generate them for themselves. Finally, the data from maintenance-rehearsal experiments have shown that continuing even the most rudimentary processing can have effects on the accessibility of memory traces.

The bottom line is that memory is improved *when subjects do more.* That is, the more processing that is devoted to an event, the better retention for it will be. An implication of this is that there are few shortcuts to good memory performance. Memory is improved by working on the material that has to be retained. However, there are qualifications to this. Not all kinds of memorial work are equally effective. For example, maintenance rehearsal, although it does influence later retention, is generally inefficient. One can greatly improve memory faster by performing fancy mnemonic tricks (e.g., imagery) than by simply repeating a word over and over. Another important qualification is that the question of what kinds of processing are optimal for later retention will depend on the nature of the memory test that will be given. There is no one processing that is best for all kinds of testing situations. A complete understanding of memory involves knowing the circumstances that prevail at test as well as those that obtained during encoding.

CHAPTER SEVEN

Repetition Paradigms

The saying "practice makes perfect" illustrates the accepted fact that repetition is crucial for learning. All other things being equal, our memory for information will depend on the number of times that we have encountered or studied it. This was discussed by numerous ancient and medieval philosophers. The role of repetition was documented empirically by Hermann Ebbinghaus (1885/1964), the first researcher to carry out a systematic series of experiments on learning and memory. Ebbinghaus showed that the retention of information (usually nonsense syllables in his studies) consistently improved as a function of the number of times that the information had been studied. In the century since the completion of Ebbinghaus's work, countless investigators have used repetition as a manipulation in experiments on learning in humans or other species. The *learning curve* has become a commonly presented figure in texts of learning and memory. Such a curve presents learning or retention as a function of number of opportunities for study. A prototypical learning curve is displayed in Fig. 7.1. The shape of this curve may be called monotonic, negatively accelerated. By "monotonic," I mean only that the curve goes in only one direction (namely, upward). By "negatively accelerated," I refer to the fact that the rate of upward movement is always slowing down. The greatest increases in learning occur as a result of the first few occurrences of information, and eventually the increases in learning that result from repetition become so small as to be undetectable.

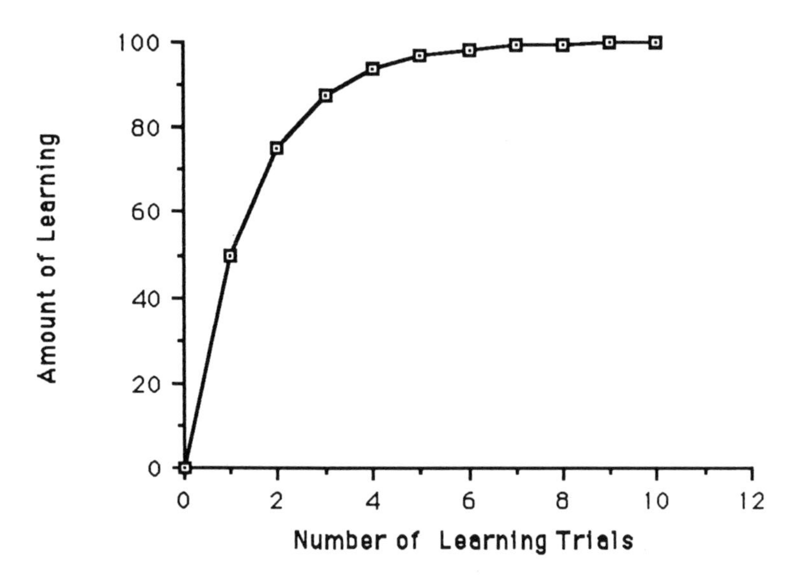

FIG. 7.1. A typical learning curve.

Since repetition has been so well studied, one would think that the mechanisms behind its effects would be well understood. This turns out to be false. Indeed, even though the theoretical issues underlying repetition effects on memory have been discussed for more than a century, there is no universally accepted resolution. In fact, there are two separate paradigms that have been developed to deal with repetition effects. Both of these paradigms will be discussed here. This chapter will first deal with the major accounts for why repetition affects memory. Then, attention will turn to a paradigm used for discriminating between these accounts, the *frequency-judgment task*. Finally, the *spacing-effect paradigm*, an analysis of the way that the distribution of repetitions influences memory, will be discussed.

THEORETICAL ACCOUNTS OF REPETITION EFFECTS IN MEMORY

Ward (1893) distinguished between two possible explanations for why repetition generally leads to an improvement in learning and memory. Ward gave these explanations the names of *functional views* and *atomistic views*. Although Ward's terminology has not been widely used, the distinction that he drew is still the major one dividing theories in this area.

Functional Views

By a functional view of repetition effects, Ward meant the idea that repetition has the effect of altering one particular representation in memory. That is, there is one trace in memory that corresponds to a particular event or concept. Every time that that event or concept or event is encountered, that trace is altered somehow. This alteration has the effect of increasing the availability of that trace.

Strength Theory. Perhaps the most obvious way to phrase this kind of approach is in terms of the strength of memory traces. According to such an approach, all traces in memory would differ along some unidimensional property that can be called trace strength. Stronger traces are assumed to be more resistant to forgetting and more easily retrieved than are weaker traces. This sort of account seems to flow naturally from the shape of the learning curve that is usually found and was favored by Ebbinghaus (1885/1964) himself. Presumably, repetition would always lead to increases in trace strength, but the magnitude of such increases would be a negatively accelerated function of repetition. This account is the traditional explanation for repetition effects. Suggestions of this approach can be found in the ancient philosophers' discussion of repetition and memory. Also, learning researchers (such as Clark Hull) from the early and middle twentieth century who based their theories primarily upon research on animals often included notions of trace strength or habit strength.

Attribute Theory. A second sort of functional view is epitomized by the theory of Underwood (1969). He held that every event is represented by a single memory trace. Part of that trace is an internal counter. Every time that the event is encountered, the counter is advanced by a certain unit. Underwood's theory was initially advanced to explain results found in experiments on ***verbal discrimination learning***. In this task, subjects are first shown a list composed of pairs of words. One member of each pair is arbitrarily chosen by the experimenter as the correct member of the pair; it may be indicated by being underlined or starred. The experimenter tells the subjects to study the list so that they will be able to remember which word in each pair is the correct one. After the list has been shown, subjects are given a test in which they are shown all the word pairs and must choose the correct item in each pair. Then, subjects are shown the list again and receive another test. This process continues until performance is perfect or until a specified number of learning trials has been reached. Subjects generally do quite well on this task even when very long lists are presented.

Underwood (1969) argued that, every time a word pair is shown, frequency counters associated with each word are incremented. In addition, subjects will most likely rehearse the correct item in each pair but not the incorrect item; this rehearsal would lead to an additional increase in that item's counter. This suggests that, on each trial, the correct word will receive a greater increase in its counter than the incorrect word. When subjects are asked to choose the correct word, they pick the one that has the greatest frequency count.

Although this theory was originally intended to explain results from the verbal-discrimination task, it can be easily applied to recognition memory as well. In a recognition experiment, subjects are given a test that consists of some stimuli that had been presented earlier and others that are new. The frequency counters of the old stimuli would be higher than those for the new items, so subjects would be able to perform this memory task by consulting the frequency counters of each test stimulus and giving a positive recognition response for those with the highest counts. If an item had been studied on repeated occasions, its frequency counter would be particularly high, and recognition of that item would be especially good. Thus, this sort of approach can offer a general explanation for repetition effects in memory.

Atomistic Views

By an atomistic view, Ward (1893) meant theories that would explain repetition effects not by a strengthening or growth of a pre-existing trace but rather by the creation of new, independent traces. Every time that we encounter the word ACCORDION, we would create a separate trace that contains information about the circumstances under which that stimulus had been encountered. When we are later asked whether we saw the word ACCORDION in a certain context, we would retrieve traces of that word and see if any of them had been formed in the context being tested. If we are memorizing a list of words and the word LAWYER occurs at several independent places on the list, we would form several traces of that word. We would be more likely to remember LAWYER than words that had only occurred once because there would be a higher probability of finding at least one of the several traces of LAWYER than of finding the one trace of a once-presented item. Thus, this sort of approach would be capable of explaining why memory improves as a function of repetition.

At least part of the philosophical basis for this approach is the notion that no event ever truly occurs more than once. Every event can be seen as a unique experience. Each of us have seen the word TABLE countless numbers of times, yet it must have been encoded very differently each of those times. Perhaps we read the word once while reading instructions on how to assemble furniture. Another time, we heard the word while having a conversation in a kitchen. Still another time, it may have been one word on a long list that we had been asked to memorize. In each of these examples, the word TABLE is occurring in a very different context and presumably carried with it a rather idiosyncratic meaning. Although the nominal stimulus (the word TABLE) has been encountered on repeated occasions, the experience that was encoded and stored by a person could be radically different. In short, this sort of atomistic view explains repetition effects in a sense by denying that repetition ever truly occurs. Rather, when a particular stimulus is experienced more than once, the contexts are always unique and the resultant trace that is formed is separate from other traces that may also contain that stimulus.

The term *atomistic view* is rarely seen nowadays, but this general approach is still very popular. (Usually, the term *multiple-trace theory* is used to refer to this approach.) The first memory theorist to develop a clear account of this type was the German scientist Richard Semon, whose life and work in the early 20th century have been discussed by Schacter (1982). Semon's work, although it was highly sophisticated and anticipated many of the concerns of contemporary memory research, unfortunately was largely ignored for many decades. Hintzman (1976, 1988) has done much to popularize the multiple-trace view among modern cognitive psychologists. A formal model that incorporates this multiple-trace approach is MINERVA 2 (Hintzman, 1988). MINERVA 2 has been applied to several memory tasks (and also other domains of cognition, notably categorization) with a high degree of success.

THE FREQUENCY-JUDGMENT PARADIGM

A central difference between functional and atomistic views is how they deal with the specific details of particular times we encounter a stimulus. Functional views claim that each occurrence of a repeated event simply strengthens a single memory trace. Since each occurrence has the same effect, the specific details of particular occurrences would be lost. On the other hand, the atomistic (multiple-trace) views claim that every occurrence produces its own trace. The specific details of each occurrence would be preserved in memory.

These approaches have often been distinguished by using the frequency-judgment task. Here, subjects are asked to judge how often (or how frequently) a particular event has occurred. Two kinds of frequency information may be tested. One kind is *background frequency*, which refers to the frequency of an event through your lifetime. The number of times that you have seen a giraffe or encountered the word KIOSK in your life would both be background frequency information. Another kind of frequency information is *situational frequency*, which refers to the number of times that an event has occurred in a particular situation. For example, subjects might be shown a list of words, on which some items occur once, others twice, and still others three times. After the list has been shown, the experimenter might give a test requiring subjects to determine how often each word had been presented on the list. The experimenter is not asking for judgments as to how many times the subjects had encountered each of these words throughout their lives. Rather, the test deals only with the frequency of the stimuli in a particular situation, namely, the laboratory list. A crucial part in a situational frequency judgment task is to keep separate the occurrences of the item in the situation being tested and other occurrences of that item.

It should also be mentioned here that there are also two ways to administer a frequency judgment test. One way is to show people each of the test stimuli individually and ask for a number to indicate the estimated number of times that that stimulus had been encountered either in everyday life (background frequency) or in a particular situation (situational frequency). Alternatively, the experimenter could show two test stimuli at a time and ask subjects to choose the one that had occurred more often; this can be called a relative-frequency test or a frequency-discrimination test.

One important fact to keep in mind about these frequency tests is that subjects often do quite well on them. For example, Attneave (1953) studied people's ability to make background frequency judgments of individual letters of the English alphabet. He found that these background frequency judgments correlated .88 with true frequency of occurrence in the English language. Howes (1954) asked college students for background frequency judgments for words and found that these judgments correlated .87 with true frequency as measured by studies of word usage. Similarly, experimenters who have studied the ability of subjects to make situational frequency judgments have often expressed astonishment at how well people perform this task (e.g., Hasher & Zacks, 1979, 1984).

How would functional and atomistic (multiple-trace) accounts explain performance in frequency judgment tasks? According to functional views, subjects would consult the memory trace for the item being tested and base a judgment on this trace. For example, in a strength account, subjects would base their judgments on the strength of the memory trace of the item being tested. If frequency estimation were required, subjects would have to translate the strength of each trace into a particular number of occurrences. If frequency discrimination was being tested, subjects would compare the strengths of the two items in a test pair and choose the stronger item as the one with the greater frequency. The attribute account would offer a similar explanation. Such an explanation would work very well as an account for how subjects could exhibit memory for background frequency. However, when this sort of approach is applied to situational frequency, problems appear. How could people give an estimate for frequency of estimation in one situation that was independent of a stimulus's overall frequency? One way to apply these functional accounts is to claim that people are not able to do that. People asked to make a situational-frequency judgment for items presented on a laboratory list would consult each stimulus's strength or frequency counter and would then give a response based on the overall frequency. This is clearly wrong. It would predict that subjects would give higher situational frequency estimates to stimuli with high background frequencies. In reality, the opposite is true; when the true situational frequency is held constant, people give higher situational estimates to items of low background frequency than to items of high background frequency (Rao, 1983).

Another way to apply the functional approach to situational frequency judgment is to allow people to create separate strengths or frequency attributes when they know that they will have to remember the situational frequency of a stimulus. For example, when people are told that they will be hearing a list of items and will be tested on their memory for the frequencies of the items, they may create a brand new frequency counter that is meant to track the situational occurrences of each stimulus. Such an approach would suggest that people would be able to judge situational frequency accurately only when they know that they will be tested on it. This prediction is also clearly false. In fact, it has been shown several times that people who expect a situational-frequency test on a list of items are no more accurate than people who are merely told to expect some sort of unspecified memory test (e.g., Hasher & Chromiak, 1977). Thus, the functional approach could not be extended to situational frequency in this way.

Another possible way to extend the functional approach to situational frequency judgment is to say that strengths and frequency attributes would be context-specific. That is, every time subjects enter a new, distinct context, they create a new trace strength or frequency attribute for each stimulus they encounter there. This sort of extension would weaken the essential assumptions of the functional approach and would blur the differences between this position and atomistic approaches. Nevertheless, this version of the functional hypothesis would make one prediction that atomistic accounts would not, namely, that subjects would not be able to separate occurrences that happen in one distinct context. That is, although subjects might be able to distinguish between background frequency and the overall situational frequency, they would not be able to discriminate among the occurrences that happened in that situation. This prediction is also false. One clear demonstration of this was provided by Hintzman and Block (1971). They showed subjects two separate lists of words in one experimental session. Some words occurred on both lists. Each word occurred 0, 2, or 5 times on the first list and 0, 2, or 5 times on the second list. After both lists had been presented, subjects were asked to give a situational frequency estimate for each list. That is, on the test, subjects would be shown a test stimulus and would have to give two responses, one indicating frequency of occurrence on the first list and the second indicating frequency of occurrence on the second list. People were quite accurate at this task, and their estimates were primarily determined by the item's frequency on the list being judged. In other words, subjects were able to give two reasonably accurate frequency judgments in one situational context. An even more extreme version of this idea is presented in Greene (1990a, Experiment 5). In that experiment, subjects were shown a list of items without being told what kind of test to expect. After the list was over, subjects were shown a stimulus accompanied by two other words. Subjects had to indicate which of the two words had occurred more often immediately before the single stimulus. (For example, on the list, subjects might see the word CART three times; once it occurred immediately after TOWN, and twice it occurred immediately after LAKE. LAKE and TOWN occurred at other places on the list so that their overall frequencies were equal. On the test, subjects would see CART accompanied by LAKE and TOWN. To be correct, they would have to choose LAKE as the word that more often immediately preceded CART.) Each subject had to answer this sort of question for 36 of the list words. Not surprisingly, this task was quite difficult. Still, subjects performed well above chance levels. Thus, people are able to make very fine distinctions in situational frequencies even within a single situation.

Where does that leave us? We have seen that the functional approach could offer a reasonable and defensible account for background frequency judgments. However, it offers no immediately obvious way in which subjects could estimate situational frequency independently of background frequency. We have considered three ways in which the functional approach could be extended to explain situational frequency judgments. Each of those three ways predicts limitations on people's ability to do the task, limitations that have been found not to hold. Thus, the functional approach seems fundamentally inadequate as an explanation for situational frequency judgment. This raises inevitable questions as to how well it really operates as an explanation for repetition effects in general.

In contrast, atomistic (multiple-trace) accounts do quite well in explaining frequency judgments. In a background-frequency task, subjects would try to retrieve all of the traces that contain the stimulus being tested and base their response on some kind of count of the traces being retrieved. In situational frequency judgments, subjects would use the situation being tested to discriminate among the relevant traces, only counting those that come from the correct context. People could thus exhibit amazing flexibility as to the frequency judgments that they could make, a prediction that has been consistently upheld in the literature.

Atomistic accounts make a further general prediction. Judgments of frequency should be influenced by any variable that influences the ability of people to retrieve the traces of an item. This influence should take two forms. First, people should believe that items whose occurrences are easily retrievable had higher frequencies than items whose occurrences are harder to retrieve. Second, people should be more accurate in their judgments of frequency when occurrences are easily retrieved than when they are not. After all, if subjects could retrieve all of the relevant traces of all of the test items, their frequency judgments should be perfectly accurate. On the other hand, if subjects are not able to retrieve any of the traces of any of the items, their performance should be at chance. This prediction is generally upheld. The magnitude and accuracy of frequency judgments are affected by variables such as level of processing (Greene, 1984; Rose & Rowe, 1976; Rowe, 1974), intentionality of learning (Greene, 1984, 1986b), and generation (Greene, 1988). As discussed in chap. 6, all of these variables have been shown to influence the retrievability of memory traces.

Categorical Frequency Estimation

Can people make frequency judgments for stimuli that they have not directly experienced? This was the question addressed by Alba, Chromiak, Hasher, and Attig (1980). They showed subjects a word list. The items on the list came from several taxonomic categories. That is, there might be a few occupations, a few animal names, a few beverages, and so forth. Each specific stimulus would be presented only once. After subjects saw the list, the experimenter gave a test in which the names of each of the taxonomic categories was shown. Subjects were told to judge how many exemplars from each category had been shown. This differs from the item frequency experiments discussed earlier in that each list stimulus is only shown once and subjects are asked to make judgments about test stimuli (the category names) that they had not seen on the list. Still, Alba et al. found that subjects were able to make these judgments of categorical frequency with good (but not perfect) accuracy.

As has been discussed, the atomistic (multiple-trace) approach has appeared to be the most promising way to explain judgments of item frequency. Could an analogous approach be used to explain how categorical frequency judgments are made? One way to do this has been suggested by Williams and Durso (1986) and Greene (1989b). According to this account, each presentation of an exemplar forms an independent trace in memory. When subjects are given a categorical frequency test, they use each category name as a cue to retrieve the traces of the exemplars that had been presented on the list. Then, the subjects count the number of retrieved traces and base their response on this count. This kind of approach states that, although subjects are being asked about the frequency of a category, the information utilized in memory consists of the traces of the specific exemplars that had been experienced.

This kind of exemplar-retrieval approach makes one very strong prediction. It implies that categorical frequency estimation is quite similar to cued recall (when category names are used as retrieval cues). The only difference occurs at the output stage. In cued recall, a subject would use the category name to retrieve the traces of the exemplars that had been presented and then write down all of the exemplars that had been accessed. In categorical frequency judgment, subjects count the number of retrieved traces and give a number as a response. This number may not be identical to the number of exemplars retrieved. Subjects may transform the counts of retrieved traces to take into account the fact that probably not all traces had been found. However, there should be a direct relationship between the number of retrieved traces and the number that is output as a response. Thus, this account predicts that any variable that facilitates cued recall of category exemplars should also lead to higher and more accurate categorical frequency estimates.

The literature generally supports this prediction. Some of the relevant examples will be reviewed here. Several experiments have examined the effects of the organization of exemplars on a list. In one condition (a *grouped* condition), all of the exemplars from a single category could occur consecutively. In a second condition (a *distributed* condition), exemplars from a category might be scattered through the list, with no two members of a single category occurring next to each other. It has consistently been found that cued recall is higher when category exemplars are grouped together, presumably because subjects find it easier to organize the list (Murphy & Puff, 1982). Thus, one would expect that categorical frequency estimates would also be higher for grouped categories than for distributed categories. The results from one such experiment (Greene, 1989b, Experiment 2) are shown in Fig. 7.2. Two, three, or four exemplars from each category were included on the list. For each subject, half of the categories were grouped and the others were distributed. Note that frequency judgments were consistently higher for the grouped categories than for the distributed categories. When measures of accuracy were ex-

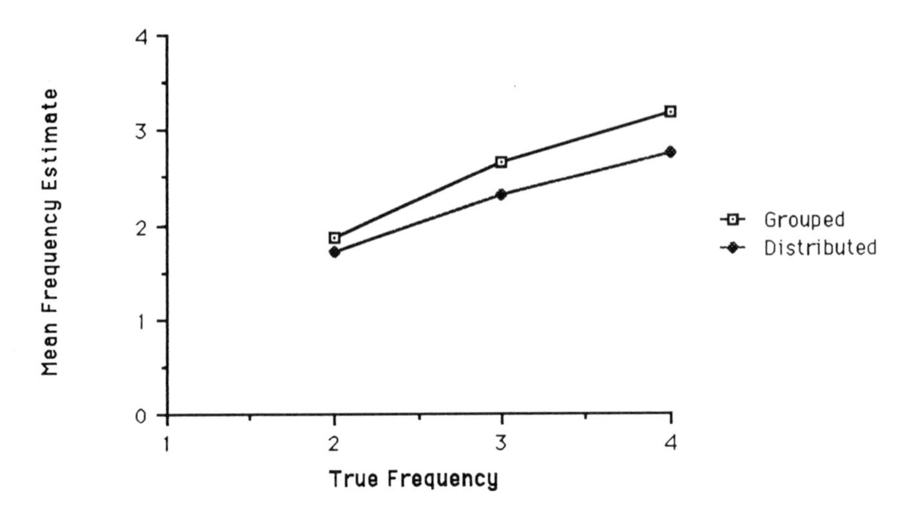

FIG. 7.2. Mean frequency estimates for grouped and distributed stimuli. From Greene, 1989b. Reprinted by permission.

amined, the conclusions were similar; estimates were closer to the true frequencies for grouped categories than for distributed categories.

Many other variables have also been shown to have parallel effects on cued recall and categorical frequency estimation. For example, generation leads to higher cued recall and higher (and more accurate) estimates (Greene, 1989b, Experiment 1). Showing subjects exemplars that were not on the list creates interference and leads to both lower cued recall and lower, more inaccurate estimates (Greene, 1989b, Experiment 3). Also, intentionality of learning can benefit both cued recall and categorical frequency estimates (Hanson & Hirst, 1988).

One more piece of evidence favoring this sort of exemplar-retrieval account comes from the examination of individual differences. Williams and Durso (1986) adopted a correlational approach and found that there was a strong relationship between the ability to recall specific exemplars and the magnitude and accuracy of the categorical frequency estimates that were given. In sum, the literature supports the claim that there is a close relationship between the ability to retrieve particular exemplars and the estimation of categorical frequency. This supports the notion that these estimates are based at least in part on the retrieval and counting of discrete traces.

There is some evidence that a process of retrieving and counting exemplars is not sufficient to explain categorical frequency estimation. Two lines of evidence have been used to assert the insufficiency of exemplar-retrieval accounts. One of these lines is not convincing upon close examination. Bruce, Hockley, and Craik (1991) showed subjects categorized lists and then asked for both cued recall and frequency estimation. They then correlated the number of items recalled from each category with the estimated frequency of occurrence of exemplars from that category. An exemplar-retrieval account would predict that strong correlations would be found between these measures even if the effects of true category frequency were statistically controlled. Bruce et al. found inconsistent results, reporting strong recall-estimation correlations in some conditions but not in others. However, the relevance of these data is undercut by the peculiar method used by Bruce et al. when calculating these correlations. Each of the 15 subjects in a condition was exposed to 24 categories on the list, and Bruce et al. treated each of the 360 (that is, 24 times 15) subject-category combinations as if it came from a different individual. This leads to violations of several of the standard assumptions of correlational analysis and renders this study largely uninterpretable.

A far sounder critique of the adequacy of the exemplar-retrieval account was reported by Watkins and LeCompte (1991). They pointed out that a strong version of the exemplar-retrieval account would claim that the only information that subjects had about category frequency would be the number of exemplars that could be retrieved. Thus, the number of exemplars that can be recalled in cued recall should be as closely related to true frequency as are the frequency estimates. Across a series of experiments, Watkins and LeCompte showed that this prediction generally did not hold. True frequencies were generally more closely related to frequency estimates than they were to the number of exemplars recalled. This suggests that frequency estimates are not entirely based on the retrieval of exemplars and that another source of frequency information must be available to help make these estimates so accurate. Watkins and LeCompte refrained from speculating as to the nature of this additional source of frequency information. Still, this work represents an important contribution to this area and is the first clear-cut evidence that the recall of specific instances might not be sufficient to explain memory for frequency.

Automaticity and Frequency Information

In the 1980s, a rather curious controversy developed in the area of frequency judgment. This controversy was sparked by the observation that subjects are often surprisingly good at estimating frequency of occurrence. This observation led Hasher and Zacks (1979, 1984) to propose that frequency information is encoded automatically. They argued that there may be certain classes of information that are so fundamental to cognition that their encoding and utilization cannot be left to chance. The human mind may have evolved to store these classes of information without any effort. Hasher and Zacks largely concentrated on frequency since they believed that it was the one example of automatically encoded information for which there was the most relevant empirical evidence.

Hasher and Zacks (1979, 1984) proposed a set of criteria for determining whether a particular kind of information is encoded automatically. One criterion is that memory for this kind of information should be above chance levels even when subjects were not expecting to be tested on that kind of information. There is considerable evidence on this point, and it supports Hasher and Zacks's claim that frequency information is automatically encoded. Subjects have repeatedly demonstrated above-chance memory for frequency information even after incidental learning of the stimuli (e.g., Greene, 1984, 1986b). (Indeed, the whole literature on people's estimates of background frequency for stimuli such as letters or words may be considered as relevant here; after all, it is unlikely that people consciously go around keeping track of how often particular words or letters are encountered.) It is possible to devise an experiment where subjects devote practically no attention to the list words and consequently perform quite poorly on a later situational-frequency test (e.g., Fisk & Schneider, 1984). However, it is reasonable to consider such demonstrations as simply establishing boundary conditions on when this criterion is met, rather than seeing them as evidence against the automaticity position.

Another criterion listed by Hasher and Zacks (1979, 1984) for automatic encoding is that practice should have no effect. A process that we have been performing automatically is presumably one that we have already carried out countless times in our life. Thus, a little more practice in the laboratory should not have any noticeable influence on the efficacy with which that process has been carried out. The evidence on this point also tends to support Hasher and Zacks; in general, practice at performing frequency-judgment tasks typically lead to no improvement in accuracy (Greene, 1989a; Zacks, Hasher, & Sanft, 1982).

A third criterion is that alterations in attentional capacity should have no influence on an automatic process. Thus, populations that differ markedly from each other in their attentional capacity should do equally well on a frequency task. Here, the evidence is decidedly more mixed. There are significant and reliable individual differences in frequency judgment, with some people doing better consistently than others (Greene, 1989a). There are many clinical populations (such as those with Korsakoff's syndrome, Huntington's disease, or Alzheimer's disease) who do quite poorly on a frequency task (Strauss, Weingartner, & Thompson, 1985). Numerous experiments have compared young adults with children and elderly adults. The evidence is somewhat ambiguous, but at least some studies have found that young adults display better accuracy at this task than other age groups (e.g., Ghatala & Levin, 1973; Kausler, Lichty, & Hakami, 1984; Warren & Mitchell, 1980; for exceptions to this pattern, see Attig & Hasher, 1980; Hasher & Zacks, 1979).

A particularly important criterion for automaticity suggested by Hasher and Zacks (1979, 1984) is that the nature of the encoding strategies carried out by subjects should have no effect. This criterion has been resoundingly disproven here. People exhibit better frequency judgments for material they learn intentionally than for material they learn incidentally. Although subjects who are told to expect a test on frequency do no better than those who are told only to expect an unspecified memory test, both groups are far more accurate than subjects who are not expecting any kind of test on the information at all (Greene, 1984). Also, instructing subjects to engage in elaborative rehearsal strategies, such as creating a sentence for each item, can lead to dramatic improvements in performance (Greene, 1986b).

In light of the material discussed so far in this chapter, we should be able to understand this picture. According to the atomistic (multiple-trace perspective), every occurrence of an event leads to the creation of a new trace, and frequency judgments are based upon the retrieval of these traces. Thus, Hasher and Zacks (1979, 1984) would be right in saying that no particular intention is needed to encode the information that is needed to remember frequency. However, the atomistic account also makes clear that frequency encoding cannot truly be automatic. Not all traces are retrieved with equal ease, and the amount of effort that was devoted to the encoding of an event will largely determine how easy it is to retrieve later. Thus, memory for frequency (like all other memory tests) will be influenced by factors such as effort, generation, encoding strategy, and intentionality of learning. In this sense, Hasher and Zack's theory clearly must be false. After the initial flurry of excitement created by their proposal, this seems to be the consensus reached in the literature (Fisk & Schneider, 1984; Greene, 1984, 1986b, 1988, 1990a; Naveh-Benjamin & Jonides, 1986).

THE SPACING-EFFECT PARADIGM

All repetitions are not created equal. That is, a piece of information studied on four occasions might be remembered better than a similar piece of information also studied on four occasions. Why could this be the case? A crucial factor is the temporal distribution of the study episodes. A piece of information studied on four occasions widely spaced apart in time will be remembered better than a similar fact studied on four occasions closer to each other. This is most commonly known as the *spacing effect*.

As with so many other aspects of memory research, analysis of the effects of the spacing of repetitions began with Ebbinghaus. He noted that "with any considerable number of repetitions a suitable distribution of them over a space of time is decidedly more advantageous than the massing of them at a single time" (1885/1964, p. 89). In subsequent decades, the spacing of repetitions became an important variable among researchers in animal learning, human motor learning, and human memory. Because so many different procedures were used, the overall picture was somewhat confusing, and researchers sometimes despaired of finding consistent advantages for spaced learning over massed learning (see, e.g., Underwood, 1961).

Among human-memory researchers, a breakthrough study was reported by Melton (1967), who employed a procedure that became a general model for many subsequent investigations. Subjects saw a list of 48 different words presented one at a time at a rate of one word every 1.5 s. Any word could occur once or twice on the list. Some of the repeated words occurred twice in a row; these are known as *massed* items. Other repeated words had their occurrences separated by one or more other words; these are the *spaced* words. After subjects received the list, they were asked for free recall. Recall was higher for twice-presented words than for once-presented words. This is just a repetition effect. More important, spaced words were recalled much more often than massed words; this is the *spacing effect*. Many subsequent investigators have found this effect, marking it as one of the most powerful and consistent phenomena in the memory literature. Melton also found that, among spaced items, recall improved as a function of the number of intervening items separating the occurrences of a repeated item. That is, even when there was at least one item intervening between repetitions, performance was better when there were many intervening items than when there were only a few. This is often called a *lag effect*. Although some subsequent investigators have also demonstrated the lag effect, there are a number of studies that have not found this phenomenon (e.g., Greene, 1990b; Toppino & Gracen, 1985). No one has systematically explored why the lag effect is such an unreliable phenomenon. In any event, there is no doubt about the reliability of the spacing effect. Spaced items are consistently remembered better than massed items. We will focus on the spacing effect here.

The spacing effect has been demonstrated on a wide variety of memory tasks, including free recall, recognition, and frequency judgment (e.g., see Greene, 1989c, for a demonstration of spacing effects on all of these tasks). Spacing effects have also been demonstrated using measures of *priming*, that is, facilitation of performance on a task by previous exposure to a stimulus. The magnitude of this facilitation was greater if the previous exposures to the stimulus had been repeated in spaced fashion than if they had been repeated in massed fashion (Greene, 1990b).

What causes these spacing effects? There have been many theories that have been proposed over the decades. They can be most easily assigned into two categories, *deficient-processing theories* and *encoding-variability theories*. These kinds of account are not necessarily mutually exclusive. Both may contain considerable truth. In fact, the literature suggests that both may be necessary.

Deficient-Processing Theories

A number of theorists (e.g., Bregman, 1967; Cuddy & Jacoby, 1982; Greeno, 1970; Hintzman, 1976; Zechmeister & Shaughnessy, 1980) have claimed that people do not process an item as fully when it is repeated in massed fashion as when it is repeated in spaced fashion. Generally, it is assumed that the second occurrence of a massed stimulus is given less attention or rehearsal than the second occurrence of a spaced item. This assumption has been made because there is evidence that subjects seem to remember very few details about the second occurrence of a massed item (Hintzman, Block, & Summers, 1973).

Why would people fail to process a massed item as thoroughly as they do a spaced item? One explanation has been suggested by Zechmeister and Shaughnessy (1980). They point out that, as subjects see a list of stimuli that they are trying to remember, they do not just rehearse the current item. Rather, they distribute their rehearsals between the current item and others. Presumably, the amount of rehearsal that a subject devotes to an item depends on how easy it seems to remember. If a subject is sure that he or she will be able to remember a particular item, they might not rehearse it as much as an item that inspires less confidence. Zechmeister and Shaughnessy found that subjects tend to overestimate the degree to which they would remember massed items. As an example, imagine a subject seeing a list of words. The word HOUSE appears, and the subject rehearses it to make sure that it will be remembered. Then, the word HOUSE appears again right after its first presentation. The subject thinks "Oh, I already know that word because I just rehearsed it, so I won't bother to rehearse it again." As a result, the subject ends up paying little attention to the second presentation of the word HOUSE. When the test on the words is given later, it might turn out that HOUSE is actually difficult to remember because it had not been rehearsed enough. In contrast, subjects might not feel overconfident when repetitions of an item are spaced apart and thus might be more likely to pay full attention to the second occurrence of a repeated stimulus.

What sort of evidence could support an account like this? One way to find supporting evidence is to see if subjects do indeed devote more rehearsal to spaced items than to massed items. An experimenter can determine this by asking subjects to do all of their rehearsing aloud and by counting up the number of rehearsals devoted to each word. Studies of this sort have indeed found that second occurrences of massed items receive fewer overt rehearsals than do second occurrences of spaced items (Ciccone & Brelsford, 1974; Rundus, 1971). A similar conclusion can be reached when subjects are allowed to pace themselves through a list presented on slides. They choose to give less exposure time to massed items than to spaced items (Shaughnessy, Zimmerman, & Underwood, 1972; Zimmerman, 1975).

Converging evidence comes from psychophysiological measures. There is a relationship between the amount of cognitive processing a person is carrying out and the size of the pupil in the person's eye. When a person is performing difficult mental processing, the pupil becomes bigger or dilated. Magliero (1983) performed a study where changes in pupil dilation were measured as subjects watched a list of words. Pupil dilation was much greater when spaced words were shown than when massed words were shown. This is consistent with the idea that subjects were carrying out greater processing on spaced repetitions than on massed repetitions.

Additional evidence in support of deficient-processing accounts of spacing effects comes from Johnston and Uhl (1976). These authors placed subjects in a dual-task situation. One task was to remember a list of words. The other task was to respond as rapidly as possible whenever a particular tone was played. The underlying logic here is that subjects should be slower in responding to the tones if they are processing the words thoroughly. It was found that subjects gave slower responses to the tones when they were being shown spaced repetitions of an item than when they were being shown massed repetitions.

Thus, several different kinds of evidence (overt rehearsals, self-pacing times, pupil dilation, and dual-task response times) support the claim that subjects do not process massed items as completely as they do spaced items. None of these pieces of evidence is necessarily convincing in isolation. Each of them requires some modification in the typical experimental procedure, and this might make them less comparable to standard laboratory memory studies. However, taken as a group, it seems hard to resist the conclusion that subjects process massed items deficiently.

Zechmeister and Shaughnessy (1980) suggested that this deficient processing of massed items reflects the rehearsal strategies that subjects adopt. One way to test this notion is by using incidental learning. If subjects see a list of words without knowing that they will be tested on it, they should not rehearse any of the items. Since there would no longer be differences in rehearsal between massed and spaced items, this account predicts that spacing effects should be eliminated when the items are learned incidentally. When recognition or frequency-judgment tests are given to subjects, the data support this prediction; spacing effects are generally absent (Greene, 1989c, 1990b).

Can we therefore conclude that the deficient-processing approach represents a satisfactory account of spacing effects in memory? The answer seems to be "no." Although there is a considerable amount of evidence that supports this approach, there are also some findings that appear inconsistent with it. In particular, it seems that one must take into account the kind of memory test that is given to subjects when trying to explain spacing effects. As we have just seen, no spacing effects are found when a recognition or frequency-judgment test is given to subjects on material that they had learned incidentally. However, spacing effects are found when subjects are asked for free recall of incidentally-learned material (Greene, 1989c; Jensen & Freund, 1981). This finding has two implications. The first is that deficient-processing approaches would not be able to explain this finding and thus cannot offer a satisfactory, comprehensive account of spacing effects. The second is that spacing effects may be due to a combination of factors, and one factor may be more prominent on some tests than on others. What other factors could be involved here? The most popular proposal is *encoding-variability theories*.

Encoding-Variability Theories

This approach can best be understood by way of an analogy. Imagine that you have an important document that you want to be able to find later. Unfortunately, your room is very messy, and you consequently often have trouble finding things. Therefore, you make copies of that document. How should you store those copies? It would not be wise to put them all at the same place. If your goal is to make sure that you would always be able to find at least one copy of the document, it would seem as if the best approach is to place each copy at a different place around the room. Then, you would be more likely to find at least one of them when you are later searching.

We have already seen that repetition leads to the creation of multiple traces of an event in memory. When subjects are asked to recall items from a list, they need only to retrieve one trace of an item to be able to recall it. It seems likely that they would be more likely to be able to retrieve at least one trace of an event if each trace was somehow distributed at a very different place in a person's memory store. Thus, we have arrived at another account of spacing effects. According to this account, spacing improves memory by increasing the likelihood that each occurrence of a repeated event would be encoded in a very different place or way in the memory system.

This sort of approach has been phrased in a number of different ways. For example, one might think of each trace as occupying a single discrete location. Traces that are created at adjacent times tend to get placed next to each other. When a person is trying to retrieve information, only a limited region in the memory system is searched. Thus, a person would be more likely to find at least one trace of a repeated event if the traces had not been created at adjacent times and thus located next to each other (Landauer, 1976). Alternatively, one might prefer not to have to make assumptions about the geographical distribution of memory traces. One could still assume that each item tends to become associated with nearby items. These interitem associations would then be used to retrieve items at the time of test. When a stimulus is repeated in massed fashion, both of its occurrences would tend to be associated with the same items. This limits the number of ways that could be used to access at least one of the traces of the repeated item. In contrast, if the item had been repeated in spaced fashion, each presentation would become associated with very different items, thus increasing the number of possible associations that could be used to retrieve at least one of these traces (Glenberg, 1979). Yet another way of phrasing this encoding-variability approach is to assume that an item might be interpreted somewhat differently every time it occurs. Even if the word has only one meaning, it might bring to mind very different images and connotations each time it is presented. Some interpretations of an event might lead to particularly memorable encodings that could be easily retrieved. If one assumes that the interpretations of an item repeated in spaced fashion are likely to be more different from each other than the interpretations given to a massed item, then the probability that the subject will form at least one very memorable encoding of an item might be greater for spaced items than for massed items (Gartman & Johnson, 1972).

These explanations are all different ways of expressing a more general point, namely, that the multiple traces formed by spaced repetitions are likely to differ from each other more in some way than are the multiple traces formed by massed repetitions. This can then be used to explain the spacing effect if one goes on to assume that the probability of retrieving at least one of two traces increases as a function of the differences between the traces. At the present time, we have no reason to favor one particular way of expressing this approach more than the others.

Greene (1989c, 1990b) concluded that the most satisfactory way of explaining spacing effects is by assuming that both the deficient-processing approach and the encoding-variability approach are true. There is considerable evidence favoring both of these approaches. Most of the studies favoring the encoding-variability approach have used a free-recall test. In free recall, there are no specific cues given to help subjects retrieve the items. Thus, factors that facilitate retrieval should have large, beneficial effects. Encoding variability seems to be such a factor, in that it increases the probability of finding at least one of the traces of an item. On the other hand, there are memory tests such as recognition and frequency judgment where subjects are given very effective retrieval cues, namely, copies of the stimuli. Thus, retrieval is not as much of a problem on these tasks as on free recall. On these cued memory tasks, performance is chiefly determined by the amount of information contained in the memory traces. That is, do the traces contain enough information to allow subjects to say confidently that a particular item occurred on the list or how often it occurred? Encoding variability, which influences the probability of finding the relevant traces would be less important here than the amount of processing, which would determine the informativeness of the traces. Thus, spacing effects found on recognition or frequency judgments generally seem best accounted for by the deficient-processing approach.

All scientists should pursue parsimony as an important goal. All of their theories should be as simple as is possible. Ideally, we would thus like to be able to explain spacing effects with only a single theoretical approach. However, the evidence suggests that we are not able to do this. At the present time, the evidence suggests that a dual-process approach offers the most satisfactory way of explaining spacing effects.

CONCLUSION

This chapter began with the discussion of the well-known effects of repetition on memory. Ward's (1893) distinction between atomistic and functional approaches was then reviewed. When frequency judgment tasks are used to discriminate between these approaches, the atomistic account is seen as the more successful of these accounts. An essential point to keep in mind, however, is that the evidence requires that some process resembling the creation of multiple traces be involved in memory. The evidence does not indicate whether this process will be sufficient to explain *all* of the effects that repetition may have on memory. One cannot rule out the possibility that some central representation of an item is being strengthened in addition to this multiple-trace process. Results reported by Watkins and LeCompte (1991) in categorical frequency estimation clearly suggest that, at least in this paradigm, the retrieving and counting of specific instances can not totally explain subjects' ability to give accurate frequency estimates. However, the literature as a whole also clearly shows that the retrieval of individual memory traces plays a large role in explaining how people estimate frequency and how repetition influences memory.

We then turned to discuss the effects of spacing repetitions on memory. In general, memory for a repeated item increases when the repetitions are not massed but rather are spaced apart in time. There is evidence suggesting that a combination of two different approaches (deficient-processing and encoding-variability approaches) will be needed to offer a satisfactory account of spacing effects.

CHAPTER EIGHT

The Eyewitness Testimony Paradigm

In some sense, all theories of memory must be theories of forgetting. That is, any theory of memory must be able to explain why we are so often unable to remember information we are trying to retrieve. For example, Sigmund Freud believed that *repression* was an important mechanism in forgetting: Some memories are associated with threatening thoughts and are therefore made inaccessible to spare us the pain that would result from remembering them. Although there is considerable anecdotal evidence supporting the existence of a repression mechanism, the experimental evidence for it is almost nonexistent (Erdelyi, 1985), so it is not widely used by memory theorists. Similarly, although many people believe that memories may decay simply as a result of the passage of time, getting evidence for such a decay process is difficult. As a result, few theories assume that a simple decay process is a major component of forgetting.

One mechanism that has consistently been shown to cause forgetting is the *loss of relevant cues*. Although we may be able to remember a certain event when we are given a particular cue, we might not be able to remember in the absence of that cue. What makes a cue relevant? Tulving (1983) has argued that only cues that are present when an event was originally encoded can later aid retrieval of that event from memory. This claim has become known as the *encoding-specificity principle*. There is now considerable evidence for at least the weaker claim that aspects of the encoding context can later serve as effective retrieval cues.

One other mechanism that has been widely implicated in forgetting is *interference*. Memories do not exist in a vacuum but rather can disrupt each other in very complex ways. Our memory for an event can be interfered with by our memories of earlier events (*proactive interference*) or by our memories for later events (*retroactive interference*). Interference has been a popular topic for memory research over many decades. Since the mid-1970s, interest in interference has taken a new turn, as psychologists have studied the ways in which people's testimony about events they have witnessed may be altered by subsequent information. We will first briefly examine the history of research in interference effects and then turn to its impact on eyewitness testimony.

THE ROLE OF INTERFERENCE IN FORGETTING

The fact that later events may cause us to forget an earlier event was first systematically studied by Muller and Pilzecker (1900). In the standard experiment, there are two groups. The experimental group learns a list, then learns a second list, and then has to recall the first list. The control group learns a list, then rests with no particular activity, and then recalls the list. The experimental group generally recalls fewer items on the list than the experimental group, a phenomenon known as *retroactive interference*. (The equivalent term *retroactive inhibition* is sometimes used.)

The study of interference became particularly widespread with the development of the method of paired-associate learning, which became popular during the 1930s. In this task, subjects receive a list composed of pairs of items (which may be numbers, words, or nonsense syllables). Memory is tested by presenting the first member (called the *stimulus term*) of each pair and requiring the subject to supply the second member (called the *response term*). One way to maximize retroactive interference is to require the subject to learn several lists that contain the same stimulus terms but different response terms. For example, the first list might contain word pairs such as DOOR–GHOST, COW–LAKE, and HOPE–ICE. The second list might contain pairs such as COW–POINT, HOPE–WALL, and DOOR–LIP. After learning the first list and then the second list, the subject is given the stimulus terms and is asked to recall the response terms of the first list. Such an experiment would be said to have an A–B, A–D design to indicate that the stimulus terms were the same on the two lists and the response terms different. Depending on the nature of the stimuli and the extent of learning of the lists, recall of the first-list responses might be quite difficult, which would be evidence for the effects of retroactive interference. In contrast, recall of the first-list responses would be much easier if different stimulus terms had been used on the two lists (an A–B, C–D design).

The large effect of retroactive interference in the A–B, A–D design led many theorists (most notably, McGeoch, 1942) to argue for a response-competition account. McGeoch assumed that the B and D response terms could coexist independently in memory. However, when subjects are given the A terms, they may end up retrieving the D terms rather than the B terms they are trying to find. In other words, possible responses are competing in memory, with the result that sometimes unwanted responses are retrieved, rather than those the person is trying to remember. McGeoch believed that response competition could offer a sufficient account for retroactive interference. An important point to emphasize about McGeoch's (1942) response-competition account is that it claims that the process of learning the A–D list has no effect on a person's memory for the A–B list. Rather, memories of the two lists can coexist independently. Retrieval failure occurs not because the A–B memories are no longer there but rather because the person ends up finding the A–D list instead.

Not all theorists accepted a pure response-competition account of retroactive interference. For example, Melton and Irwin (1940) argued that subjects *unlearn*, or weaken, the A–B associations as they are learning the A–D list. According to Melton and Irwin, the two lists do not exist independently in memory but rather the process of learning the second list leads to a diminishing of the first list in memory. This unlearning process was meant to be complementary to a response competition account. That is, Melton and Irwin believed that a theory must include both response-competition and unlearning processes to offer a satisfactory account of recognition memory.

A number of approaches have been taken to determine whether a response-competition account could offer a satisfactory explanation of retroactive interference or if another process such as unlearning is also needed. One such approach has been to use a recognition test. That is, at the time of test, a subject is shown each stimulus term and is given a set of alternatives. Included in the set of alternatives is the B-term (that is, the first-list response). The D-term (the second-list response) is not included. Subjects must choose the first-list response from the set of alternatives. In other words, this is like a multiple-choice test. Since the second-list response is not included as a possible choice, it should not compete with the first-list response. Response competition should therefore be minimized. Is retroactive interference found in a situation where there is little response competition? To determine this, numerous investigators have compared multiple-choice performance for subjects in the A–B, A–D design (where large retroactive interference is found in recall) with subjects in the A–B, C–D design (where no stimuli occur on both lists and much less interference is found in recall). If response competition (or related notions, such as response-set suppression; see Postman, Stark, & Fraser, 1968) were solely responsible for retroactive interference, there should be no difference between these two conditions. Unfortunately, the data are not as clear as the reasoning for the experiment. Postman (1976) reviewed several relevant experiments and concluded that there was no evidence for retroactive interference in multiple-choice testing; there were no consistent significant differences between A–B, A–D subjects and A–B, C–D subjects. On the other hand, Chandler (1989), when reviewing these same studies, pointed out that the A–B, A–D subjects consistently scored lower than the A–B, C–D subjects, although the difference was usually small and not statistically significant. Therefore, the data do not yield an absolute answer. However, it does seem fair to conclude that there is at most only a very small amount of retroactive interference (if any) found when response competition is eliminated. Therefore, some sort of response competition seems to underlie most (and possibly all) of retroactive interference.

This has been a very limited review of interference effects. I have not tried to untangle all of the convoluted theories that have been proposed here or to specify the exact mechanisms that underlie concepts such as "response competition" or "unlearning." I have also not tried to review the literature on *proactive interference*, interference caused by information learned previously, although this is clearly an important factor in forgetting (Underwood, 1957; for a more complete review of interference effects, see Crowder, 1976). However, the literature that has been reviewed here does suggest how fragile memory is in the face of subsequent events that might cause interference. It is to the consequences of this fragility in more real-life settings to which we now turn.

INTERFERENCE EFFECTS IN EYEWITNESS TESTIMONY

Elizabeth Loftus initiated modern research on interference effects on memory for realistic information. Her work began with studies of the ways in which the phrasing of a question may alter how people answer. For example, when people watch a film of an automobile accident and are subsequently given a series of questions to answer, they are more likely to answer "yes" if they are asked "Did you see the broken headlight?" than when asked "Did you see a broken headlight?". This effect of question phrasing was found regardless of whether there was in fact any broken headlight in the film (Loftus & Zanni, 1975). Use of the word "the" implies that there was a broken headlight, and this makes subjects more likely to respond as if they remembered it. Similarly, Loftus (1975) asked some subjects "Do you get headaches frequently and, if so, how often?". These subjects reported an average of 2.2 headaches per week. She asked other subjects the same question but with the word "occasionally" substituted for the word "frequently." These subjects reported an average of only 0.71 headaches per week. Since subjects were assigned randomly to the two groups, it is improbable that people in one group actually did have considerably more headaches than people in the other group. Rather, it seems likely that subjects responded with a higher number in the "frequently" group than in the "occasionally" group only because the question in the former group seemed to presuppose that it would be a high number.

Studies such as these illustrate that people's responses can be influenced by the wording of a question. Although this is an important observation in its own right, the basis of this effect could not be determined by studies of this type. For example, it is possible that subjects' memories for an event are not influenced by the wording of a question but rather that subjects simply tried to give the answer that the experimenter seemed to want. For example, when asked "Did you see the broken headlight?", subjects could make the inference that a broken headlight had been shown and that perfectly attentive viewers would have seen it. Subjects might thus be motivated to answer positively. Alternatively, it is possible that the wording of a question not only changes people's responses but may actually fundamentally alter the representation of the event in memory.

To choose between these possibilities, one must determine whether the wording of a question will alter not only people's answer to that question but also how they answer other questions. Loftus and Palmer (1974) attempted to determine this. They showed subjects a film of an automobile accident. Subjects then had to answer questions about the accident. Some subjects received the question "About how fast were the cars going when they smashed each other?". These subjects reported an average estimated speed of 10.5 miles per hour. Other subjects received the same question but with the more neutral word "hit" in place of the word "smashed." These subjects reported an average estimated speed of only 8.0 miles per hour. So far, this is just one more demonstration of how the wording of a question can influence the answers that are given. The novel aspect of this experiment is that subjects were required to return 1 week later and answer more questions about the film. The crucial question in this second session was "Did you see any broken glass?". (In reality, there was no broken glass shown in the film.) However, subjects who had been asked to estimate the cars' speed when they "smashed" were much more likely to remember seeing broken glass than subjects who had received the "hit" version of the speed-estimation question. This holds even though there is no direct relationship between the speed-estimation question and the broken-glass question and a week passed between the asking of these two questions.

How should one explain Loftus and Palmer's (1974) findings? They argued that memory traces may be permanently altered by subsequent information. In the case of their experiment, hearing references to the cars' "smashing" each other led people to reinterpret the accident in their minds as being more serious. This reinterpretation brought about a permanent transformation of their memory about the accident. When subjects were later asked if they remembered seeing broken glass, they would base their responses not on their original memory of the film (which is effectively gone). Rather, their responses would be based on their transformed memories, which depict a more serious accident. Since broken glass is more likely to be found after a serious accident than after a minor one, these subjects were more likely to claim to having seen broken glass than subjects who received the less serious "hit" wording.

Loftus (1975) made a similar point using a different technique. In this study, Loftus studied how people's memories could be altered by false presuppositions. In one experiment, subjects watched a film of eight demonstrators disrupting a classroom. Immediately after viewing the film, subjects were given a questionnaire about the film. For some subjects, the questionnaire included the question "Was the leader of the four demonstrators who entered the classroom a male?" Other subjects received that question with the word "twelve" substituted for "four." In either case, the question is misleading as there were actually eight demonstrators. However, subjects were not asked to verify the number but were given a question that presupposed that the misleading information was correct. One week later, subjects were asked to return to the laboratory and were asked a series of questions, including "How many demonstrators did you see entering the classroom?". Those subjects who had received the question presupposing the presence of 12 demonstrators overestimated the true number of demonstrators when asked. Subjects who had received the question presuming that there were only four demonstrators tended to underestimate the true number of demonstrators.

In a similar experiment, Loftus (1975) asked subjects to watch a film and answer questions about it. One question was "How fast was the car going while traveling along the country road?". Other subjects received the question in the form "How fast was the car going when it passed the barn while traveling along the country road?". (In reality, there was no barn.) A week later, subjects returned to the laboratory and answered questions about the film. Among those questions was one that asked them whether they remembered seeing a barn. Since there was no barn, one would expect people to answer "no" and, in fact, almost all of the subjects who had received the first version of the question the previous week answered negatively. However, subjects were much more likely to answer positively if they had received the second form of the question, the version that had presupposed the existence of the barn.

Loftus, Miller, and Burns (1978) carried on this line of research. Subjects saw 30 slides, one of which depicted a red Datsun at a stop sign. Immediately after the last slide, subjects were asked to answer 20 questions. For some subjects, one of the questions was "Did another car pass the red Datsun while it was stopped at the stop sign?". For these subjects, there was no misleading suggestion implicit in the question. Other subjects received a question that was identical except that it referred to a yield sign, rather than a stop sign; these subjects were thus exposed to a misleading inference. After subjects completed all 20 questions, they were given an unrelated filler task to perform for 20 min. Then, they were given a forced-choice recognition test. They were shown a pair of slides at a time, one of which had been shown earlier and the other which was new. Subjects were asked to choose the slide in each pair that had been shown earlier. In the crucial test pair, one slide depicted the Datsun at the stop sign. The other slide depicted the Datsun at a yield sign. The correct choice included the stop sign, and subjects who had not been exposed to misleading information were generally able to respond correctly; they chose the stop-sign slide 75% of the time. However, subjects who had been asked the misleading question earlier chose the correct slide only 41% of the time, which was significantly lower than the chance-guessing level of 50%. Again, exposure to a misleading suggestion altered subjects' responses to a later question.

Loftus (1977) showed that even subjects' memory for so basic an attribute as color is not immune from interference. She showed subjects a series of 30 slides, each shown for 3 s. The series depicted the unfolding of an accident involving a red car. One slide depicted a green car passing the red car. Immediately after seeing the slides, subjects were given 12 questions. Some subjects received the question "Did the blue car that drove past the accident have a ski rack on the roof?". Other subjects received that question with the misleading word "blue" omitted. After answering these questions, subjects performed an unrelated task for 20 min. Then, they were shown 30 color strips and asked to pick the one that matched the color of the car that passed the accident. Subjects tended to pick a bluer shade if they had gotten the misleading "blue" question earlier than if they had received the neutral question. For the misled subjects, it is almost as if the memory for the true color had blended with the color implied in the misleading question. A similar finding was presented by Weinberg, Wadsworth, and Baron (1983), who found that subjects' reports of the color of a traffic sign can be changed by subsequent misleading information. What these studies illustrate is the vulnerability of eyewitness testimony. What subjects report they have seen will be influenced not only by how that question is asked but also by how earlier statements and questions were expressed.

An interesting aspect of this effect of misleading information is that it does not lead subjects to be more hesitant than would be true otherwise. Subjects who are exposed to misinformation and who are then inaccurate on a later recognition test of the original event respond as rapidly on their recognition judgments as do subjects who were not misinformed (Cole & Loftus, 1979). Also, these misled subjects have as much confidence in their often-mistaken recognition judgments as nonmisled subjects who are considerably more accurate (Loftus, Donders, Hoffman, & Schooler, 1989).

Once the interfering effects of misleading information had been established beyond question, attention turned to defining the conditions that are necessary for it to occur. An important one is that the discrepancy between the original event and the misleading subsequent information must not be blatant. Subjects will not be affected by information that they realize is false as they are reading it. In the successful misinformation studies discussed here, the misinformation is introduced subtly as a secondary part of a question. For example, in Loftus's (1977) color-shifting experiment, when subjects are asked the question "Did the blue car that drove past the accident have a ski rack on the roof?", their attention is directed to trying to remember whether a ski rack was present. The fact that this question is misleading since it refers to a green car as blue may easily escape notice. The subtle aspects of the misinformation process is crucial. A direct question (e.g., "Was the car that drove past the accident blue?") has no effect on later memory for the original event. Similarly, when the misinformation is made obvious and blatant, it has little interfering effect (Loftus, 1979b). Also, subjects who process the misinformation carefully may be able to ignore it. For example, Tousignant, Hall, and Loftus (1986) had subjects watch an event and then read a misleading text about that event before having a recognition test on the event. Subjects who read the text more slowly and carefully were more likely to realize as they were reading that the text contradicted the original event. These subjects were less likely to show any interference effect due to the misinformation. Also, people with particularly good memories are more resistant to interference than other people (Powers, Andriks, & Loftus, 1979). Presumably, subjects who are good at remembering are especially likely to notice when a misleading text contradicts the original event and thus to make a point of paying little attention to the text.

How should one explain these data? Loftus's preferred solution is the *substitution hypothesis*. According to this account (articulated most fully perhaps in Loftus & Loftus, 1980), later information can overwrite established memories. Information that is learned subsequent to an event can be substituted for parts of the memory trace of that event. In other words, our memory for an event and later knowledge that we acquire about that event can become merged. This will have two consequences for behavior. The first is that we will have difficulty discriminating between our memory for the original event and our memory for the later information we learned about that event. A second consequence is that some of the aspects of the original trace will be overwritten by later information and therefore be permanently lost. Once this overwriting process occurs, there is no way to undo it.

This substitution hypothesis flies in the face of how most psychologists think about memory. Loftus and Loftus (1980) polled both psychologists and nonpsychologists and found that large majorities in both groups rejected the possibility of this substitution process. Most psychologists and nonpsychologists stated that they believed that, once information is stored in long-term memory, it remains there permanently. These people would thus believe that forgetting reflects not the absence of relevant memory traces but rather the inability to locate the needed information. When asked what evidence supported this belief in the permanence of memory, many cited cases when memories that could not be retrieved under one set of circumstances were later recalled under different circumstances (such as hypnosis, brain stimulation, or even just a change of physical surroundings). However, as Loftus and Loftus point out, accepting the evidence that suggests that some examples of forgetting are due to retrieval failure does not force us to conclude that all cases of forgetting are due to retrieval failure. It would be impossible for anyone to ever prove the permanent storage of all memories with our current methods.

Loftus and Loftus (1980) argued that the research on the effects of misleading information on eyewitness testimony is evidence against the notion of permanent storage. They claimed that the misinformation led to a permanent erasure of some aspects of the original memory. They cited evidence that suggests that the original event is literally absent from the memories of misled subjects. For example, subjects were no more accurate in their recognition of the original event when they were highly motivated (by being paid up to $85 for accuracy) than when they were less motivated (Loftus, 1979a). Allowing subjects to have second guesses among three alternatives also does not help to overcome the effects of the misleading information (Loftus, 1979a). Loftus and Loftus reasoned that, if the original information still existed in memory, subjects would surely recall it when properly motivated or when given a second opportunity.

Remember that this misinformation effect is only found when the misinformation subtly contradicts one's memory for the original event. More blatant and direct contradictions cause little interference. Loftus's substitution hypothesis assumes that subjects are able to prevent the substitution process from happening if they are aware that they are encountering false information. Thus, warning subjects before they read the misleading text that it may not be accurate greatly reduces the interfering effect of this misinformation. Subjects are looking out for misinformation and would not allow it to overwrite their memory for the original event. However, once the substitution process has occurred, it cannot be undone. If subjects are only warned about the possibility of misleading information after they have read the misinformation but before having their memory for the original information tested, a strong misinformation effect is still found. Warnings only reduce misinformation effects if they are given before the subject reads the misleading information, not after (E. Greene, Flynn, & Loftus, 1982). (There is some evidence that a sufficiently strong and specific warning may reduce interference somewhat even if it is only given after the misleading information has been presented; see Christiaansen & Ochalek, 1983.)

When one considers Loftus's substitution hypothesis in the light of the literature on interference effects reviewed earlier, one can see that she is proposing a variation of an unlearning account of retroactive interference in her paradigm. Memory failure is not just attributed to competition between several possible responses, one based on the original event and the other based on the later misleading information. Rather, she feels that the original event is unlearned in part when the person encounters the later misinformation. This unlearning process is left rather vague by Loftus but would presumably bear little resemblance to the speculations that Melton and Irwin (1940) and other interference theorists made about unlearning. Metcalfe (1990) has given a quantitative model of what such a substitution process might look like. However, Loftus's account would share with the earlier theories the notion that conflicting memories can not coexist independently but that the newer one leads to an elimination of the older one.

THE BIASED-GUESSING INTERPRETATION

Since Loftus's substitution account does conflict with the way in which most people think about memory, it was perhaps inevitable that researchers would begin to propose other accounts for these data, accounts that allow for the coexistence of the original event and the misleading information (e.g., Bekerian & Bower, 1983; Shaughnessy & Mand, 1982). The most influential alternative explanation for the effects of misinformation was proposed by McCloskey and Zaragoza (1985). They argued that perhaps presenting misleading postevent information had no effect on subjects' memory for the original event. Rather, misleading postevent information might simply alter subjects' strategies when they are unable to remember the original event and are forced to guess. This could lead misled subjects to make more errors than subjects who were not misled. However, this would not necessarily reflect better memory in the latter subjects.

Let us consider the reasoning of McCloskey and Zaragoza (1985) in depth. As was done by those authors, we will concentrate on one particular design used in many studies by Loftus and others in this area; the basic argument, however, extends to variations on this design. In this design, there are two groups, a control group and an experimental group. Both groups watch the event depicted on film or slides. Then, the experimental group is exposed to subtly misleading information; the control group is not exposed to such information. Both groups are then given a forced-choice recognition test. On the crucial test pair, subjects are forced to choose between an accurate depiction of the event and a false depiction that is consistent with the misleading information that the experimental group received. The general finding is that the experimental group does not perform as accurately on the critical test pair as does the control group.

To follow McCloskey and Zaragoza's (1985) reasoning, consider the control group. Let us say that 50% of the control subjects remember the original event accurately. All of these subjects should respond accurately. The remaining subjects are forced to choose between the two alternatives. Such guessing should be random, which means that half of the people who guess should choose the correct option. This would mean that, if 50% of the control subjects remember the original event, 75% of the subjects in this group should make the correct choice.

McCloskey and Zaragoza (1985) went on to assume that experimental subjects, those who were exposed to the misleading information, would be no less likely to remember the original event accurately than the control subjects. To continue this hypothetical example, this would mean that 50% of the experimental subjects could remember the event. What about the other experimental subjects? They would not be able to remember the original event and would be forced to guess. However, at least some of these subjects would remember the misleading information that they had been exposed to. Since these subjects would have no reason to doubt the accuracy of the misleading information, they may base their guesses on it and choose the recognition alternative that is consistent with the misleading information. In other words, when experimental subjects cannot remember the original event and are forced to guess, they would tend to choose the incorrect alternative more often than the correct one. This would mean that experimental subjects would not be correct as often as control subjects even if one assumes that both groups are equally likely to remember the original event.

Let us consider how this account would explain the results of one particular study by Loftus et al. (1978) that we have already discussed. In this study, subjects originally saw a Datsun stopped at a stop sign. Subjects in the experimental group (but not subjects in the control group) received a question later that implied that the Datsun was stopped at a yield sign. On a subsequent recognition test, subjects had to choose between slides that depicted the Datsun stopped at either a stop sign or a yield sign. Subjects in the control group were more likely to pick the stop-sign slide than subjects in the experimental group. McCloskey and Zaragoza (1985) argued that perhaps memory is unaffected by the misleading information. However, all of the subjects in the control group who remember the stop sign (and half of the subjects who do not remember it) will be correct. In contrast, in the experimental group, any subjects who do not remember the stop sign but do remember receiving a later question about a yield sign will presumably choose the yield-sign slide and thus be incorrect.

According to McCloskey and Zaragoza (1985), only those subjects who remember seeing the stop sign and do not remember receiving a question about a yield sign are guaranteed to be correct. Those subjects who do not remember either will be forced to guess randomly and will be right half the time. Those subjects who do not remember the stop sign but who do remember the yield-sign question will probably choose the incorrect alternative. Those subjects who remember both the stop sign and the yield-sign question will be caught in a conflict. Some of these subjects might decide that the experimenter who asked the questions should know what is on the slides and therefore choose the yield sign. In short, even when memory for the stop sign is the same in the control and experimental (misled) groups, the proportion correct on a recognition test will not necessarily be the same.

Although McCloskey and Zaragoza (1985) dealt at length only with this one design, their arguments extend to other types of experiments used by Loftus and her colleagues. McCloskey and Zaragoza claimed that the basic problem with the designs used by Loftus and her colleagues was that they always placed subjects from the experimental group in a conflict between two alternatives, each of which they may have reason to believe is correct. In other words, the standard designs are inadequate to determine the existence of a substitution process because subjects in the experimental group are faced with a situation of high response competition. To get evidence for substitution, response competition must be reduced or eliminated. McCloskey, Zaragoza, and their colleagues have explored three designs that meet this requirement.

Modified Recognition Test

McCloskey and Zaragoza (1985) introduced a small but important change in the design used by earlier researchers in this area. This change concerned only the recognition test. Rather than requiring subjects to choose between the original stimulus and an alternative that is consistent with the misinformation given to the misled group, all subjects have to choose between the original stimulus and a novel stimulus. For example, subjects might see a series of slides, one of which depicts a man holding a hammer. Then, subjects read a narrative about the slides. For the subjects in the experimental (misled) group, the narrative refers to the wrench that the man was holding. The subjects in the control group do not receive any reference to a specific tool in the narrative. At the time of test, all subjects are forced to choose between a slide showing a hammer and a slide showing a screwdriver. If Loftus's substitution account is correct, then the control subjects should be more accurate than the misled subjects, because the reference to the wrench in the narrative would have overwritten the misled subjects' memory for the hammer. Misled subjects would then be less likely to remember the hammer and be more likely to have to guess randomly between the two alternatives. On the other hand, McCloskey and Zaragoza's (1985) biased-guessing account would predict that misleading information should have no effect on performance. According to this account, misleading information has its effect by biasing subjects to choose the recognition alternative consistent with the misleading information. However, since neither alternative is consistent with the misleading information, this bias should not effect performance. On this modified recognition test, subjects who remember the hammer from the original slides should be correct. Those from either group who do not remember it should guess randomly and have a 50% chance of being correct. Since McCloskey and Zaragoza assume that the misleading information does not affect memory for the original item, performance should be equal between the two groups.

A technical point should be made here. As pointed out by Lindsay (1990) among others, the biased-guessing account would not be disproven even if misled subjects scored below control subjects in this modified-recognition test. If subjects remember both the original event and the misleading suggestion, they would not necessarily always choose the original event even when the misleading suggestion is not given as a response option. Possibly, the conflict that subjects feel as they recall the two contradictory pieces of information might lead them to doubt the reliability of their memory and to guess instead, sometimes picking the incorrect response alternative. Thus, the biased-guessing account would predict that misinformation should have a smaller effect on the modified-recognition test than on the original version of the recognition test where subjects must choose between the correct and misleading stimuli. This account does not necessarily predict that the misinformation effect would go away entirely, although that would be particularly striking evidence in support.

McCloskey and Zaragoza (1985) reported a series of six experiments, using a variety of stimuli and procedures. All of them employed the modified recognition test, and they all yielded the same result; there was no difference on this test between the control subjects and the experimental (misled) subjects. This null effect has since been replicated several times (e.g., Bowman & Zaragoza, 1989; Loftus et al., 1989). This finding is inconsistent with the substitution account. McCloskey and Zaragoza concluded that the evidence favored the biased-guessing account. Thus, they argued that the exposure of subjects to subtle misleading postevent information does not impair memory for the original event.

Loftus et al. (1989) have found that misled subjects respond more slowly than control subjects on the modified test, although their accuracy was equivalent. These reaction-time differences are consistent with a biased-guessing account. Misled subjects who remember the misinformation but not the original stimulus may at first be startled to see that there is no recognition alternative consistent with the misinformation. It may take a little more time for them to decide that they have to guess randomly. However, once they do respond, these subjects are as accurate as subjects who had not received misleading information.

There are several limitations on our conclusions that should be mentioned here. One such limitation deals with developmental differences. Ceci, Ross, and Toglia (1987) used children (averaging around 4 years of age) as subjects. When they tested children in experiments similar to those performed by McCloskey and Zaragoza (1985), they found small but significant advantages for the control subjects over the misled subjects. This may mean that children's memories might be more vulnerable to substitution from subsequent information than are the memories of adults. However, since the modified-recognition test is just one way of studying interference in the absence of response competition, considerably more research should be done before we conclude that the memories of children follow different principles than the memories of adults. Moreover, as noted above, the biased-guessing account is not disproven when small misinformation effects are found in the modified-recognition test.

Chandler (1989) reported a series of experiments that used a very different procedure than the one used by McCloskey and Zaragoza (1985), although Chandler considered these experiments to be a refutation of the biased-guessing approach. Chandler showed subjects a series of nature pictures that they were asked to memorize. Then, subjects saw a second series of pictures, some of which were similar to a picture in the first series. As subjects were viewing this second set, they had to indicate which were similar to pictures from the first series. Finally, subjects were given a forced-choice recognition test in which they had to choose between a picture from the first series and a new, related picture. Chandler compared recognition accuracy for pictures that had been followed by a similar picture in the second set with accuracy for control pictures that were not similar to any stimuli in the second set. Small but significant differences were found favoring the pictures not followed by similar pictures. Chandler considered this to be a challenge to McCloskey and Zaragoza's conclusions, although the procedures are so dissimilar that this claim should be viewed skeptically. Moreover, additional research must be done before we know whether idiosyncratic aspects of Chandler's procedure (e.g., instructing subjects to compare pictures in the second set with those in the first set) are responsible for these effects.

All of the studies discussed so far have used forced-choice recognition tests; that is, subjects were given a set of two alternatives and had to choose the one that they believed was correct. For the sake of completeness, it should be noted that several experimenters have also used yes–no recognition tests, in which subjects are shown test stimuli one at a time and have to indicate whether each one had been shown earlier. Unfortunately, these studies have found somewhat inconsistent results (Belli, 1989; Pirolli & Mitterer, 1984; Tversky & Tuchin, 1989). Moreover, these studies do not discriminate between the predictions of the substitution and biased-guessing accounts (Zaragoza & McCloskey, 1989), so they will not be discussed further.

In general, research using the modified-recognition test has supported McCloskey and Zaragoza's (1985) biased-guessing account over Loftus's (1979a) substitution account. However, conclusions based on only one design must always be viewed with caution. Therefore, proponents of the biased-guessing account turned to other procedures to gain additional evidence for their conclusions.

Cued-Recall Test

Zaragoza, McCloskey, and Jamis (1987) designed a cued-recall test that would minimize the possibility that misleading postevent information would bias the responses that subjects use as guesses. To use one example of how this worked, subjects saw a series of slides. One slide depicted a can of Coke on a desk. Then, subjects read a narrative that described the sequence. The narrative referred to a can of Planter's peanuts that was on the desk (for the misled experimental subjects) or simply to a can (for subjects in the control group). Then, all subjects were given a cued-recall test about the slide sequence. One question could ask what brand of soft drink was on the desk. The cued-recall questions were phrased so that the misleading information presented in the narrative could not be used as a possible response. Thus, subjects would be incorrect only if they did not remember the brand and were not able to guess correctly. Since the biased-guessing approach claims that the misleading information had no effect on the original memory for the can and since seeing a reference to Planter's peanuts should not bias subjects to name a particular brand of soft drink as a guess, this account would predict no difference between the control and experimental conditions. In contrast, Loftus's (1979a) substitution hypothesis would claim that the misleading information could eliminate the original event from the subjects' memories and should therefore impair cued recall.

Zaragoza et al. (1987) report two experiments using a variety of stimuli. Both experiments revealed equivalent levels of cued recall for the control and experimental groups. This finding is in agreement with the results from the modified-recognition test that favored the biased-guessing account.

Source-Recognition Test

Zaragoza and Koshmider (1989) developed another test to compare the biased-guessing and substitution accounts. As in previous experiments, subjects would see a series of slides. (To use a specific example of a critical stimulus, one slide may depict a man holding a hammer.) Then, subjects had to read a narrative that may conflict with the slide (e.g., by referring to a screwdriver) or that may not conflict. Finally, subjects were given a test in which they were shown slides. For each test slide, subjects had to make one of four responses. They had to respond *saw* only if they specifically remembered seeing that particular item in the slide sequence. They had to respond *read* if they did not remember seeing the item on the original slides but did remember reading about it in the narrative. They were told to respond *consistent* if the item in the slide was consistent with what they remembered about the event even if they did not remember where the item came from. Finally, the response *inconsistent* was to be used if the item in the slide contradicted what they remembered about the event.

Subjects were tested both on the original slides and also on slides that were consistent with the misinformation given in the misled condition. The most important finding was that there was no difference between the control and misled conditions in how often they responded *saw*. When the original test slide was shown, the *saw* response was the most common response and was used equally often in the two conditions. When a test slide that was consistent with the misleading information was shown, the *saw* response was rarely used in either condition. In the misled condition, the most common response to the misleading test slide was *read*, showing that subjects are able to discriminate between stimuli they saw and those they only read about in the narrative.

This study is particularly important because it demonstrates that misleading information had no effect at all on memory performance when subjects knew that they had to indicate only whether they specifically remembered seeing a test stimulus. Similar results have been reported by Lindsay and Johnson (1989a). Thus, studies using this sort of source-recognition test present strong evidence that the original information was not overwritten by the subsequent misleading information. This directly contradicts the claims of the substitution hypothesis but is entirely consistent with a biased-guessing account.

CONCLUSIONS

We have seen results from three different paradigms, all of which support the biased-guessing account of McCloskey and Zaragoza (1985), rather than the substitution account of Loftus (1979a). Probably no one of these paradigms is definitive: It is rare in psychology that a single experimental procedure can lead to the decisive rejection of a theory. However, the agreement between the three paradigms offers strong support for the biased-guessing account. Also, there are other scattered findings that appear inconsistent with the substitution account, at least as originally expressed by Loftus. For example, Lindsay and Johnson (1989b) reported a reversed misinformation effect: Misleading information can impair memory for a set of slides even when the misleading information is presented *before* the slides, rather than afterward. If Loftus's original findings of interference were really due to later information being substituted for earlier information, it would have been impossible for misinformation to overwrite memory for stimuli that had not been presented yet. (However, see Chandler, 1991, for a failure to find this kind of backward interference in a different sort of memory task.)

Loftus and Loftus (1980) presented this work on interference in eyewitness testimony as evidence against the permanence of human memory. If the substitution account were correct, then the fact that memories can be overwritten by later information would surely be inconsistent with the principle that memory traces are stored permanently in the human brain. However, now that the weight of the evidence has swung against the substitution account, this argument no longer holds. Thus, there is no convincing evidence against the belief that memory traces are permanent. It should be noted that the converse is likewise true. As Loftus and Loftus have documented, there is no convincing evidence against the belief that memory traces are not permanent. Thus, one should keep an open mind on this question, which may turn out to be one that is unanswerable through the use of psychological experiments.

We have seen that a kind of response-competition theory, the biased-guessing account (McCloskey & Zaragoza, 1985), seems to be the best account for the effects of misleading information on eyewitness memory. Other mechanisms may also play a role at times. For example, logically, it seems quite likely that, when subjects encounter both an event and a misleading description of that event, they may at times have trouble distinguishing between the two memories and may be confused as to which memory to base their response on. Lindsay (1990) has shown that an experiment may be constructed where such source confusions may be a source of error (although these source confusions do not seem to be common using typical experimental procedures; see Zaragoza & Koshmider, 1989). Note, however, that even this source-confusion process is a kind of response competition. Thus, response competition seems to be the primary (and possibly the exclusive) cause of response errors in this eyewitness-testimony paradigm. Interestingly, when we reviewed the classic literature on retroactive interference at the beginning of this chapter, we also concluded that response competition appeared to be the major cause of forgetting there. Thus, although the two literatures have used tasks that are quite distinct, they have led to very similar conclusions.

No matter what kind of theoretical conclusion is reached here, there are strong practical conclusions that may be drawn. The central one is the amazing fragility of eyewitness testimony. Information that a witness learns about later, the sorts of questions that are asked, even the way in which a question is phrased—all of these may have dramatic effects on how that witness reports the event. The way that a question is asked about one aspect of an event may contaminate the answers that are given concerning very different aspects. The line of research that was initiated by Loftus and her colleagues has raised disturbing questions about the validity of eyewitness testimony and the effectiveness of judicial proceedings that rely on such testimony as their primary source of evidence. These questions persist no matter what theoretical account one uses for explaining these phenomena. Whether you believe in Loftus's substitution approach or McCloskey and Zaragoza's biased-guessing approach, the bottom line is that a witness will often be inaccurate and may report memories that are based not on the original event but on subsequently learned information. The finding that misled subjects have as much confidence in their mistaken judgments as nonmisled subjects do in their accurate judgments (Loftus et al., 1989) is particularly worrisome. People (such as jurors) who have to evaluate the trustworthiness of eyewitness testimony thus cannot depend on the amount of confidence expressed by the witness as an indicator of its reliability. Perhaps as a result of this, when mock-jury experiments have been conducted, jurors have been quite poor at distinguishing between accurate testimony and incorrect testimony biased by misinformation (Schooler, Gerhard, & Loftus, 1986).

As a consequence of this line of research, psychologists have sometimes been called as expert witnesses in trials in which the principal evidence comes from eyewitnesses to an event. The purpose of this testimony by psychologists is to warn jurors of the unreliability of eyewitness testimony. This application of this research has not escaped criticism (McCloskey & Egeth, 1983). All that psychologists can usually offer in courtrooms are vague, probabilistic statements about memory errors based on laboratory experiments that would not match any one real-life situation closely. It is not clear that such testimony really helps jurors to be better at discriminating between accurate and inaccurate eyewitness reports. Still, it is worthwhile for all of us to keep in mind that memory is a fragile thing and that what we report is not necessarily what we saw.

CHAPTER NINE

Implicit Memory Tasks: Paradigms in the Making

The previous eight chapters dealt with the major paradigms that have dominated memory research over the last three decades. This chapter will deal with memory tasks that have become widely studied only over the last few years. Whereas previous chapters have discussed established paradigms, this chapter will discuss paradigms that are still being created. There are several trepidations about attempting this. One can discuss an established paradigm (such as partial-report superiority or memory-scanning) and feel reasonably confident that the conclusions one reaches will still be defensible for a reasonable period of time. So much is known about these tasks that it seems unlikely that our basic beliefs about them will be easily overthrown in a period of time. However, if the research area that one is discussing is relatively new, still rather poorly understood, and being studied by a shockingly large proportion of researchers in the field, one can have no such confidence.

Such is the case when one writes about implicit memory. Although one can trace precursors of this line of research to the dawn of the experimental study of memory, it became recognized as a separate domain of research only in the mid-1980s. Currently, there is no theoretical account that pretends to be a satisfactory explanation for all of the findings in this area. Moreover, research in this topic is proceeding at a feverish pace: I doubt that any researcher will deny that it is by far the most heavily studied area in cognitive psychology at present.

What follows is a presentation of the central tasks in this area. The emphasis will be on the major findings that aroused interest in this area. The interested reader is also encouraged to consult one of the several excellent review articles that have appeared on this topic (particularly, Roediger, 1990b, for a review centered around his theoretical account; Schacter, 1987, for a review that includes a discussion of work in philosophy that anticipated some of the psychological findings; and Shimamura, 1986, for a review devoted entirely to the application of implicit memory tasks to the study of amnesia).

THE CONCEPT OF IMPLICIT MEMORY

Traditionally, psychologists have studied human memory by presenting lists of stimuli to subjects and then giving them a test on the lists. To perform well on the tests, subjects must be able to bring previous experiences to mind, realize that these experiences correspond to the ones that are required for the test, and then respond appropriately. In other words, conscious awareness of the past is required. However, it is true that a person's behavior may often be influenced by a past experience without that person necessarily trying to retrieve that experience. Indeed, a person may even be unaware of the past event that is governing a behavior.

Hermann Ebbinghaus, the first person to engage in the extended experimental study of human memory, was aware of this. He noted that there were many times when a past experience is brought to mind (either voluntarily or involuntarily) and we immediately recognize it as a memory corresponding to a specific past event. However, there are other times when our behavior is influenced by a previous event without that sort of conscious recognition. "Most of these experiences remain concealed from consciousness and yet produce an effect which is significant and which authenticates their previous experience" (Ebbinghaus, 1885/1964, p. 2).

Graf and Schacter (1985) introduced terms that will be helpful. *Explicit memory tasks* are those in which subjects are asked by the experimenter to recollect a past experience (such as the presentation of a list). Recall and recognition tests are common explicit memory tasks. In contrast, *implicit memory tasks* are those tasks in which subjects are not specifically asked to recollect a past experience but on which performance may be influenced by a recent past experience. The reader should note that we will use the terms *explicit* and *implicit* only to refer to tasks, not necessarily to different kinds of memory experiences or systems. Indeed, determining if and when explicit and implicit tasks measure different experiences or systems has been one of the chief activities in this area. Also, it should be mentioned that Johnson and Hasher's (1987) terms *direct memory tests* and *indirect memory tests* have occasionally been used to refer to explicit and implicit tasks, respectively; this terminology has not been as widely used as the implicit/explicit distinction, so the latter set of terms will be used here. Let us turn now to some concrete examples of implicit memory tasks.

COMMON IMPLICIT MEMORY TASKS

Perceptual Identification

Jacoby and his colleagues popularized one such implicit task, the perceptual-identification task. In this task, subjects are visually shown a list of words, one at a time. Shortly thereafter, subjects are then put into a perception task: Words are presented briefly, and subjects have to identify each one. However, the words are flashed so quickly that subjects have a hard time knowing which words had been shown. Some of the words in this perception phase had also been shown earlier on the list; these are the *primed* words. Other words in this perception phase had not been shown earlier; these are the *unprimed* words. The basic finding here is that subjects find it easier to identify the primed words than the unprimed words. For example, in one representative experiment (Jacoby, 1983, Experiment 1), subjects were able to identify 61% of the primed words and 34% of the unprimed words.

Notice here that subjects are not told to use their memory for the list to help them identify the words. In fact, (as was the case for some of the subjects in the Jacoby, 1983, experiment), they may even be told that the perception phase is entirely separate from the list and that none of the list words will be used in the perception phase. Nevertheless, subjects still find it easier to identify words that they had seen recently than to identify unprimed words. The experience of encountering these words on a list had a significant effect on their performance on a later task. This is why this identification task may be considered a memory test. During the perception phase, subjects are not being asked to remember the list items. However, their behavior during the perception phase has been influenced by the list, as demonstrated by the fact that they find it easier to perceive primed words than unprimed words.

Of course, it is possible that subjects are just treating the perception phase as if it were a recognition test on the list words. That is, perhaps subjects think that they will do better on the perception phase if they rely on their memory for the list words and therefore they try to think of the list words as they are being flashed words. In short, perhaps subjects are relying on their conscious memory for the words to help them in the perception phase.

Jacoby and his colleagues have gone to considerable lengths to rule out the possibility that subjects are employing an explicit memory strategy. The logic here is to take variables that have been shown many times to affect standard explicit memory tasks. If subjects are relying on their effortful retrieval of the list words to help them in the perception phase, then variables that influence effortful retrieval (as indexed by standard explicit memory tasks) should also influence this perceptual-identification task.

For example, Jacoby and Dallas (1981, Experiment 1) studied the effects of levels of processing. In the first phase of the experiment, subjects saw a list of words one at a time, each one accompanied by a question. For some words, the question dealt with the physical properties of the word (e.g., "Does it contain the letter E?"). For other words, the question dealt with the meaning of the word (e.g., asking whether it would fit into a particular sentence). In the second phase of the experiment, subjects received either a recognition test or a perceptual-identification test. Subjects who received the recognition test were able to recognize .50 of the words that had been accompanied by a physical-property question on the list and .86 of the words that had been accompanied by a meaning question on the list. This is simply a replication of the standard levels-of-processing effect on recognition memory (e.g., Craik & Tulving, 1975) that had been discussed in chap. 6. Of greater interest is the effect of question type on perceptual identification. In this test, subjects were able to identify .80 of the words that had been processed physically on the list and .82 of the words that had been processed meaningfully on the list, a small and nonsignificant difference. (In this experiment, unprimed words were identified 65% of the time.) Thus, the level of processing that is carried out on list items has a big effect on recognition but little or no effect on perceptual identification. If subjects were using the same processes on both tasks, then one would expect level of processing to have identical effects on the two lists. The fact that level of processing does not have similar effects on recognition and perceptual identification suggests that subjects were using very different processes on the two tests.

Jacoby and Dallas (1981, Experiment 2) also examined the effects of generation. In this experiment, subjects again saw a list. Some items on the list were words spelled normally. Other words were presented as anagrams; that is, their letters were mixed up, and the subject had to solve the anagram to identify the word (e.g., unscrambling OHUES to identify the word HOUSE). Obviously, it takes considerably more effort to generate a word from an anagram than simply to read it. After the list was presented, subjects were again placed into a second phase where they received either a recognition test on the words or a perceptual identification test. Subjects who received the former test recognized .62 of the words that they had read normally in the first phase and .75 of the words that they had generated from anagrams, a replication of the generation effect (Slamecka & Graf, 1978) discussed in chap. 6. Subjects receiving the other test identified .79 of the words that they had read and .74 of the words that they had generated in the first phase. There was a significant difference between the *read* and *generated* conditions on both tests, but this difference went in opposite directions. Generated words were easier to recognize, but read words exhibited greater priming in perceptual identification.

When I have tested subjects in a perceptual-identification task and talked with them afterward, they rarely report trying to use their memory for the list items to help them identify the words. Each word is flashed so quickly that subjects feel that either they are able to identify it immediately or else they have no idea. This is consistent with the finding that variables such as level of processing or generation may have opposite effects on perceptual identification and recognition. Subjects report that some words just seem to "pop out" more than other words although all of them are presented equally briefly. Witherspoon and Allan (1985) obtained empirical support for this observation by asking subjects to estimate the duration of the presentation of each word. Subjects believed that primed words were shown longer than unprimed words, even though in reality the average durations were equal. However, since primed words appeared to be much clearer, subjects mistakenly believed that they had been presented for a longer period of time.

We have seen evidence that perceptual identification and recognition may be somewhat independent, as indicated by the fact that some variables may influence the two measures differently. They are not necessarily entirely independent, however. It is possible under some circumstances for perceptual identification to be based upon explicit retrieval processes similar to those used in recognition or recall (Whitlow, 1990). The converse is also true: Under some circumstances, recognition may be based on perceptual identification. Subjects may be aware that a previously seen stimulus will be easier to perceive than a new stimulus and may use this knowledge when making recognition judgments. Test stimuli that can be perceived most easily may be more likely to be judged as having been shown earlier. Whittlesea, Jacoby, and Girard (1990) report evidence that subjects do follow this strategy under some circumstances. Whittlesea et al. demonstrated this by manipulating the visual clarity of stimuli presented on the recognition test. Subjects were more likely to respond positively in recognition to those stimuli that were presented most clearly on the test.

Completion Tasks

A number of implicit memory tasks have been developed involving partial cuing of stimuli. In these tasks, subjects see a list of items. Then, they are placed in a test where they are shown partial stimuli and must indicate how to complete them. This task is easier when the partial stimuli correspond to items presented on the list.

One representative experiment here was reported by Tulving, Schacter, and Stark (1982). Subjects saw a list of 96 words. Then, either 1 hour later or 1 week later, subjects were shown word fragments, sets of words and spaces that could be completed to form only one word in the English language. (For example, the fragment A--A--IN could only be completed to form the word ASSASSIN; a collection of word fragments, each of which could be completed in only one way, is given by Gibson & Watkins, 1988.) Some of the fragments could be completed with words that had been presented earlier on the list. Tulving et al. found that .46 of these primed fragments were completed correctly, compared with .31 of the unprimed fragments that did not correspond to list words. Significant priming was found both at the 1-hr and 1-week retention intervals. (Later research indicated that the amount of priming found in fragment completion declines over time, though only gradually; see Sloman, Hayman, Ohta, Law, & Tulving, 1988.)

Some investigators used a slightly different form of word completion. Again, subjects see a list of words. At the time of test, they are given sets of three letters (often called *word stems*) that are the initial letters for many common words. Subjects are asked to give the first word that pops into mind that begins with those three letters. For example, if subjects saw a list of words that included the word CAMPUS, one of the stems that they might receive would be CAM. Seeing the word CAMPUS on the list makes subjects much more likely to use that to complete the stem CAM than other possible responses, such as CAMP, CAMERA, or CAMPAIGN. These priming effects can occur on stem completion even when the subject is not aware that there is any relationship at all between the completion test and the list that had been presented earlier (Bowers & Schacter, 1990).

Graf and Mandler (1984, Experiment 3) utilized this task in a particularly clever way. They were interested in comparing an implicit memory task and an explicit memory task that were as similar as possible. In the implicit version, subjects received the three-letter stems and were told to complete each *with the first word to pop into mind*. In the explicit version, subjects are told that they are in a cued-recall task and to use the word stems to remember words that had been shown on the list; each stem should be completed *only with a word from the list*. The stems are the same for the implicit and explicit versions; all that differs is the instructions. Graf and Mandler found that subjects were able to follow each of these instructions. Moreover, when given the implicit completion instructions, they utilized different processes than when given the explicit cued-recall instructions. This was indicated by the fact that level of processing of the list items had a large effect on cued recall but no effect on implicit completion. (This pattern whereby levels of processing affects an explicit task but not an implicit task is the same as was found in the Jacoby & Dallas, 1981, perceptual identification experiment discussed earlier.) Greene (1986d) used the same comparison of stem completion and cued recall (using the word stems as cues) and found that rehearsal time and intentionality of learning affected cued recall but not completion.

The implicit tasks discussed so far have used words. However, it is possible to use other sorts of stimuli. For example, in the picture-completion task of Hirshman, Snodgrass, Mindes, and Feenan (1990), subjects are shown fragments of a line drawing depicting a common object. Subjects are able to name the depicted object more easily if they had seen it earlier.

Homophone Spelling

Homophones are sets of two or more words that sound the same but have different spellings and meanings. For example, PAIN–PANE and STEAL–STEEL are both pairs of homophones. Several experimenters (e.g., Eich, 1984; Greene, 1990b; Jacoby & Witherspoon, 1982) have used homophones to measure implicit memory.

We shall use Eich's (1984) experiment as an example. Each subject was tested individually. The subject was given stereo headphones to wear. Over the right speaker was played an essay. The subject's task was to shadow the essay (that is, repeat it word for word as it was being played). The subject was also told that a test would later be given on the essay. Over the left speaker was played a number of letters and words in the same voice as the essay. The experimenter told the subject to pay as little attention as possible to the material being presented on the left speaker. Some of the unattended stimuli presented on the left speaker were homophones, preceded by biasing words. For example, among the letters and words presented on the unattended left channel would be the word "taxi," followed immediately by the homophone "fare." Then, subjects might hear the word "movie," followed by the homophone "reel." In all cases, the biasing words were chosen to be consistent with the less common spelling of the homophone. While this material was being presented on the left channel, subjects were trying to concentrate on the essay presented on the right channel. In this kind of experiment, subjects are usually able to focus on one channel to the point where they claim to be entirely unaware of the stimuli presented on the other channel.

After this initial phase of the experiment was completed, subjects were given two tests. The first test was a recognition test for words presented on the left channel. Subjects exhibited no recognition memory at all for these words; their performance was at chance. The second test was a spelling test. The subject heard a list of words and had to spell them. The homophones presented in the first phase of the experiment were included in this spelling test; subjects were told to give the first spelling that came to mind for words that had more than one correct spelling. The crucial finding is that hearing the less common meaning of the homophone biased on the unattended channel led subjects to spell the homophones that way even though subjects exhibited no recognition memory at all for the homophones.

Two important points were made in this section. The first simply is the presentation of another implicit test, homophone spelling. When a word has more than one spelling, a previous exposure may lead people to spell it in a way consistent with how it had been presented earlier. The second point is that this effect will be found even for stimuli that the subject did not pay attention to and exhibits no recollection for, as measured on an explicit memory test. In earlier sections, we saw that an implicit memory test may be somewhat independent of recognition memory; that is, a variable that affects recognition memory may have no effect or even an opposite effect on an implicit test. The Eich (1984) experiment takes this comparison one step further by illustrating that an implicit memory test may be influenced by previous events for which the subjects exhibit absolutely no recognition memory.

Judgment Tasks

Another class of implicit memory tests involves showing subjects a list of stimuli. Then, they are presented pairs of items. In each pair is one stimulus that had been presented on the list and one that had not been presented earlier. Subjects are asked to make some sort of choice between the stimuli, a choice that subjects are unable to base on any real grounds. Implicit memory for the list is demonstrated if subjects tend to choose the member in each pair that had been presented earlier.

A classic experiment was carried out by Kunst-Wilson and Zajonc (1980). They showed subjects a series of unusual shapes (octagons). Each octagon was shown five times for 1 ms. Under these circumstances, subjects typically report that the stimuli were shown too quickly to be truly seen. A test phase followed in which subjects were shown pairs of octagons, one that had been shown earlier and one new. When subjects were asked for a recognition judgment, that is, to choose the member in each pair that had been shown earlier, they performed essentially at chance (.47, not significantly different from the level of .50 that would be expected if they were choosing randomly). However, when subjects are asked to choose which one of the two that they *like* better, subjects picked the previously shown octagon on .60 of the trials, a figure that was significantly higher than .50. These octagons were all plain, and subjects probably found little reason to prefer one to another. However, when forced to make these preference judgments, they relied on some dimension that was affected by whether the stimulus had been shown previously. Thus, these judgments of liking or preference can be considered an implicit memory measure. As in the case of the Eich (1984) homophone-spelling experiment, the Kunst-Wilson and Zajonc study demonstrates that an implicit memory task may be affected by an experience which subjects are not able to recognize. Later studies found further evidence that preference judgments and recognition involved different processes. The amount of attention paid to a stimulus when it was first presented affected later recognition but did not affect the tendency for subjects to choose previously seen stimuli in preference judgment (Seamon, Brody, & Kauff, 1983). Also, the duration of the initial presentation of a stimulus affected later recognition but did not influence later preference judgments (Seamon, Marsh, & Brody, 1984).

Preference judgments are not the only kind of decisions that can be influenced by a previous experience. Mandler, Nakamura, and van Zandt (1987) showed subjects a set of octagons, each one shown five times at 2 ms each. Then, some subjects were given a forced-choice recognition test. As in the Kunst-Wilson and Zajonc (1980), these subjects did not exhibit above-chance recognition memory; they correctly chose the previously shown octagon on only .47 of the trials, which did not differ significantly from .50. Other subjects were asked for preference judgments and chose the previously shown octagon on .62 of the test trials, replicating the Kunst-Wilson and Zajonc study. The new twist here is that other subjects were asked for brightness or darkness judgments. That is, pairs of octagons were shown, one old one and one new one. Some subjects were asked to pick the octagon in each pair that appeared brighter; others were asked to pick the octagon in each pair that appeared darker. (In reality, each octagon was equally bright, so there was no objective basis to make a choice.) Both the brightness-judgment and darkness-judgment subjects chose the previously seen octagon in .60 of the pairs, a number that was significantly higher than the proportion of octagons recognized but did not differ significantly from the proportion chosen by the subjects making preference judgments. Thus, brightness and darkness judgments, like preference judgments, may indicate the presence of memory for stimuli even when recognition memory is at chance levels.

Other Implicit-Memory Tests

Reviewed here have been the most common implicit memory tests. However, since any test that is influenced by a previous episode without specifically requiring recollection of that episode may be considered an implicit test, one may find numerous other tasks that have been used in one or a few experiments. For example, Smith and Branscombe (1988) primed categories of personality traits and employed subjects' usage of the primed categories. Jacoby and Whitehouse (1989) used judgments of fame as a measure of implicit memory. When subjects encounter a novel name in an experiment, they are likely to judge later that it is the name of a famous person, presumably because the name seems familiar.

Particularly interesting are those cases where measures have been used for many years before the implicit/explicit distinction became popular but, in retrospect, can be considered implicit tasks. Even the earliest memory measure, Ebbinghaus's (1885/1964) savings method, can be viewed this way. In the savings method, the subject has to learn a sequence of items so that they can be recited in order perfectly from memory. The amount of time it takes to achieve this mastery of the list is recorded. At a later time, the subject is asked to relearn the sequence. If it takes less time to relearn the sequence than it did to learn it originally (that is, if the original learning leads to a saving of time on this second occasion), then some kind of memory is indicated for the sequence. It should be noted that the subject is not explicitly asked to remember the first experience of learning the list while the list is being relearned. Since no conscious awareness of remembering the earlier learning is required, this savings technique can be considered an implicit memory test. Classifying the savings technique this way sheds light on findings that this technique may demonstrate learning even for material the subject is no longer able to recognize (e.g., MacLeod, 1988), just as other implicit tests may reveal memory for unrecognizable stimuli.

Other tasks that may be retrospectively classified as implicit memory tasks include those developed to study memory in infants. For example, Fagan (1973) showed 6-month-old infants a series of black-and-white photographs of human faces. Then, at a later time (up to 2 weeks after the presentation of the faces), the infants were given a test. They were shown pairs of faces. In each of these pairs, one face had been shown earlier, and one was entirely novel. The amount of time that the infants spent looking at each of the faces was recorded. The basic finding is that infants spent more time looking at the novel faces than at the old faces, thus demonstrating some form of memory for the faces that had been shown earlier. This sort of task became known as an "infant recognition memory test," but it is no such thing. After all, the infants are not being asked specifically to recollect a particular episode in their lives. Rather, the experimenter is measuring how their behavior is influenced by a previous event. This means that this sort of test meets the definition of implicit tests. Whether these infant tests are measuring the same memory processes as do standard implicit tests in adults has not yet been established.

DISSOCIATIONS AND PARALLELS BETWEEN IMPLICIT AND EXPLICIT MEMORY TESTS

We have already seen that there are many variables that can be shown to have different (or even opposite effects) on an implicit test and an explicit test. Such variables already discussed include level of processing (Graf & Mandler, 1984; Jacoby & Dallas, 1981), generation (Jacoby & Dallas, 1981), intentionality of learning (Greene, 1986d), and duration of rehearsal interval (Greene, 1986d). Many more examples from other studies could have been cited (see Schacter, 1987). Each of these studies can be considered an example of a *functional dissociation*, that is, a demonstration that two dependent variables may be influenced in different ways by an experimental manipulation. It is the number and variety of these functional dissociations that have led researchers to the conclusion that implicit and explicit measures may be based on different systems or processes.

Not every experiment has led to the discovery of a functional dissociation. There are manipulations that appear to have parallel effects on implicit and explicit tests. For example, being tested in the same psychological environment as the stimuli were originally presented in benefits both implicit and explicit tests (Jacoby, 1983). When stimuli are repeated on a presentation list, memory improves as a function of the distance or spacing between the repetitions of an item; these spacing effects appear to be quite similar for many implicit and explicit tests (Greene, 1990b). There is also some evidence that directed forgetting (that is, instructing subjects to remember some items and forget others) has similar effects on implicit and explicit tests (MacLeod, 1989; but see Paller (1990) for conflicting evidence).

Functional dissociations were not the only findings that inspired interest in the differences between implicit and explicit tests. For the sake of historical accuracy, one should note that findings of *stochastic independence* also played a part. In these experiments, subjects were shown a list of items. Then, each subject received two tests, one implicit and one explicit. The order of the two tests was usually counterbalanced between subjects. For example, Tulving et al. (1982) showed subjects a list of words and then tested them on recognition and fragment completion. Tulving et al. were interested in whether one could use the results of one test to predict how subjects would do on the other. If a particular subject got a particular item correct on one test, would that subject be likely to get that same item correct on the other test? Tulving et al., basically found independence; that is, one test was entirely uninformative as to how a subject would do on a particular item on the other test. However, subsequent investigators did not always find similar results, sometimes reporting strong dependence between implicit and explicit tests (e.g., Graf & Mandler, 1984; Greene, 1986d). Moreover, there are severe statistical problems that complicate analyses such as these (Hintzman & Hartry, 1990), so studies of this type are not nearly as decisive as they first appeared. They will therefore not be discussed further here.

IMPLICIT MEMORY TESTS IN SPECIAL POPULATIONS

An important reason why there has been so much interest in implicit memory tests since the mid-1980s is that evidence was found that groups of people who show substantial deficits in their memory performance when measured with explicit tests may appear unimpaired when implicit tests are employed. Such groups of people include amnesics, the elderly, and young children.

Amnesia

A person is diagnosed as having amnesia when some kind of brain damage causes severe problems in remembering, even though other cognitive functions such as perception or language are relatively unimpaired. When an amnesic is presented with a list of items and is subsequently tested for recall or recognition, performance is much worse than it is for control subjects matched with the amnesics for personal characteristics such as age and education level. The classic account of amnesia proposed that these people were unable to form new long-term memories (e.g., Baddeley & Warrington, 1970).

Some of the first work challenging this view of a global memory deficit in amnesia was reported by Warrington and Weiskrantz (1968, 1970). In these experiments, amnesic and control subjects were given a list of words to remember. When memory for the list was tested with a standard explicit test such as free recall or recognition, the amnesic patients performed much worse than did the controls. However, when subjects were provided with word stems and encouraged to guess how to complete each of these stems to form a word, amnesic patients were as likely to respond with list words as were control subjects. This finding was rather surprising, and the correct interpretation for it was unclear for many years. However, subsequent research indicated that the crucial factor behind when amnesic patients are able to display normal memory for recent experiences is the wording of the instructions. When subjects are given explicit memory instructions, that is, when they are told specifically to recollect a particular recent episode, amnesic patients do quite poorly. However, when implicit memory instructions are given, when subjects are not told that they are in a test for memory of particular events but are instead just encouraged to do a task such as word completion as well as possible, amnesic patients perform much more like controls (Graf, Squire, & Mandler, 1984; Shimamura, 1986).

Completion tasks are not the only implicit tests on which amnesics perform normally. Jacoby and Witherspoon (1982) compared the performance of college students and amnesic patients on a homophone-spelling task. In the first phase of this experiment, subjects heard questions that biased the less common spelling of a homophone (e.g., "Name a musical instrument that employs a reed."). In the second phase of the experiment, subjects were tested on their memory for the homophones. When an explicit task, recognition, was given, the college students performed much better than did the amnesics. However, when a spelling test was given and subjects were encouraged to give each homophone the first spelling that came to mind, amnesic patients showed no sign of a memory impairment; they were no less likely than college students to spell each homophone in accordance with the way that it had been biased in the first phase.

Other implicit memory tests on which amnesic patients demonstrate normal memory abilities include perceptual identification of words (Cermak, Talbot, Chandler, & Wolbarst, 1985) and preference judgment (Johnson, Kim, & Risse, 1985). Moreover, this pattern has been demonstrated in people who developed amnesia as a result of a number of different kinds of brain injury. Thus, the finding that amnesic patients perform poorly on explicit memory tasks but at an approximately normal level on implicit tasks has wide generality (Shimamura, 1986).

Age Differences

Young adults typically do considerably better on standard explicit memory tasks than do either children or elderly adults. There has been interest in the question of whether implicit tests show a similar pattern.

There are some practical problems in making comparisons here. For example, elderly subjects may have problems in sensory acuity that may complicate comparisons with young adults (particularly on tests such as perceptual identification that place heavy demands on sensory abilities). Also, since the most common implicit tests all use verbal materials, one may not be able to transfer them easily to studies of young children, who may not have mastered reading.

Despite these complications, there are several studies that have compared implicit-memory performance by young adults with performance by the elderly (e.g., Light & Singh, 1987) or by young children (e.g., Parkin & Streete, 1988). The overall conclusion from these studies appears to be that whatever changes occur over the life-span are rather small and inconsistent (Graf, 1990). Just as implicit memory seems generally preserved in amnesia, it seems to change little as a function of age.

Populations Showing Parallel Effects on Explicit and Implicit Tests

Not every population that is impaired on explicit memory tests performs normally on implicit tests. One exception involves Alzheimer's disease, a disorder affecting chiefly elderly adults. Patients with this disorder may show little or no priming at all on implicit tests, suggesting that their memory deficits are more general than those associated with amnesia or normal age development (e.g., Butters, Heindel, & Salmon, 1990). Similarly, patients who are diagnosed with clinical depression may exhibit deficits on implicit measures that are at least as large as their deficits on explicit tests (Elliott & Greene, 1992). Thus, a complete picture of the distinction between implicit and explicit tasks must deal with clinical populations that show similar impairments on both kinds of test, as well as those populations who are impaired on one kind but not on the other.

THEORETICAL ACCOUNTS OF THE IMPLICIT–EXPLICIT DISTINCTION

The only thing that a clear majority of researchers would be able to agree on concerning theories in this area is that there is no account that is able to offer a satisfactory explanation for all of the findings here. The theories that have been offered tend to fall into three categories, and one's choice as to which approach is most promising depends more on one's taste than upon empirical evidence.

Activation Approach.

Although the notion of activation had played roles in many previous theories, it was probably Anderson and Bower (1973) who popularized this concept as an explanatory device in contemporary cognitive psychology.

According to this account, the cognitive system consists of a large number of interconnected units (called *nodes*), each representing some elementary concept. Each node has a resting level of excitation or activation. When a concept is encountered in everyday life, two things happen. First, the node representing that concept is elevated in activation, with that activation spreading to related concepts. Second, the person forms a "time tag" that becomes associated to the activated node. That tag includes information about the time and situation in which the node had become active. When a person is given an explicit memory test for stimuli encountered in the laboratory, he or she relies on these time tags to determine which stimuli had been presented in that context.

Graf and Mandler (1984) applied this approach to implicit memory. They assumed that a node that had become activated would more readily leap into mind than an inactive node. Thus, an activated node would be more available to use as a response on implicit tests. Since the instructions given on implicit tests do not ask the subject to only use responses from a certain context (e.g., a memorized list), there is no need for the subject to consult the node's time tag. Thus, implicit tests would largely be influenced by the activation level of a node, while explicit tests would depend on subjects being able to access and interpret the time tag of that node.

Since this account sees different processes as playing a role on explicit and implicit tests, it could easily explain why experimental manipulations can have different effects on the two kinds of test. It could also explain why populations such as amnesics could be impaired on explicit tests but normal on implicit tests. These people would have lost the ability to form or to retrieve time tags, but the process of activation would still be happening normally. Perhaps most strikingly, this account captures the essence of the difference between implicit and explicit tests. That is, implicit tests do not require the subject to know why a particular word comes to mind easily; on explicit tests, it is precisely this judgment as to why a word pops into mind that is the central problem.

Still, there are several serious problems with this approach. One central problem stems from findings that performance on implicit tests is very sensitive to changes in psychological context. Subjects are more likely to use items from a list as responses on an implicit test if the test context is as similar as possible to the context present when the list was studied (Allen & Jacoby, 1990; Jacoby, 1983). In this, implicit tests resemble explicit tests, where similar findings had been reported for many decades. However, if implicit tests are meant to be a pure test of the activation level of a node, why should the context matter (since contextual information is not contained in the node at all but only in an associated time tag)?

Another serious problem concerns the duration of activation. When activation was first proposed as a psychological construct, it was generally assumed that the activation level of a node stays elevated for at most a few seconds at a time. This short-lived nature of priming was used to explain many phenomena (see Neely, 1977). However, priming on implicit tests may be found many days or weeks after a list was presented (e.g., Sloman et al., 1988; Tulving et al., 1982). It is hard to imagine an activation process that demonstrates such persistence.

Multiple Memory Systems Approach

Another approach that has been taken to the distinction between implicit and explicit tests is to argue that there are entirely separate memory systems, one supporting performance on explicit tests and one supporting performance on implicit tests. Each of these systems may involve different parts of the brain and could function even when the other system is damaged. This approach offers a very straightforward explanation for why populations of people, such as amnesics, may be impaired on one kind of test and not on the other. Similarly, if one assumes that the system supporting implicit performance matures faster and is more resistant to disruption in old age, one would be able to account for the findings that suggest that implicit tasks are affected less by age than are explicit tasks. Also, the many functional dissociations that have been found could be easily explained: If different systems are involved, there is no reason why a particular experimental manipulation should have similar effects on explicit and implicit tests.

The first question that must be dealt with from a multiple-systems approach is to define exactly what these systems are. Some authors (e.g., Cermak et al., 1985; Tulving, 1983) postulated the existence of separate *episodic* and *semantic* memory systems. Episodic memory would contain information about particular events that happened in one's life; it is, in a sense, autobiographical. Semantic memory, on the other hand, would contain general world knowledge that is stored independently of particular times and places. According to such an approach, explicit tasks require retrieval of episodic memories, and implicit tasks measure changes that happen in the semantic system. Although the episodic–semantic distinction gained a fair amount of attention, there is considerable empirical evidence against the hypothesis that these two kinds of information are stored in independent systems (e.g., McKoon, Ratcliff, & Dell, 1986). Thus, this approach has lost favor as a way of explaining differences between explicit and implicit tasks.

A more promising approach is that *declarative* and *procedural* information are stored in separate systems in the brain (e.g., Squire, 1987).

Declarative information is verbalizable knowledge; it would include both semantic and episodic information. Procedural information consists of mental skills and operations. Put crudely, if a piece of information involves ***knowing that*** a certain statement is true or false, it would be declarative knowledge; if it involves ***knowing how*** to do something, it would be procedural. According to this view, explicit tests measure information stored in declarative memory. Priming in implicit tests would reflect changes occurring in procedural memory; for example, perceiving a word on a list would lead to the storage of more knowledge about how to perceive it, thereby facilitating the perceptual identification of the word.

The multiple-systems approach tends to be particularly favored by researchers working in the neurological tradition. One proponent of this viewpoint has phrased his views strongly:

> The battle over multiple memory systems is over, and the multiple-systems view has won. . . . The outcome was (or, for nonbelievers, is going to be) what it was, because the general idea of multiple memory systems fits the biological orientation of our day, and biology matters more than does psychology right now. (E. Tulving, quoted in Roediger, 1990a)

Certainly, researchers working in the neurosciences are trained to seek separable modules of cognition. Indeed, if no separation of cognitive abilities in the brain were possible, if the mind performed all of its activities in a holistic, molar manner, the neurosciences would lose much of their reason for being. It has been known for over a century that extreme molarity is *not* a property of the human brain; it is possible to localize some cognitive abilities in particular areas of the brain, and damage to one of these areas may lead to a very narrow cognitive deficit. This does not necessarily mean, however, that memory is appropriate for this sort of approach. Certainly finding that a patient with brain damage is impaired on one task but not another is not sufficient until a detailed analysis of the demands of the two tasks has been completed. The multiple-systems approach was originally inspired by the finding that brain-damaged patients could be found who were impaired on explicit tests but not on implicit tests. However, now there is evidence that brain damage may lead to decrements on some explicit tests but not others and decrements on some implicit tests but not others (Heindel, Salmon, Shults, Walicke, & Butters, 1989). Indeed, Roediger (1990a) has estimated that neuropsychologists would have to postulate at least 20 different memory systems to account for the patterns of dissociations already found in brain-damaged patients. Although it may turn out that many separate memory systems have indeed evolved, considerably more evidence is needed before parsimony is entirely abandoned.

One line of evidence is particularly troublesome for the multiple-systems approach. If explicit and implicit tests reflect independent systems, there is no reason why normal subjects who do well on one kind of test should do well on the other. One would expect that explicit tests should be correlated more closely with each other than they are with implicit tests, and vice versa. However, studies that have examined correlations between explicit and implicit tests have not verified this prediction. There are some implicit tests that correlate more closely with explicit tests than with other implicit tests, and there are explicit tests that correlate more closely with implicit tests than with other explicit tests (Elliott & Greene, 1992; Perruchet & Baveaux, 1989; Witherspoon & Moscovitch, 1989). This suggests that simple multiple-system theories are unlikely to be correct. More complex multiple-system theories postulating several systems underlying implicit tests and several systems underlying explicit tests are still tenable. However, an alternative approach is to abandon the notion of multiple systems entirely.

Processing Approaches

There are several researchers (mostly studying normal populations of subjects and working in the tradition of cognitive psychology) who argue that implicit and explicit tests should be viewed not as reflecting separate systems but rather as demanding different kinds of information from memory (e.g., Blaxton, 1989; Jacoby, 1983; Roediger, 1990a, 1990b). This approach begins with the observation that explicit tests are particularly sensitive to the meaning of stimuli. Words that are processed physically, that is, merely as sets of letters, are recalled and recognized quite poorly; it is only when stimuli are processed meaningfully that high levels of recall or recognition are achieved (e.g., Craik & Tulving, 1975). Thus, most standard explicit tests can be considered *conceptually driven*, or meaning-driven, tests. In contrast, the standard implicit tests most heavily studied (i.e., perceptual identification, completion tests) deal with the physical properties of the stimuli. For example, when one tests a subject in perceptual identification, the meaning of the stimuli is never discussed; rather, the subject simply has to identify what pattern of letters was flashed. Moreover, the chief difficulty of the task is a perceptual one, namely, to perceive correctly the stimulus that was flashed so quickly. Thus, the most common implicit tests can be considered *data-driven*, or perception-driven, tests.

Theorists adopting a processing approach here also note the principle that memory for an event is improved to the extent that the conditions at test match those present during the original learning or encoding of the event. This principle has been called either the *encoding-specificity principle* or the *principle of transfer-appropriate processing*. Thus, if the test that a subject is given deals primarily with meaning (that is, if it is conceptually driven), performance will be best if that subject had primarily concentrated on meaning while originally encoding the stimuli. If the test that is given deals primarily with the perceptual or physical aspects (that is, if it is data-driven), performance will be best if the subject had concentrated on the physical properties of the stimuli while encoding the material.

According to this viewpoint, it is possible to find variables that have differing effects on explicit and implicit tasks not because they are using different memory systems but rather because they are testing different kinds of information (all of which may be involved in one system). For example, Jacoby (1983) showed that stimulus generation had opposite effects on recognition and perceptual identification. Recognition was better for words that the subject had had to generate, while perceptual identification was better for words that the subject merely had to read. According to this processing approach, generation led to better recognition because it led to greater conceptual elaboration than did reading. On the other hand, reading a word in isolation is basically a perceptual (or data-driven) process. It matches better with the perceptual-identification task than does generation. Therefore, reading led to greater priming on this task than did generation.

An important aspect of this sort of processing account is that there is no necessary relationship between the explicit or implicit nature of a memory test and the kind of processing (conceptually driven or data-driven) that it requires. One could devise an explicit memory test that deals with the perceptual aspects of stimuli. For example, consider an experiment where subjects see a list of words, half in uppercase letters and half in lowercase letters, and are later asked to indicate the case that each of the words had been presented in. This is an explicit memory test because subjects are specifically being asked about a particular episode. However, the test deals with the physical properties of the stimuli. Thus, this would be a data-driven explicit test. Similarly, one could create a conceptually driven implicit test. One such test was devised by Blaxton (1989), who showed subjects a list of words and later gave them a series of general-knowledge questions, some of which could be answered with list words. Subjects exhibited priming (that is, they were more likely to answer a general-knowledge question if the answer had been presented on the list than if it had not). However, since this test involved the meaning of the list words, it is a conceptually driven test. According to the processing approach, the properties of a memory test depend not on whether it is implicit or explicit but rather whether it is conceptually driven or data-driven. Blaxton (1989) found evidence to support this claim.

The processing approach has been very successful in accounting for the research in this area (see Roediger, 1990b, for a summary of evidence supporting this approach). However, it has several shortcomings. It does not offer a particularly convincing explanation for why performance on implicit tests is spared in amnesia. Amnesics show normal performance not only on standard data-driven implicit tests but also on conceptually driven implicit tests (Shimamura, 1986). This suggests that, at least as far as amnesia is concerned, whether a test is data-driven or conceptually driven is irrelevant. What does matter is whether a test is implicit or explicit. This pattern runs counter to predictions that would be made by this processing account.

Moreover, the processing approaches seem to ignore the central distinction between explicit and implicit tests. Explicit tests depend on a conscious awareness that a particular memory has been retrieved. Without that conscious awareness that a particular stimulus had been experienced in a certain time and place, subjects would be unlikely to give it as a response. Implicit tests do not depend on conscious awareness and are generally unaffected by whether or not the subject becomes consciously aware (Bowers & Schacter, 1990). The processing approach does not say anything at all about consciousness. At best, it could make the assumption that consciousness is related to conceptually driven processing and not to data-driven processing, but there is little evidence for this. A theoretical position that ignores what is perhaps the defining attribute of implicit memory tests seems inherently unsatisfactory.

CONCLUSION

In recent years, there has been an explosion of empirical knowledge gained about implicit memory tasks. Unfortunately, this explosion has not yet been accompanied by the development of a satisfactory theoretical account. The three major theoretical approaches that have been developed all have strengths and weaknesses. Tulving and Schacter (1990) propose that a combination of these approaches might be needed. However, as of now, such combinations are more complicated but no more successful than the original approaches taken individually (Roediger, 1990b).

This frustrating state of affairs on a theoretical level should not blind us to the tremendous increase in knowledge that we have gained in a short time in this area. An entire new class of memory tests has been developed, and this class differs in fundamental ways from the tests primarily used by memory researchers for decades. We now know more about what populations such as amnesics and the elderly are able to do, in addition to knowing what they are unable to do. Concepts such as "consciousness" have made a welcome return to the core of memory research. Given the feverish pace of current research in this area, we can look forward to many interesting findings here in the years to come.

References

Adelson, E. H., & Jonides, J. (1980). The psychophysics of iconic storage. *Journal of Experimental Psychology: Human Perception and Performance, 6*, 486–493.

Alba, J. W., Chromiak, W., Hasher, L., & Attig, M. S. (1980). Automatic encoding of category size information. *Journal of Experimental Psychology: Human Learning and Memory, 6*, 370–378.

Allen, S. W., & Jacoby, L. L. (1990). Reinstating study context produces unconscious influences of memory. *Memory & Cognition, 18*, 270–278.

Anders, T. R., Fozard, J. L., & Lillyquist, T. D. (1972). Effects of age upon retrieval from short-term memory. *Developmental Psychology, 6*, 214–217.

Anderson, J. R., & Bower, G. H. (1973). *Human associative memory*. Washington, DC: Winston.

Atkinson, R. C., & Shiffrin, R. M. (1968). Human memory: A proposed system and its control processes. In K. W. Spence & J. T. Spence (Eds.), *The psychology of learning and motivation* (Vol. 2, pp. 89–105). New York: Academic Press.

Attig, M., & Hasher, L. (1980). The processing of frequency of occurrence by adults. *Journal of Gerontology, 35*, 66–69.

Attneave, F. (1953). Psychological probability as a function of experienced frequency. *Journal of Experimental Psychology, 46*, 81–86.

Aube, M., & Murdock, B. (1974). Sensory stores and high-speed scanning. *Memory & Cognition, 2*, 27–33.

Averbach, E., & Coriell, A. S. (1961). Short-term memory in vision. *Bell System Technical Journal, 40*, 309–328.

Ayres, T. J., Jonides, J., Reitman, J. S., Egan, J. C., & Howard, D. A. (1979). Differing suffix effects for the same physical suffix. *Journal of Experimental Psychology: Human Learning and Memory, 5*, 315–321.

Baddeley, A. D. (1978). The trouble with levels: A re-examination of Craik and Lockhart's framework for memory research. *Psychological Review, 85*, 139–152.

Baddeley, A. D. (1990). *Human memory: Theory and practice*. Boston: Allyn & Bacon.

Baddeley, A. D., & Ecob, J. R. (1973). Reaction time and short-term memory: Implications of repetition effects for the high-speed exhaustive scan hypothesis. *Quarterly Journal of Experimental Psychology, 25*, 229–240.

Baddeley, A. D., & Hitch, G. J. (1977). Recency re-examined. In S. Dornic (Ed.), *Attention and performance* (Vol. 6, pp. 647–667). Hillsdale, NJ: Lawrence Erlbaum Associates.

Baddeley, A. D., & Hull, A. (1979). Prefix and suffix effects: Do they have a common basis? *Journal of Verbal Learning and Verbal Behavior, 18*, 129–140.

Baddeley, A. D., & Scott, D. (1971). Short-term forgetting in the absence of proactive interference. *Quarterly Journal of Experimental Psychology, 23*, 275–283.

Baddeley, A. D., & Warrington, E. K. (1970). Amnesia and the distinction between long- and short-term memory. *Journal of Verbal Learning and Verbal Behavior, 9*, 176–189.

Balota, D. A., Cowan, N., & Engle, R. W. (1990). Suffix interference in the recall of linguistically coherent speech. *Journal of Experimental Psychology: Learning, Memory, and Cognition, 16*, 446–456.

Balota, D. A., & Duchek, J. M. (1986). Voice-specific information and the 20-second delayed-suffix effect. *Journal of Experimental Psychology: Learning, Memory, and Cognition, 12*, 509–516.

Balota, D. A., & Engle, R. W. (1981). Structural and strategic factors in the stimulus suffix effect. *Journal of Verbal Learning and Verbal Behavior, 20*, 346–357.

Banks, W. P., & Barber, G. (1977). Color information in iconic memory. *Psychological Review, 84*, 536–546.

Bartlett, F. C. (1932). *Remembering*. Cambridge, England: Cambridge University Press.

Begg, I., & Snider, A. (1987). The generation effect: Evidence for generalized inhibition. *Journal of Experimental Psychology: Learning, Memory, and Cognition, 13*, 553–563.

Bekerian, D. A., & Bowers, J. M. (1983). Eyewitness testimony: Were we misled? *Journal of Experimental Psychology: Learning, Memory, and Cognition, 9*, 139–145.

Belli, R. F. (1989). Influences of misleading postevent information: Misinformation interference and acceptance. *Journal of Experimental Psychology: General, 118*, 72–85.

Bennett, R. W. (1975). Proactive interference in short-term memory: Fundamental forgetting processes. *Journal of Verbal Learning and Verbal Behavior, 14*, 123–144.

Bird, C. P., & Campbell, P. L. (1982). Orienting tasks and release from proactive inhibition. *American Journal of Psychology, 95*, 251–265.

Biederman, I., & Stacy, E. W. (1974). Stimulus probability and stimulus set size in memory scanning. *Journal of Experimental Psychology, 102*, 1100–1107.

Bjork, R. A., & Whitten, W. B. (1974). Recency-sensitive retrieval processes in long-term free recall. *Cognitive Psychology, 6*, 173–189.

Blaxton, T. A. (1989). Investigating dissociations among memory measures: Support for a transfer appropriate processing framework. *Journal of Experimental Psychology: Learning, Memory, and Cognition, 15*, 657–668.

Bliss, J. C., Crane, H. D., Mansfield, P. K., & Townsend, J. T. (1966). Information available in brief tactile presentations. *Perception & Psychophysics, 1*, 273–283.

Bowers, J. S., & Schacter, D. L. (1990). Implicit memory and test awareness. *Journal of Experimental Psychology: Learning, Memory, and Cognition, 16*, 404–416.

Bowman, L. L., & Zaragoza, M. S. (1989). Similarity of encoding context does not influence resistance to memory impairment following misinformation. *American Journal of Psychology, 102*, 249–264.

Bradley, M. M., & Glenberg, A. M. (1983). Strengthening associations: Duration, attention, or relations? *Journal of Verbal Learning and Verbal Behavior, 22*, 650–666.

Brannelly, S., Tehan, G., & Humphreys, M. S. (1989). Retrieval plus scanning: Does it occur? *Memory & Cognition, 17*, 712–722.

Bregman, A. S. (1967). Distribution of practice and within-trials interference. *Canadian Journal of Psychology, 21*, 1–14.

Breitmeyer, B. G., & Ganz, L. (1976). Implications of sustained and transient channels for theories of visual pattern masking, saccadic suppression, and information processing. *Psychological Review, 83*, 1–36.

Broadbent, D. E. (1958). *Perception and communication*. New York: Pergamon.

Broadbent, D. E. (1984). The Maltese cross: A new simplistic model for memory. *Behavioral and Brain Sciences, 7*, 55–94.

Broadbent, D. E., & Broadbent, M. H. P. (1981). Recency effects in visual memory. *Quarterly Journal of Experimental Psychology, 3A*, 1–15.

Broadbent, D. E., Vines, R., & Broadbent, M. H. P. (1978). Recency effects in memory as a function of modality of intervening events. *Psychological Research, 40*, 5–13.

Brodie, D. A., & Prytulak, L. S. (1975). Free recall curves: Nothing but rehearsing some items more or recalling them sooner? *Journal of Verbal Learning and Verbal Behavior, 14*, 549–563.

Brown, H. L., & Kirsner, K. (1980). A within-subjects analysis of the relationship between memory span and processing rate in short-term memory. *Cognitive Psychology, 12*, 177–187.

Brown, J. (1958). Some tests of the decay theory of immediate memory. *Quarterly Journal of Experimental Psychology, 10*, 12–21.

Bruce, D., Hockley, W. E., & Craik, F. I. M. (1991). Availability and category-frequency estimation. *Memory & Cognition, 19*, 301–312.

Burns, D. J. (1990). The generation effect: A test between single- and multifactor theories. *Journal of Experimental Psychology: Learning, Memory, and Cognition, 16*, 1060–1067.

Butters, N., Heindel, W. C., & Salmon, D. P. (1990). Dissociation of implicit memory in dementia: Neurological implications. *Bulletin of the Psychonomic Society, 28*, 359–366.

Bryant, D. J. (1990). Implicit associative responses influence encoding in memory. *Memory & Cognition, 18*, 348–358.

Campbell, R., & Dodd, B. (1980). Hearing by eye. *Quarterly Journal of Experimental Psychology, 32*, 85–99.

Campbell, R., Dodd, B., & Brasher, J. (1983). The sources of visual recency: Movement and language in serial recall. *Quarterly Journal of Experimental Psychology, 35A*, 571–587.

Cantor, J., & Engle, R. W. (1989). The influence of concurrent load on mouthed and vocalized modality effects. *Memory & Cognition, 17*, 701–711.

Cavanaugh, J. P. (1972). Relation between the immediate memory span and the memory search rate. *Psychological Review, 79*, 525–530.

Ceci, S. J., Ross, D. F., & Toglia, M. P. (1987). Suggestibility of children's memory: Psycholegal implications. *Journal of Experimental Psychology: General, 116*, 38–49.

Cermak, L. S., Talbot, N., Chandler, K., & Wolbarst, L. R. (1985). The perceptual priming phenomenon in amnesia, *Neuropsychologia, 23*, 615–622.

Chandler, C. C. (1989). Specific retroactive interference in modified recognition tests: Evidence for an unknown cause of interference. *Journal of Experimental Psychology: Learning, Memory, and Cognition, 15*, 256–265.

Chandler, C. C. (1991). How memory for an event is influenced by repeated events: Interference in modified recognition tests. *Journal of Experimental Psychology: Learning, Memory, and Cognition, 17*, 115–125.

Chiang, A., & Atkinson, R. C. (1976). Individual differences and inter-relationships among a select set of cognitive skills. *Memory & Cognition, 4*, 661–672.

Chow, S. L. (1985). Iconic store and partial report. *Memory & Cognition, 13*, 256–264.

Chow, S. L. (1986). Iconic memory, location information, and partial report. *Journal of Experimental Psychology: Human Perception and Performance, 12*, 455–465.

Christiaansen, R. E., & Ochalek, K. (1983). Editing misleading information from memory: Evidence for the coexistence of original and post-event information. *Memory & Cognition, 11*, 467–475.

Ciccone, D. S., & Brelsford, J. W. (1974). Interpresentation lag and rehearsal mode in recognition memory. *Journal of Experimental Psychology, 103*, 900–906.

Clifton, C., Jr. (1973). Must overlearned lists be scanned? *Memory & Cognition, 1*, 121–123.

Clifton, C., Jr., & Birenbaum, S. (1970). Effects of serial position and delay of probe in a memory scan task. *Journal of Experimental Psychology, 86*, 69–76.

Cofer, C. N., & Davidson, E. H. (1968). Proactive interference in STM for consonant units of two sizes. *Journal of Verbal Learning and Verbal Behavior, 7*, 268–270.

Cole, W. G., & Loftus, E. F. (1979). Incorporating new information into memory. *American Journal of Psychology, 92*, 413–425.

Coltheart, M. (1980). Iconic memory and visible persistence. *Perception & Psychophysics, 27*, 183–228.

Coltheart, M. (1984). Sensory memory: A tutorial review. In H. Bouma & D. G. Bouwhuis (Eds.), *Attention and performance: Control of language processes* (Vol. 10). Hillsdale, NJ: Lawrence Erlbaum Associates.

Conrad, R. (1964). Acoustic confusions in immediate memory. *British Journal of Psychology, 55*, 75–84.

Conrad, R., & Hull, A. J. (1968). Input modality and the serial position curve in short-term memory. *Psychonomic Science, 10*, 135–136.

Conway, M. A., & Gathercole, S. E. (1987). Modality and long-term memory. *Journal of Memory and Language, 26*, 341–361.

Corballis, M. C. (1966). Rehearsal and decay in immediate recall of visually and aurally presented items. *Canadian Journal of Psychology, 20*, 43–51.

Corballis, M. C., Kirby, J., & Miller, A. (1972). Access to elements of a memorized list. *Journal of Experimental Psychology, 94*, 185–190.

Corballis, M. C., Murray, J. E., & Connolly, G. (1989). Memory scanning: Are fixed and varied sets scanned concurrently or successively? *Journal of Experimental Psychology: Learning, Memory, and Cognition, 15*, 1175–1184.

Corman, C. N., & Wickens, D. D. (1968). Retroactive inhibition in short-term memory. *Journal of Verbal Learning and Verbal Behavior, 7*, 16–19.

Craik, F. I. M. (1969). Modality effects in short-term memory. *Journal of Verbal Learning and Verbal Behavior, 8*, 658–664.

Craik, F. I. M. (1970). The fate of primary memory items in free recall. *Journal of Verbal Learning and Verbal Behavior, 9*, 143–148.

Craik, F. I. M., & Levy, B. A. (1970). Semantic and acoustic information in primary memory. *Journal of Experimental Psychology, 86*, 77–82.

Craik, F. I. M., & Lockhart, R. S. (1972). Levels of processing: A framework for memory research. *Journal of Verbal Learning and Verbal Behavior, 11*, 671–684.

Craik, F. I. M., & Tulving, E. (1975). Depth of processing and the retention of words in recognition memory. *Journal of Experimental Psychology: General, 104*, 268–294.

Crowder, R. G. (1967). Prefix effects in immediate memory. *Canadian Journal of Psychology, 21*, 450–461.

Crowder, R. G. (1970). The role of one's own voice in immediate memory. *Cognitive Psychology, 1*, 157–178.

Crowder, R. G. (1971). The sound of vowels and consonants in immediate memory. *Journal of Verbal Learning and Verbal Behavior, 10*, 587–596.

Crowder, R. G. (1973). Precategorical acoustic storage for vowels of short and long duration. *Perception & Psychophysics, 13*, 502–506.

Crowder, R. G. (1976). *Principles of learning and memory*. Hillsdale, NJ: Lawrence Erlbaum Associates.

Crowder, R. G. (1978a). Mechanisms of backward masking in the stimulus suffix effect. *Psychological Review, 85*, 502–504.

Crowder, R. G. (1978b). Memory for phonologically uniform lists. *Journal of Verbal Learning and Verbal Behavior, 17*, 73–89.

Crowder, R. G. (1982a). The demise of short-term memory. *Acta Psychologica, 50*, 291–323.

Crowder, R. G. (1982b). Disinhibition of masking in auditory sensory memory. *Memory & Cognition, 10*, 424–433.
Crowder, R. G. (1986). Auditory and temporal factors in the modality effect. *Journal of Experimental Psychology: Learning, Memory, and Cognition, 12*, 268–275.
Crowder, R. G. (1989). Modularity and dissociations in memory systems. In H. L. Roediger III and F. I. M. Craik (Eds.), *Varieties of memory and consciousness: Essays in honour of Endel Tulving*. Hillsdale, NJ: Lawrence Erlbaum Associates.
Crowder, R. G., & Greene, R. L. (1987). On the remembrance of times past: The irregular list technique. *Journal of Experimental Psychology: General, 116*, 265–278.
Crowder, R. G., & Morton, J. (1969). Precategorical acoustic storage (PAS). *Perception & Psychophysics, 5*, 365–373.
Crowder, R. G., & Raeburn, V. P. (1970). The stimulus suffix effect with reversed speech. *Journal of Verbal Learning and Verbal Behavior, 9*, 342–345.
Crutcher, R. J., & Healy, A. F. (1989). Cognitive operations and the generation effect. *Journal of Experimental Psychology: Learning, Memory, and Cognition, 15*, 669–675.
Cuddy, L. J., & Jacoby, L. J. (1982). When forgetting helps memory: An analysis of repetition effects. *Journal of Verbal Learning and Verbal Behavior, 21*, 451–467.
Dallett, K. M. (1965). "Primary memory": The effects of redundancy upon digit repetition. *Psychonomic Science, 3*, 237–238.
Daniels, A. H. (1895). The memory after-image and attention. *American Journal of Psychology, 6*, 558–564.
Dark, V. J., & Loftus, G. R. (1976). The role of rehearsal in long-term memory performance. *Journal of Verbal Learning and Verbal Behavior, 15*, 479–490.
Darwin, C. J., Turvey, M. T., & Crowder, R. G. (1972). An auditory analogue of the Sperling partial report procedure: Evidence for brief auditory storage. *Cognitive Psychology, 3*, 255–267.
Dempster, F. N. (1985). Proactive interference in sentence recall: Topic-similarity effects and individual differences. *Memory & Cognition, 13*, 81–89.
DeRosa, D. V., & Tkacz, S. (1976). Memory scanning of organized visual material. *Journal of Experimental Psychology: Human Learning and Memory, 2*, 688–694.
Dick, A. O. (1969). Relations between the sensory register and short-term storage in tachistoscopic recognition. *Journal of Experimental Psychology, 82*, 279–284.
Dick, A. O. (1970). Visual processing and the use of redundant information in tachistoscopic recognition. *Canadian Journal of Psychology, 24*, 133–141.
Dick, A. O. (1971). On the problem of selection in short-term visual (iconic) memory. *Canadian Journal of Psychology, 25*, 250–263.
Dick, A. O. (1974). Iconic memory and its relation to perceptual processing and other memory mechanisms. *Perception & Psychophysics, 16*, 575–596.
Diener, D. (1988). Absence of the set-size effect in memory-search tasks in the absence of a preprobe delay. *Memory & Cognition, 16*, 367–376.
Dillon, R. F. (1973). Locus of proactive interference effects in short-term memory. *Journal of Experimental Psychology, 99*, 75–81.
DiLollo, V. (1977). Temporal characteristics of iconic memory. *Nature, 267*, 241–243.
Donders, F. C. (1868/1969). Over de snelheid van psuchische processen. Onderzoekingen gedann in het Psysiologish Laboratorium der Utrechtsche Hoogeschool: 1868-1869. (W. G. Koster, Trans.). *Acta Psychologica, 30*, 412–431.
Duncan, J. (1983). Perceptual selection based on alphanumeric class: Evidence from partial report. *Perception & Psychophysics, 33*, 533–547.
Ebbinghaus, H. (1885/1964). *Memory: A contribution to experimental psychology*. New York: Dover.
Ebbinghaus, H. (1902). *Grundzuge der psychologie*. Leipzig: Von Veit.

Efron, R. (1970). Effect of stimulus duration on perceptual onset and offset latencies. *Perception & Psychophysics, 8*, 231–234.

Eich, E. (1984). Memory for unattended events: Remembering with and without awareness. *Memory & Cognition, 12*, 105–111.

Elliott, C. L., & Greene, R. L. (1992). Implicit memory in clinical depression. *Journal of Abnormal Psychology, 12*.

Elliott, L. A., & Strawhorn, R. J. (1976). Interference in short-term memory from vocalization: Aural versus visual modality differences. *Journal of Experimental Psychology: Human Learning and Memory, 2*, 705–711.

Elliott, M. L., Geiselman, R. E., & Thomas, D. J. (1981). Modality effects in short-term recognition memory. *American Journal of Psychology, 94*, 85–98.

Engle, R. W., Cantor, J., & Turner, M. (1989). Modality effects: Do they fall on deaf ears? *Quarterly Journal of Experimental Psychology, 41A*, 273–292.

Engle, R. W., Fidler, D. S., & Reynolds, L. H. (1981). Does echoic memory develop? *Journal of Experimental Child Psychology, 32*, 459–473.

Erdelyi, M. H. (1985). *Psychoanalysis: Freud's cognitive psychology*. New York: Freeman.

Erdmann, B., & Dodge, R. (1898). *Psychologische Untersuchungen uber das Lesen auf experimenteller Grundlage*. Halle, Germany: Niemeyer.

Eriksen, C. W., Hamlin, R. M., & Daye, C. (1973). Aging adults and rate of memory scan. *Bulletin of the Psychonomic Society, 1*, 259–260.

Eriksen, C. W., & Johnson, H. J. (1970). Storage and decay characteristics of nonattended auditory stimuli. *Journal of Experimental Psychology, 68*, 28–36.

Eriksen, C. W., & Rohrbaugh, J. W. (1970). Visual masking in multielement displays. *Journal of Experimental Psychology, 83*, 147–154.

Eysenck, M. W. (1982). Incidental learning and orienting tasks. In C. R. Puff (Ed.), *Handbook of research methods in human memory and cognition* (pp. 197–228). New York: Academic Press.

Fagan, J. F. (1973). Infants' delayed recognition memory and forgetting. *Journal of Experimental Child Psychology, 16*, 424–450.

Farrell, J. E. (1984). Visible persistence of moving objects. *Journal of Experimental Psychology: Human Perception and Performance, 10*, 502–511.

Fischler, I., Rundus, D., & Atkinson, R. C. (1970). Effects of overt rehearsal procedures on free recall. *Psychonomic Science, 19*, 249–250.

Fisher, R. P., & Craik, F. I. M. (1977). Interaction between encoding and retrieval operations in cued recall. *Journal of Experimental Psychology: Human Learning and Memory, 3*, 701–711.

Fisk, A. D., & Schneider, W. (1984). Memory as a function of attention, level of processing, and automatization. *Journal of Experimental Psychology: Learning, Memory, and Cognition, 10*, 181–197.

Forrin, B., & Cunningham, K. (1973). Recognition time and serial position of probed item in short-term memory. *Journal of Experimental Psychology, 99*, 272–279.

Frankish, C., & Turner, J. (1984). Delayed suffix effects at very short delays. *Journal of Experimental Psychology: Learning, Memory, and Cognition, 10*, 767–777.

Fuchs, A. H., & Melton, A. W. (1974). Effects of frequency of presentation and stimulus length on retention in the Brown-Peterson paradigm. *Journal of Experimental Psychology, 103*, 629–637.

Gardiner, J. M., Craik, F. I. M., & Birtwistle, J. (1972). Retrieval cues and release from proactive inhibition. *Journal of Verbal Learning and Verbal Behavior, 11*, 778–783.

Gardiner, J. M., & Gregg, V. H. (1979). When auditory memory is not overwritten. *Journal of Verbal Learning and Verbal Behavior, 18*, 705–719.

Gardiner, J. M., Gregg, V. H., & Hampton, J. A. (1988). Word frequency and generation effects. *Journal of Experimental Psychology: Learning, Memory, and Cognition, 14*, 687–693.

Gardiner, J. M., & Hampton, J. A. (1985). Semantic memory and the generation effect: Some tests of the lexical activation hypothesis. *Journal of Experimental Psychology: Learning, Memory, and Cognition, 11*, 732–741.

Gardiner, J. M., & Rowley, J. M. (1984). A generation effect with numbers rather than words. *Memory & Cognition, 12*, 443–445.

Gartman, L. M., & Johnson, N. F. (1972). Massed versus distributed repetition of homographs: A test of the differential-encoding hypothesis. *Journal of Verbal Learning and Verbal Behavior, 11*, 801–805.

Ghatala, E. S., & Levin, J. L. (1973). Developmental differences in frequency judgments of words and pictures. *Journal of Experimental Child Psychology, 16*, 495–507.

Gibson, J. M., & Watkins, M. J. (1988). A pool of 1,086 words with unique two-letter fragments. *Behavior Research, Methods, Instruments, & Computers, 19*, 370–376.

Gilmore, G. C., Allan, T. M., & Royer, F. L. (1986). Iconic memory and aging. *Journal of Gerontology, 41*, 183–190.

Gillund, G., & Shiffrin, R. M. (1984). A retrieval model for both recognition and recall. *Psychological Review, 91*, 1–67.

Glanzer, M. (1972). Storage mechanisms in recall. In G. Bower & J. T. Spence (Eds.), *The psychology of learning and motivation* (Vol. 5, pp. 129–193). New York: Academic Press.

Glanzer, M., & Adams, J. K. (1985). The mirror effect in recognition memory. *Memory & Cognition, 13*, 8–20.

Glanzer, M., & Cunitz, A. R. (1966). Two storage mechanisms in free recall. *Journal of Verbal Learning and Verbal Behavior, 5*, 351–360.

Glanzer, M., & Meinzer, A. (1967). The effects of intralist activity on free recall. *Journal of Verbal Learning and Verbal Behavior, 6*, 928–935.

Glass, A. L. (1984). Effect of memory set on reaction time. In J. R. Anderson & S. M. Kosslyn (Eds.), *Tutorials in learning and memory: Essays in honor of Gordon Bower*. San Francisco: Freeman.

Glenberg, A. M. (1979). Component-levels theory of the effects of spacing of repetitions on recall and recognition. *Memory & Cognition, 7*, 95–112.

Glenberg, A. M. (1984). A retrieval account of the long-term modality effect. *Journal of Experimental Psychology: Learning, Memory, and Cognition, 10*, 16–31.

Glenberg, A. M. (1987). Temporal context and recency. In D. S. Gorfein & R. R. Hoffman (Eds.), *Memory and learning: The Ebbinghaus centennial conference* (pp. 173–190). Hillsdale, NJ: Lawrence Erlbaum Associates.

Glenberg, A. M., & Adams, F. (1978). Type 1 rehearsal and recognition. *Journal of Verbal Learning and Verbal Behavior, 17*, 455–463.

Glenberg, A. M., & Bradley, M. M. (1979). Mental contiguity. *Journal of Experimental Psychology: Human Learning and Memory, 5*, 88–97.

Glenberg, A. M., Bradley, M. M., Kraus, T. A., & Renzaglia, G. J. (1983). Studies of the long-term recency effect: Support for a contextually guided retrieval hypothesis. *Journal of Experimental Psychology: Learning, Memory, and Cognition, 9*, 231–255.

Glenberg, A. M., Bradley, M. M., Stevenson, J. A., Kraus, T. A., Tkachuk, M. J., Gretz, A. L., Fish, J. H., & Turpin, B. M. (1980). A two-process account of long-term serial position effects. *Journal of Experimental Psychology: Human Learning and Memory, 6*, 355–369.

Glenberg, A. M., & Fernandez, A. (1988). Evidence for auditory temporal distinctiveness: Modality effects in order and frequency judgments. *Journal of Experimental Psychology: Learning, Memory, and Cognition, 14*, 728–739.

Glenberg, A. M., Mann, S., Altman, L., Forman, T., & Procise, S. (1989). Modality effects in the coding and reproduction of rhythms. *Memory & Cognition, 17*, 373–383.

Glenberg, A. M., Smith, S. M., & Green, C. (1977). Type 1 rehearsal: Maintenance and more. *Journal of Verbal Learning and Verbal Behavior, 16*, 339–352.

Glenberg, A. M., & Swanson, N. G. (1986). A temporal distinctiveness theory of recency and modality effects. *Journal of Experimental Psychology: Learning, Memory, and Cognition, 12*, 3–15.

Glucksberg, S., & Cowan, G. N. (1970). Memory for nonattended auditory material. *Cognitive Psychology, 1*, 149–156.

Gorfein, D. S. (1970). Effects of intralist activity on free recall performance. *Psychonomic Science, 20*, 331–333.

Gorfein, D. S. (1987). Explaining context effects on short-term memory. In D. S. Gorfein & R. R. Hoffman (Eds.), *Memory and learning: The Ebbinghaus centennial conference* (pp. 153–172). Hillsdale, NJ: Lawrence Erlbaum Associates.

Gorfein, D. S., & Jacobson, D. E. (1973). Memory search in a Brown-Peterson short-term memory paradigm. *Journal of Experimental Psychology, 99*, 82–87.

Graf, P. (1990). Life-span changes in implicit and explicit memory. *Bulletin of the Psychonomic Society, 28*, 353–358.

Graf, P., & Mandler, G. (1984). Activation makes words more accessible, but not necessarily more retrievable. *Journal of Verbal Learning and Verbal Behavior, 23*, 553–568.

Graf, P., & Schacter, D. A. (1985). Implicit and explicit memory for new associations in normal and amnesic subjects. *Journal of Experimental Psychology: Learning, Memory, and Cognition, 11*, 501–518.

Graf, P., Squire, L. R., & Mandler, G. (1984). The information that amnesic patients do not forget. *Journal of Experimental Psychology: Learning, Memory, and Cognition, 10*, 164–178.

Greenberg, S. N., & Engle, R. W. (1983). Voice change in the stimulus suffix effect: Are the effects structural or strategic? *Memory & Cognition, 11*, 551–556.

Greene, E., Flynn, M., & Loftus, E. F. (1982). Inducing resistance to misleading information. *Journal of Verbal Learning and Verbal Behavior, 21*, 207–219.

Greene, R. L. (1984). Incidental learning of event frequency. *Memory & Cognition, 12*, 90–95.

Greene, R. L. (1985). Constraints on the long-term modality effect. *Journal of Memory and Language, 24*, 526–541.

Greene, R. L. (1986a). A common basis for recency effects in immediate and delayed recall. *Journal of Experimental Psychology: Learning, Memory, and Cognition, 12*, 413–418.

Greene, R. L. (1986b). Effects of intentionality and strategy on memory for frequency. *Journal of Experimental Psychology: Learning, Memory, and Cognition, 12*, 489–495.

Greene, R. L. (1986c). Sources of recency effects in free recall. *Psychological Bulletin, 99*, 221–228.

Greene, R. L. (1986d). Word stems as cues in recall and completion tasks. *Quarterly Journal of Experimental Psychology, 38A*, 663–673.

Greene, R. L. (1987). Stimulus suffixes and visual presentation. *Memory & Cognition, 15*, 497–503.

Greene, R. L. (1988). Generation effects in frequency judgment. *Journal of Experimental Psychology: Learning, Memory, and Cognition, 14*, 298–304.

Greene, R. L. (1989a). Immediate serial recall of mixed-modality lists. *Journal of Experimental Psychology: Learning, Memory, and Cognition, 15*, 266–274.

Greene, R. L. (1989b). Negative practice effects on frequency discrimination. *American Journal of Psychology, 102*, 225–232.

Greene, R. L. (1989c). On the relationship between categorical frequency estimation and cued recall. *Memory & Cognition, 17*, 235–239.

Greene, R. L. (1989d). Spacing effects in memory: Evidence for a two-process account. *Journal of Experimental Psychology: Learning, Memory, and Cognition, 15*, 371–377.

Greene, R. L. (1990a). Memory for pair frequency. *Journal of Experimental Psychology: Learning, Memory, and Cognition, 16*, 110–116.

Greene, R. L. (1990b). Spacing effects on implicit memory tests. *Journal of Experimental Psychology: Learning, Memory, and Cognition, 16*, 1004–1011.

Greene, R. L., & Crowder, R. G. (1984a). Effects of semantic similarity on long-term recency. *American Journal of Psychology, 97*, 441–449.

Greene, R. L., & Crowder, R. G. (1984b). Modality and suffix effects in the absence of auditory stimulation. *Journal of Verbal Learning and Verbal Behavior, 23*, 371–382.

Greene, R. L., & Crowder, R. G. (1986). Recency effects in delayed recall of mouthed stimuli. *Memory & Cognition, 14*, 355–360.

Greene, R. L., & Crowder, R. G. (1988). Memory for serial position: Effects of spacing, vocalization, and stimulus suffixes. *Journal of Experimental Psychology: Learning, Memory, and Cognition, 14*, 740–748.

Greene, R. L., Elliott, C. L., & Smith, M. D. (1987). When do interleaved suffixes improve recall? *Journal of Memory and Language, 27*, 560–571.

Greene, R. L., & Samuel, A. G. (1986). Recency and suffix effects in serial recall of musical stimuli. *Journal of Experimental Psychology: Learning, Memory, and Cognition, 12*, 517–524.

Greeno, J. G. (1970). Conservation of information-processing capacity in paired-associate learning. *Journal of Verbal Learning and Verbal Behavior, 9*, 581–586.

Gunter, B., Berry, C., & Clifford, B. R. (1981). Proactive interference effects with television news items: Further evidence. *Journal of Experimental Psychology: Learning, Memory, and Cognition, 7*, 480–487.

Haber, R. N. (1970). Visual information storage. In *Visual search*. Washington, DC: National Academy of Sciences.

Haber, R. N. (1983). The impending demise of the icon: A critique of the concept of iconic storage in visual information processing. *Behavioral and Brain Sciences, 6*, 1–54.

Haber, R. N., & Standing, L. (1969). Direct measures of short-term visual storage. *Quarterly Journal of Experimental Psychology, 21*, 43–54.

Haith, M. M. (1971). Development changes in visual information processing and short-term visual memory. *Human Development, 14*, 249–261.

Halford, G. S., Mayberry, M. T., & Bain, J. D. (1988). Set-size effects in primary memory: An age-related capacity limitation? *Memory & Cognition, 16*, 480–487.

Hanley, M. J., & Scheirer, C. J. (1975). Proactive inhibition in memory scanning. *Journal of Experimental Psychology: Human Learning and Memory, 1*, 81–83.

Hanson, C., & Hirst, W. (1988). Frequency encoding of token and type information. *Journal of Experimental Psychology: Learning, Memory, and Cognition, 14*, 289–297.

Harris, G. J., & Fleer, R. E. (1974). High speed memory scanning in mental retardates: Evidence for a central processing deficit. *Journal of Experimental Child Psychology, 17*, 452–459.

Hasher, L., & Chromiak, W. (1977). The processing of frequency information: An automatic mechanism? *Journal of Verbal Learning and Verbal Behavior, 16*, 173–184.

Hasher, L., & Zacks, R. T. (1979). Automatic and effortful processes in memory. *Journal of Experimental Psychology: General, 108*, 356–388.

Hasher, L., & Zacks, R. T. (1984). Automatic processing of fundamental information: The case of frequency of occurrence. *American Psychologist, 39*, 1372–1388.

Heindel, W. C., Salmon, D. P., Shults, C. W., Walicke, P. A., & Butters, N. (1989). Neuropsychological evidence for multiple implicit systems: A comparison of Alzheimer's, Huntington's, and Parkinson's disease patients. *Journal of Neuroscience, 9*, 582–587.

Hellyer, S. (1962). Frequency of stimulus presentation and short-term decrement in recall. *Journal of Experimental Psychology, 64*, 650.

Hill, J. W., & Bliss, J. C. (1968). Modeling a tactile sensory register. *Perception & Psychophysics, 4*, 91–101.

Hintzman, D. L. (1969). Apparent frequency as a function of frequency and the spacing of repetitions. *Journal of Experimental Psychology, 80*, 139–145.

Hintzman, D. L. (1976). Repetition and memory. In G. H. Bower (Ed.), *The psychology of learning and motivation* (Vol. 11, pp. 47–91). New York: Academic Press.

Hintzman, D. L. (1988). Judgments of frequency and recognition memory in a multiple-trace model. *Psychological Review, 95*, 528–551.

Hintzman, D. L., & Block, R. A. (1971). Repetition and memory: Evidence for a multiple-trace hypothesis. *Journal of Experimental Psychology, 88*, 297–306.

Hintzman, D. L., Block, R. A., & Summers, J. J. (1973). Contextual associations and memory for serial position. *Journal of Experimental Psychology, 97*, 220–229.

Hintzman, D. L., & Hartry, A. L. (1990). Item effects in recognition and fragment completion: Contingency relations vary for different subsets of words. *Journal of Experimental Psychology: Learning, Memory, and Cognition, 16*, 955–969.

Hirshman, E., & Bjork, R. A. (1988). The generation effect: Support for a two-factor theory. *Journal of Experimental Psychology: Learning, Memory, and Cognition, 14*, 484–494.

Hirshman, E., Snodgrass, J. G., Mindes, J., & Feenan, K. (1990). Conceptual priming in fragment completion. *Journal of Experimental Psychology: Learning, Memory, and Cognition, 16*, 634–647.

Hoving, K. L., Morin, R. E., & Konick, D. S. (1970). Recognition reaction time and size of the memory set: A developmental study. *Psychonomic Science, 21*, 247–248.

Howes, D. (1954). On the interpretation of word frequency as a variable affecting speed of recognition. *Journal of Experimental Psychology, 48*, 106–112.

Hunt, E. (1978). Mechanics of verbal ability. *Psychological Review, 85*, 104–130.

Hunt, E., Frost, N., & Lunneborg, C. (1973). Individual differences in cognition: A new approach to cognition. In G. Bower (Ed.), *The psychology of learning and motivation* (Vol. 7). New York: Academic Press.

Hyde, T. S., & Jenkins, J. J. (1969). Differential effects of incidental tasks on the organization of recall of a list of highly associated words. *Journal of Experimental Psychology, 82*, 472–480.

Intraub, H., & Nicklos, S. (1985). Levels of processing and picture memory: The physical superiority effect. *Journal of Experimental Psychology: Learning, Memory, and Cognition, 11*, 284–298.

Jacoby, L. L. (1978). On interpreting the effects of repetition: Solving a problem versus remembering a solution. *Journal of Verbal Learning and Verbal Behavior, 17*, 649–667.

Jacoby, L. L. (1983). Remembering the data: Analyzing interactive processes in reading. *Journal of Verbal Learning and Verbal Behavior, 22*, 485–508.

Jacoby, L. L., & Dallas, M. (1981). On the relationship between autobiographical memory and perceptual learning. *Journal of Experimental Psychology: General, 110*, 306–340.

Jacoby, L. L., & Whitehouse, K. (1989). An illusion of memory: False recognition influenced by unconscious perception. *Journal of Experimental Psychology: General, 118*, 126–135.

Jacoby, L. L., & Witherspoon, D. (1982). Remembering without awareness. *Canadian Journal of Psychology, 32*, 300–324.

Jensen, T. D., & Freund, J. S. (1981). Persistence of the spacing effect in incidental free recall: The effect of external list comparisons. *Bulletin of the Psychonomic Society, 18*, 183–186.

Johnson, M. K., & Hasher, L. (1987). Human learning and memory. *Annual Review of Psychology, 38*, 631–668.

Johnson, M. K., Kim, J. K., & Risse, G. (1985). Do alcoholic Korsakoff's syndrome patients acquire affective reactions? *Journal of Experimental Psychology: Learning, Memory, and Cognition, 11*, 22–36.

Johnston, W. A., & Uhl, C. N. (1976). The contribution of encoding effort and variability to the spacing effect on free recall. *Journal of Experimental Psychology: Human Learning and Memory, 2*, 153–160.

Jones, W. P., & Anderson, J. R. (1982). Semantic categorization and high-speed scanning. *Journal of Experimental Psychology: Learning, Memory & Cognition, 8*, 237–242.

Jones, W. P., & Anderson, J. R. (1987). Short- and long-term memory retrieval: A comparison of the effects of information load and relatedness. *Journal of Experimental Psychology: General, 116*, 137–153.

Kallman, H. J., & Cameron, P. (1989). Enhanced recency effects with changing-state and primary-linguistic stimuli. *Memory & Cognition, 17*, 318–328.

Kallman, H. J., & Massaro, D. W. (1983). Backward masking, the suffix effect, and preperceptual storage. *Journal of Experimental Psychology: Learning, Memory and Cognition, 9*, 312–327.

Kausler, D. H., Lichty, W., & Hakami, M. K. (1984). Frequency judgments for distractor items in a short-term memory task: Instructional variation and adult age differences. *Journal of Verbal Learning and Verbal Behavior, 23*, 660–668.

Keppel, G., & Underwood, B. J. (1962). Proactive inhibition in short-term retention of single items. *Journal of Verbal Learning and Verbal Behavior, 1*, 153–161.

Kincaid, J. P., & Wickens, D. D. (1970). Temporal gradient of release from proactive inhibition. *Journal of Experimental Psychology, 86*, 313–316.

Klatzky, R. L., & Smith, E. E. (1972). Stimulus expectancy and retrieval from short-term memory. *Journal of Experimental Psychology, 94*, 101–107.

Kolers, P. A. (1979). A pattern-analyzing basis of recognition. In L. S. Cermak & F. I. M. Craik (Eds.), *Levels of processing in human memory*. Hillsdale, NJ: Lawrence Erlbaum Associates.

Kolers, P. A., & Ostry, D. J. (1974). Time course of loss of information regarding pattern analyzing operations. *Journal of Verbal Learning and Verbal Behavior, 13*, 599–612.

Kolers, P. A., & Roediger, H. L. III. (1984). Procedures of mind. *Journal of Verbal Learning and Verbal Behavior, 23*, 425–449.

Koppenaal, L., & Glanzer, M. (1990). An examination of the continuous distractor task and the "long-term recency effect." *Memory & Cognition, 18*, 183–195.

Krakow, R. A., & Hanson, V. L. (1985). Deaf signers and serial recall in the visual modality: Memory for signs, fingerspelling, and print. *Memory & Cognition, 13*, 265–272.

Kristofferson, M. W. (1972a). Effects of practice on character-classification performance. *Canadian Journal of Psychology, 26*, 54–60.

Kristofferson, M. W. (1972b). When item recognition and visual search functions are similar. *Perception & Psychophysics, 12*, 379–384.

Kroll, N. E. A., & Kellicutt, M. H. (1972). Short-term recall as a function of covert rehearsal and of intervening task. *Journal of Verbal Learning and Verbal Behavior, 11*, 196–204.

Krueger, L. E. (1970). Effects of stimulus probability on two-choice reaction time. *Journal of Experimental Psychology, 84*, 377–379.

Kuhn, T. S. (1962). *The structure of scientific revolutions*. Chicago: University of Chicago Press.

Kunst-Wilson, W. R., & Zajonc, R. B. (1980). Affective discrimination of stimuli that cannot be recognized. *Science, 207*, 557–558.

Landauer, T. K. (1962). Rate of implicit speech. *Perceptual and Motor Skills, 15*, 646.

Landauer, T. K. (1976). Memory without organization: Properties of a model with random storage and undirected retrieval. *Cognitive Psychology, 7*, 495–531.

Lewis-Smith, M. Q. (1975). Short-term memory as a processing deficit. *American Journal of Psychology, 88*, 605–626.

Light, L. L., & Singh, A. (1987). Implicit and explicit memory in young and old adults. *Journal of Experimental Psychology: Learning, Memory, and Cognition, 13*, 531–541.

Lindsay, D. S. (1990). Misleading suggestions can impair eyewitness' ability to remember event details. *Journal of Experimental Psychology: Learning, Memory, and Cognition, 16*, 1077–1083.

Lindsay, D. S., & Johnson, M. K. (1989a). The eyewitness suggestibility effect and memory for source. *Memory & Cognition, 17*, 349–358.

Lindsay, D. S., & Johnson, M. K. (1989b). The reversed suggestibility effect. *Bulletin of the Psychonomic Society, 27*, 111–113.

Lively, B. L. (1972). Speed/accuracy trade-off and practice as determinants of stage durations in a memory search task. *Journal of Experimental Psychology, 96*, 97–103.

Lively, B. L., & Sanford, B. J. (1972). The use of category information in a memory search task. *Journal of Experimental Psychology, 93*, 379–385.

Lockhart, R. S., & Craik, F. I. M. (1990). Levels of processing: A retrospective commentary on a framework for memory research. *Canadian Journal of Psychology, 44*, 87–112.

Loess, H. (1964). Proactive inhibition in short-term memory. *Journal of Verbal Learning and Verbal Behavior, 3*, 362–368.

Loess, H., & Waugh, N. C. (1967). Short-term memory and intertrial interval. *Journal of Verbal Learning and Verbal Behavior, 6*, 455–460.

Loftus, E. F. (1975). Leading questions and the eyewitness report. *Cognitive Psychology, 7*, 560–572.

Loftus, E. F. (1977). Shifting human color memory. *Memory & Cognition, 5*, 696–699.

Loftus, E. F. (1979a). *Eyewitness testimony*. Cambridge, MA: Harvard University Press.

Loftus, E. F. (1979b). Reactions to blatantly contradictory information. *Memory & Cognition, 7*, 368–374.

Loftus, E. F., Donders, K., Hoffman, H. G., & Schooler, J. W. (1989). Creating new memories that are quickly accessed and confidently held. *Memory & Cognition, 17*, 607–616.

Loftus, E. F., & Loftus, G. R. (1980). On the permanence of stored information in the human brain. *American Psychologist, 35*, 409–420.

Loftus, E. F., Miller, D. G., & Burns, H. J. (1978). Semantic integration of verbal information into a visual memory. *Journal of Experimental Psychology: Human Learning and Memory, 4*, 19–31.

Loftus, E. F., & Palmer, J. C. (1974). Reconstruction of automobile destruction: An example of the interaction between memory and language. *Journal of Verbal Learning and Verbal Behavior, 13*, 585–589.

Loftus, E. F., & Zanni, G. (1975). Eyewitness testimony: The influence of the wording of a question. *Bulletin of the Psychonomic Society, 5*, 86–88.

Loftus, G. R., & Patterson, K. K. (1975). Components of short-term proactive interference. *Journal of Verbal Learning and Verbal Behavior, 14*, 105–121.

Long, G. M. (1980). Iconic memory: A review and critique of the study of short-term visual storage. *Psychological Review, 88*, 785–820.

Long, G. M., & Beaton, R. J. (1982). The case for peripheral persistence: Effects of target and background luminance on a partial-report task. *Journal of Experimental Psychology: Human Perception and Performance, 8*, 383–391.

Lorsbach, T. C. (1990). Buildup of proactive inhibition as a function of temporal spacing and adult age. *American Journal of Psychology, 103*, 21–36.

MacDonald, J., & McGurk, H. (1978). Visual influences on speech perception processes. *Perception & Psychophysics, 24*, 253–257.

MacLeod, C. M. (1975). Release from proactive interference: Insufficiency of an attentional account. *American Journal of Psychology, 88*, 459–465.

MacLeod, C. M. (1988). Forgotten but not gone: Savings for pictures and words in long-term memory. *Journal of Experimental Psychology: Learning, Memory, and Cognition, 14*, 195–212.

MacLeod, C. M. (1989). Directed forgetting affects both direct and indirect tests of memory. *Journal of Experimental Psychology: Learning, Memory, and Cognition, 15*, 13–21.

Magliero, A. (1983). Pupil dilation following pairs of identical and related to-be-remembered words. *Memory & Cognition, 11*, 609–615.

Maki, R. H., & Schuler, J. (1980). Effects of rehearsal duration and level of processing on memory for words. *Journal of Verbal Learning and Verbal Behavior, 19*, 36–45.

Mandler, G., Nakamura, Y., & van Zandt, B. J. S. (1987). Nonspecific effects of exposure on stimuli that cannot be recognized. *Journal of Experimental Psychology: Learning, Memory, and Cognition, 13*, 646–648.

Manning, S. K. (1980). Tactual and visual alphanumeric suffix effects. *Quarterly Journal of Experimental Psychology, 32*, 257–267.

Manning, S. K., & Gmuer, B. A. (1985). Visual suffix effects on the Optacon: A test of changing state, primary linguistic, and attentional theories. *Bulletin of the Psychonomic Society, 23*, 1–4.

Manning, S. K., & Robinson, I. I. (1989). Recency and suffix effects as a function of auditory confusability and set size. *American Journal of Psychology, 102*, 495–510.

Marcel, A. J. (1976). Negative set effects in character classification: A response-retrieval view of reaction time. *Quarterly Journal of Experimental Psychology, 29*, 31–48.

Marmurek, H. H. C. (1983). Negative recency in final free recall: Encoding or retrieval. *American Journal of Psychology, 96*, 17–35.

Marshall, P. H., & Werder, P. R. (1972). The effects of the elimination of rehearsal on primacy and recency. *Journal of Verbal Learning and Verbal Behavior, 11*, 649–653.

Massaro, D. W. (1976). Preperceptual processing in dichotic listening. *Journal of Experimental Psychology: Human Learning and Memory, 2*, 331–339.

Masterman, M. (1970). The nature of a paradigm. In I. Lakatos & A. Musgrave (Eds.), *Criticism and the growth of knowledge*. Cambridge: Cambridge University Press.

McClelland, J. L. (1979). On the time relations of mental processes: An examination of systems of processes in cascade. *Psychological Review, 86*, 287–330.

McCloskey, M., & Egeth, H. E. (1983). Eyewitness identification: What can a psychologist tell a jury? *American Psychologist, 38*, 550–563.

McCloskey, M., & Zaragoza, M. (1985). Misleading postevent information and memory for events: Arguments and evidence against memory impairment hypothesis. *Journal of Experimental Psychology: General, 114*, 381–387.

McDaniel, M. A., Waddill, P. A., & Einstein, G. O. (1988). A contextual account of the generation effect: A three-factor theory. *Journal of Memory and Language, 27*, 521–536.

McElroy, L. A., & Slamecka, N. J. (1982). Memorial consequences of generating nonwords: Implications for semantic-memory interpretations of the generation effect. *Journal of Verbal Learning and Verbal Behavior, 21*, 249–259.

McGeoch, J. A. (1942). *The psychology of human learning*. New York: Longmans, Green.

McKoon, G., Ratcliff, R., & Dell, G. S. (1986). A critical evaluation of the semantic/episodic distinction. *Journal of Experimental Psychology: Learning, Memory, and Cognition, 12*, 295–306.

Melton, A. W. (1967). Repetition and retrieval from memory. *Science, 158*, 532.

Melton, A. W., & Irwin, J. M. (1940). The influence of degree of interpolated learning on retroactive inhibition and the overt transfer of specific responses. *American Journal of Psychology, 53*, 173–203.

Metcalfe, J. (1990). Composite holographic associative recall model (CHARM) and blended memories in eyewitness testimony. *Journal of Experimental Psychology: General, 119*, 145–160.

Merikle, P. M. (1980). Selection from visual persistence by perceptual groups and category membership. *Journal of Experimental Psychology: General, 109*, 279–295.

Mewhort, D. J. K., Campbell, A. J., Marchetti, F. M., & Campbell, J. I. D. (1981). Identification, localization, and "iconic" memory: An evaluation of the bar-probe task. *Memory & Cognition, 9*, 50–67.

Mewhort, D. J. K., & Leppman, K. P. (1985). Information persistence: Testing spatial and identity information with a voice probe. *Psychological Research, 47*, 51–58.

Mewhort, D. J. K., Marchetti, F. M., Gurnsey, R., & Campbell, A. J. (1984). Information persistence: A dual buffer model for initial visual processing. In H. Bouma & D. G. Bouwhuis (Eds.), *Attention and performance: Control of language processes* (Vol. 10, pp. 287–298). Hillsdale, NJ: Lawrence Erlbaum Associates.

Meyer, D. E., Schvaneveldt, R. W., & Ruddy, M. G. (1975). Loci of contextual effects on visual word recognition. In P. M. A. Rabbitt & S. Dornic (Eds.), *Attention and performance* (Vol. 5, pp. 98–118). London: Academic Press.

Miller, G. A. (1956). The magical number seven plus or minus two: Some limits on our capacity for processing information. *Psychological Review, 63*, 81–97.

Miller, J., & Hardzinski, M. (1981). Case specificity of the stimulus probability effect. *Memory & Cognition, 9*, 205–216.

Miller, J., & Pachella, R. G. (1973). Locus of the stimulus probability effect. *Journal of Experimental Psychology, 101*, 227–231.

Mitchell, D. B., & Hunt, R. R. (1989). How much "effort" should be devoted to memory? *Memory & Cognition, 17*, 337–348.

Modigliani, V., & Hedges, D. G. (1987). Distributed rehearsals and the primacy effect in single-trial free recall. *Journal of Experimental Psychology: Learning, Memory, and Cognition, 13*, 426–436.

Monsell, S. (1978). Recency, immediate recognition memory, and reaction time. *Cognitive Psychology, 10*, 465–501.

Moray, N., Bates, A., & Barnett, T. (1965). Experiments on the four-eared man. *Journal of the Acoustical Society of America, 38*, 196–201.

Morris, C. D., Bransford, J. D., & Franks, J. J. (1977). Levels of processing versus transfer appropriate processing. *Journal of Verbal Learning and Verbal Behavior, 16*, 519–533.

Morton, J., Crowder, R. G., & Prussin, H. A. (1971). Experiments with the stimulus suffix effect. *Journal of Experimental Psychology, 91*, 169–190.

Morton, J., Marcus, S. M., & Ottley, P. (1981). The acoustic correlates of "speechlike": A use of the suffix effect. *Journal of Experimental Psychology: General, 110*, 568–593.

Muller, G. E., & Pilzecker, A. (1900). Experimentalle Beitrage zur Lehre vom Gedachtnis. *Zeitschrift fur Pshchologie, 1*, 1–300.

Murdock, B. B., Jr. (1961). The retention of individual items. *Journal of Experimental Psychology, 62*, 618–625.

Murdock, B. B., Jr. (1962). The serial position effect in free recall. *Journal of Experimental Psychology, 64*, 482–488.

Murdock, B. B., Jr. (1965). Effect of subsidiary task on short-term memory. *British Journal of Psychology, 56*, 413–419.

Murdock, B. B., Jr. (1967). Recent developments in short-term memory. *British Journal of Psychology, 58*, 421–433.

Murdock, B. B., Jr., & Walker, K. D. (1969). Modality effects in free recall. *Journal of Verbal Learning and Verbal Behavior, 8*, 665–676.

Murphy, M. D., & Puff, C. R. (1982). Free recall: Basic methodology and analysis. In C. R. Puff (Ed.), *Handbook of research methods in human memory and cognition* (pp. 99–128). New York: Academic Press.

Murray, D. J. (1966). Vocalization-at-presentation and immediate recall, with varying recall methods. *Quarterly Journal of Experimental Psychology, 21*, 263–276.

Muter, P. (1980). Very rapid forgetting. *Memory & Cognition, 8*, 174–179.

Nairne, J. S. (1983). Associative processing during rote rehearsal. *Journal of Experimental Psychology: Learning, Memory, and Cognition, 9*, 3–20.

Nairne, J. S. (1988). A framework for interpreting recency effects in immediate serial recall. *Memory & Cognition, 16*, 343–352.

Nairne, J. S. (1990). A feature model of immediate memory. *Memory & Cognition, 18*, 251–269.

Nairne, J. S., & Crowder, R. G. (1982). On the locus of the stimulus suffix effect. *Memory & Cognition, 10*, 350–357.

Nairne, J. S., & McNabb, W. L. (1985). More modality effects in the absence of sound. *Journal of Experimental Psychology: Learning, Memory, and Cognition, 11*, 596–604.

Nairne, J. S., Pusen, C. P., & Widner, R. L. (1985). Representation in the mental lexicon: Implications for theories of the generation effect. *Memory & Cognition, 13*, 183–191.

Nairne, J. S., & Walters, V. L. (1983). Silent mouthing produces modality- and suffix-like effects. *Journal of Verbal Learning and Verbal Behavior, 22*, 475–483.

Nairne, J. S., & Widner, R. L. (1988). Familiarity and lexicality as determinants of the generation effect. *Journal of Experimental Psychology: Learning, Memory, and Cognition, 14*, 694–699.

Nakajima, Y., & Sato, K. (1989). Distractor difficulty and the long-term recency effect. *American Journal of Psychology, 102*, 511–521.

Naveh-Benjamin, M., & Jonides, J. (1986). On the automaticity of frequency coding: Effects of competing task load, encoding strategy, and intention. *Journal of Experimental Psychology: Learning, Memory, and Cognition, 12*, 378–386.

Neely, J. H. (1977). Semantic priming and retrieval from lexical memory: Roles of inhibitionless spreading activation and limited-capacity attention. *Journal of Experimental Psychology: General, 106*, 226–254.

Neisser, U. (1967). *Cognitive psychology*. New York: Appleton-Century-Crofts.

Neisser, U. (1976). *Cognition and reality*. San Francisco: Freeman.

Nelson, T. O. (1977). Repetition and depth of processing. *Journal of Verbal Learning and Verbal Behavior, 16*, 151–171.

Nickerson, R. S. (1972). Binary-classification reaction time: A review of some studies of human information-processing capabilities. *Psychonomic Monograph Supplements, 4*, 275–318.

Nipher, F. E. (1878). On the distribution of errors in numbers written from memory. *Transactions of the Academy of Science of St. Louis, 3*, CCX–CCXI.

Norman, D. A. (1969). Memory while shadowing. *Quarterly Journal of Experimental Psychology, 21*, 85–93.

O'Neil, M. E., Sutcliffe, J. A., & Tulving, E. (1976). Retrieval cues and release from proactive inhibition. *American Journal of Psychology, 89*, 535–543.

Pachella, R. G. (1974). The interpretation of reaction time in information-processing research. In B. H. Kantowitz (Ed.), *Human information processing: Tutorials in performance and cognition*. Hillsdale, NJ: Lawrence Erlbaum Associates.

Paller, K. A. (1990). Recall and stem-completion priming have different electrophysiological correlates and are modified differentially by directed forgetting. *Journal of Experimental Psychology: Learning, Memory, and Cognition, 16*, 1021–1032.

Parkin, A. J., & Streete, S. (1988). Implicit and explicit memory in young children and adults. *British Journal of Psychology, 79*, 361–369.

Pashler, H. (1984). Evidence against late selection: Stimulus quality effects in previewed displays. *Journal of Experimental Psychology: Human Perception and Performance, 10*, 429–448.

Payne, D. G., Neely, J. H., & Burns, D. J. (1986). The generation effect: Further tests of the lexical activation hypothesis. *Memory & Cognition, 14*, 246–252.

Pellegrino, J. W., Siegel, A. W., & Dhawan, M. (1976). Differential distraction effects in short-term and long-term retention of pictures and words. *Journal of Experimental Psychology: Human Learning and Memory, 2*, 541–547.

Penney, C. G. (1985). Elimination of the suffix effect on preterminal list items with unpredictable list length: Evidence for a dual model of suffix effects. *Journal of Experimental Psychology: Learning, Memory, and Cognition, 11*, 229–247.

Perruchet, P., & Baveaux, P. (1989). Correlational analyses of explicit and implicit memory performance. *Memory & Cognition, 17*, 77–86.

Peterson, L. R., & Peterson, M. R. (1959). Short-term retention of individual verbal items. *Journal of Experimental Psychology, 58*, 193–198.

Pirolli, P. L., & Mitterer, J. O. (1984). The effect of leading questions on prior memory: Evidence for the coexistence of inconsistent memory traces. *Canadian Journal of Psychology, 38*, 135–141.

Poltrock, S. E., & MacLeod, C. M. (1977). Primacy and recency in the continuous distractor paradigm. *Journal of Experimental Psychology: Human Learning and Memory, 3*, 560–571.

Posner, M. I. (1967). Short-term memory systems in human information processing. In A. F. Sanders (Ed.), *Attention and performance* (pp. 267–284). Amsterdam: North Holland.

Postman, L. (1976). Interference theory revisited. In J. Brown (Ed.), *Recall and recognition* (pp. 157–181). New York: Wiley.

Postman, L., & Phillips, L. W. (1965). Short-term temporal changes in free recall. *Quarterly Journal of Experimental Psychology, 17*, 132–138.

Postman, L., Stark, K., & Fraser, J. (1968). Temporal changes in interference. *Journal of Verbal Learning and Verbal Behavior, 7*, 672–694.

Powers, P. A., Andriks, J. L., & Loftus, E. F. (1979). Eyewitness accounts of females and males. *Journal of Applied Psychology, 64*, 339–347.

Proctor, R. W., & Fagnani, C. A. (1978). Effects of distractor-stimulus modality in the Brown-Peterson distractor task. *Journal of Experimental Psychology: Human Learning and Memory, 4*, 676–684.

Puckett, J. M., & Kausler, D. H. (1984). Individual differences and models of memory span: A role for memory search rate. *Journal of Experimental Psychology: Learning, Memory, and Cognition, 10*, 72–82.

Purcell, D. G., & Stewart, A. L. (1971). The two-flash threshold: An evaluation of critical duration and visual persistence hypotheses. *Perception & Psychophysics, 9*, 61–64.

Raaijmakers, J. G. W. (1982). A note on the measurement of primary memory capacity. *Journal of Experimental Psychology: Learning, Memory, and Cognition, 8*, 343–352.

Raeburn, V. P. (1974). Priorities in item recognition. *Memory & Cognition, 2*, 663–669.

Rao, K. V. (1983). Word frequency effect in situational frequency estimation. *Journal of Experimental Psychology: Learning, Memory, and Cognition, 9*, 73–81.

Ratcliff, R. (1978). A theory of memory retrieval. *Psychological Review, 85*, 59–108.

Ratcliff, R. (1985). Theoretical interpretations of the speed and accuracy of positive and negative responses. *Psychological Review, 92*, 212–255.

Raymond, B. (1969). Short-term storage and long-term storage in free recall. *Journal of Verbal Learning and Verbal Behavior, 8*, 567–574.

Reed, A. V. (1976). List length and the time course of recognition in immediate memory. *Memory & Cognition, 4*, 16–30.

Reitman, J. S. (1971). Mechanisms of forgetting in short-term memory. *Cognitive Psychology, 2*, 185–195.

Reitman, J. S. (1974). Without surreptitious rehearsal, information in short-term memory decays. *Journal of Verbal Learning and Verbal Behavior, 13*, 365–377.

Roberts, L. A. (1986). Modality and suffix effects in memory for melodic and harmonic musical materials. *Cognitive Psychology, 18*, 123–157.

Roediger, H. L. III. (1990a). Implicit memory: A commentary. *Bulletin of the Psychonomic Society, 28*, 373–380.

Roediger, H. L. III (1990b). Implicit memory: Retention without remembering. *American Psychologist, 45*, 1043–1056.

Rose, R. J., & Rowe, E. J. (1976). Effects of orienting task and spacing of repetitions on frequency judgments. *Journal of Experimental Psychology: Human Learning and Memory, 2*, 142–152.

Rostron, A. B. (1974). Brief auditory storage: Some further observations. *Acta Psychologica, 38*, 471–482.

Routh, D. A., & Lifschutz, A. J. (1975). An asymmetrical effect of similarity in the attenuation of stimulus suffix interference. *Journal of Verbal Learning and Verbal Behavior, 14*, 95–104.

Rowe, E. J. (1974). Depth of processing in a frequency judgment task. *Journal of Verbal Learning and Verbal Behavior, 13*, 638–643.

Rundus, D. (1971). Analysis of rehearsal processes in free recall. *Journal of Experimental Psychology, 89*, 63–77.

Rundus, D. (1977). Maintenance rehearsal and single-level processing. *Journal of Verbal Learning and Verbal Behavior, 16*, 665–681.

Rundus, D. (1980). Maintenance rehearsal and long-term recency. *Memory & Cognition, 8*, 226–230.

Rundus, D., & Atkinson, R. C. (1970). Rehearsal processes in free recall: A procedure for direct observation. *Journal of Verbal Learning and Verbal Behavior, 9*, 99–105.

Russ-Eft, D. (1979). Proactive interference: Build-up and release for individual words. *Journal of Experimental Psychology: Learning, Memory, and Cognition, 5*, 422–434.

Sakitt, B. (1976). Iconic memory. *Psychological Review, 83*, 257–276.

Sakitt, B., & Appelman, I. B. (1978). The effects of memory load and the contrast of the rod signal on partial report superiority in a Sperling task. *Memory & Cognition, 6*, 562–567.

Sakitt, B., & Long, G. M. (1979). Spare the rod and spoil the icon. *Journal of Experimental Psychology: Human Perception and Performance, 5*, 19–30.

Salter, D., & Colley, J. G. (1977). The stimulus suffix: A paradoxical effect. *Memory & Cognition, 5*, 257–262.

Schab, F. R., & Crowder, R. G. (1989). Accuracy of temporal coding: Auditory-visual comparisons. *Memory & Cognition, 17*, 384–397.

Schacter, D. L. (1982). *Stranger behind the engram: Theories of memory and the psychology of science*. Hillsdale, NJ: Lawrence Erlbaum Associates.

Schacter, D. L. (1987). Implicit memory: History and current status. *Journal of Experimental Psychology: Learning, Memory, and Cognition, 13*, 501–518.

Schmidt, S. R., & Cherry, K. (1989). The negative generation effect: Delineation of a phenomenon. *Memory & Cognition, 17*, 359–369.

Schneider, W., & Shiffrin, R. M. (1977). Controlled and automatic human information processing: 1. Detection, search, and attention. *Psychological Review, 84*, 1–66.

Schooler, J. W., Gerhard, D., & Loftus, E. F. (1986). Qualities of the unreal. *Journal of Experimental Psychology: Learning, Memory, and Cognition, 12*, 171–181.

Seamon, J. G. (1972). Imagery codes and human information retrieval. *Journal of Experimental Psychology, 96*, 468–470.

Seamon, J. G., Brody, N., & Kauff, D. M. (1983). Affective discrimination of stimuli that are not recognized: Effects of shadowing, masking, and cerebral laterality. *Journal of Experimental Psychology: Learning, Memory, and Cognition, 9*, 544–555.

Seamon, J. G., Marsh, R. L., & Brody, N. (1984). Critical importance of exposure duration for affective discrimination of stimuli that are not recognized. *Journal of Experimental Psychology: Learning, Memory, and Cognition, 10*, 465–469.

Seamon, J. G., & Murray, P. (1976). Depth of processing in recall and recognition memory: Differential effects of stimulus meaningfulness and serial position. *Journal of Experimental Psychology: Human Learning and Memory, 2*, 680–687.

Seamon, J., & Wright, C. (1976). Generative processes in character classification: Evidence for a probe encoding set. *Memory & Cognition, 4*, 96–102.

Sebrechts, M. M., Marsh, R. L., & Seamon, J. G. (1989). Secondary memory and very rapid forgetting. *Memory & Cognition, 17*, 693–700.

Shand, M. A., & Klima, E. S. (1981). Nonauditory suffix effects in congenitally deaf signers of American Sign Language. *Journal of Experimental Psychology: Human Learning and Memory, 7*, 464–474.

Shaughnessy, J. J., & Mand, J. L. (1982). How permanent are memories of real-life events? *American Journal of Psychology, 95*, 51–63.

Shaughnessy, J. J., Zimmerman, J., & Underwood, B. J. (1972). Further evidence on the MP-DP effect in free recall learning. *Journal of Verbal Learning and Verbal Behavior, 11*, 1–12.

Shepard, R. N. (1967). Recognition memory for words, sentences, and pictures. *Journal of Verbal Learning and Verbal Behavior, 6*, 156–163.

Shiffrin, R. M. (1970). Memory search. In D. Norman (Ed.), *Models of human memory* (pp. 375–447). New York: Academic Press.

Shiffrin, R. M., & Schneider, W. (1977). Controlled and automatic human information processing: 2. Perceptual learning, automatic attending, and a general theory. *Psychological Review, 84*, 127–190.

Shimamura, A. P. (1986). Priming effects in amnesia: Evidence for a dissociable memory function. *Quarterly Journal of Experimental Psychology, 38A*, 619–644.

Sipe, S., & Engle, R. W. (1986). Echoic memory processes in good and poor readers. *Journal of Experimental Psychology: Learning, Memory, and Cognition, 12*, 402–412.

Slamecka, N. J., & Fevreiski, J. (1983). The generation effect when generation fails. *Journal of Verbal Learning and Verbal Behavior, 22*, 153–163.

Slamecka, N. J., & Graf, P. (1978). The generation effect: Delineation of a phenomenon. *Journal of Experimental Psychology: Human Learning and Memory, 4*, 592–604.

Slamecka, N. J., & Katsaiti, L. T. (1987). The generation effect as an artifact of selective displaced rehearsal. *Journal of Memory and Language, 26*, 589–607.

Sloman, S. A., Hayman, C. A. G., Ohta, N., Law, J., & Tulving, E. (1988). Forgetting in primed fragment completion. *Journal of Experimental Psychology: Learning, Memory, and Cognition, 14*, 223–239.

Smith, E. E., Barresi, J., & Gross, A. E. (1971). Imaginal versus verbal coding and the primary-secondary memory distinction. *Journal of Verbal Learning and Verbal Behavior, 10*, 597–603.

Smith, E. R., & Branscombe, N. R. (1988). Category accessibility as implicit memory. *Journal of Experimental Social Psychology, 24*, 490–504.

Smith, T. L. (1896). On muscular memory. *American Journal of Psychology, 4*, 453–490.

Smith, W. G. (1895). The relation of attention to memory. *Mind, 4*, 47–73.

Sperling G. (1960). The information available in brief visual presentations. *Psychological Monographs, 74* (Whole No. 11).

Sperling, G. (1967). Successive approximations to a model for short-term memory. *Acta Psychologica, 27*, 285–292.

Spoehr, K. T., & Corin, W. J. (1978). The stimulus suffix effect as a memory coding phenomenon. *Memory & Cognition, 6*, 583–589.

Squire, L. R. (1987). *Memory and brain*. New York: Oxford University Press.

Stadler, M. A., & Logan, G. D. (1989). Is there a search in fixed-set memory search? *Memory & Cognition, 17*, 723–728.

Stanovich, K. E., & Pachella, R. G. (1977). Encoding, stimulus-response compatibility, and stages of processing. *Journal of Experimental Psychology: Human Perception and Performance, 3*, 411–421.

Sternberg, R. J. (1977). *Intelligence, information processing, and analogical reasoning: The componential analysis of human abilities*. Hillsdale, NJ: Lawrence Erlbaum Associates.

Sternberg, S. (1966). High-speed scanning in human memory. *Science, 153*, 652–654.

Sternberg, S. (1969a). Memory-scanning: Mental processes revealed by reaction-time experiments. *American Scientist, 57*, 421–457.

Sternberg, S. (1969b). The discovery of processing stages: Extensions of Donders' method. *Acta Psychologica, 30*, 276–315.

Sternberg, S. (1975). Memory scanning: New findings and current controversies. *Quarterly Journal of Experimental Psychology, 27*, 1–32.

Stigler, S. M. (1978). Some forgotten work on memory. *Journal of Experimental Psychology: Human Learning and Memory, 4*, 1–4.

Strauss, M. E., Weingartner, H., & Thompson, K. (1985). Remembering words and how often they occurred in memory-impaired patients. *Memory & Cognition, 13*, 507–510.

Sumby, W. H. (1963). Word frequency and serial position effects. *Journal of Verbal Learning and Verbal Behavior, 1*, 443–450.

Swinney, D. A., & Taylor, O. L. (1971). Short-term memory recognition search in aphasia. *Journal of Speech and Hearing Research, 14*, 578–588.

Tardif, T., & Craik, F. I. M. (1989). Reading a week later: Perceptual and conceptual factors. *Journal of Memory and Language, 28*, 107–125.

Theios, J., Smith, P., Haviland, S., Traupmann, J., & Moy, M. (1973). Memory scanning as a serial self-termination process. *Journal of Experimental Psychology, 97*, 323–326.

Theios, J., & Walter, D. G. (1974). Stimulus and response frequency and sequential effects in memory scanning reaction times. *Journal of Experimental Psychology, 102*, 1092–1099.

Toppino, T. C., & Gracen, T. F. (1985). Lag effect and differential organization theory: Nine failures to replicate. *Journal of Experimental Psychology: Learning, Memory, and Cognition, 11*, 185–191.

Tousignant, J. P., Hall, D., & Loftus, E. F. (1986). Discrepancy detection and vulnerability to misleading postevent information. *Memory & Cognition, 14*, 329–338.

Townsend, J. T. (1971). A note on the identifiability of parallel and serial processes. *Perception & Psychophysics, 10*, 161–163.

Townsend, J. T. (1990). Serial vs. parallel processing: Sometimes they look like Tweedledum and Tweedledee but they can (and should) be distinguished. *Psychological Science, 1*, 46–54.

Townsend, V. M. (1973). Loss of spatial and identity information following a tachistoscopic exposure. *Journal of Experimental Psychology, 98*, 113–118.

Treisman, A. M., Russell, R., & Green, J. (1975). Brief visual storage of shape and movement. In P. M. A. Rabbitt & S. Dornic (Eds.), *Attention and performance 5* (pp. 699–721). London: Academic Press.

Treisman, M., & Rostron, A. B. (1972). Brief auditory storage: A modification of Sperling's paradigm applied to audition. *Acta Psychologica, 36*, 161–170.

Tulving, E. (1976). Ecphoric processes in recall and recognition. In J. Brown (Ed.), *Recall and recognition*. New York: Wiley.

Tulving, E. (1983). *Elements of episodic memory*. Oxford, England: Oxford University Press.

Tulving, E., & Colotla, V. (1970). Free recall of trilingual lists. *Cognitive Psychology, 1*, 86–98.

Tulving, E., & Schacter, D. L. (1990). Priming and human memory systems. *Science, 247*, 301–305.

Tulving, E., Schacter, D. L., & Stark, H. (1982). Priming effects in word-fragment completion are independent of recognition memory. *Journal of Experimental Psychology: Learning, Memory, and Cognition, 8*, 336–342.

Turner, M. L., LaPointe, L. B. Cantor, J., Reeves, C. H., Griffeth, R. H., & Engle, R. W. (1987). Recency and suffix effects found with auditory presentation and with mouthed visual presentation: They're not the same thing. *Journal of Memory and Language, 13*, 430–447.

Turvey, M. T., Brick, P., & Osborn, J. (1970). Proactive interference in short-term memory as a function of prior-item retention interval. *Quarterly Journal of Experimental Psychology, 22*, 142–147.

Tversky, B., & Tuchin, M. (1989). A reconciliation of the evidence on eyewitness testimony: Comments on McCloskey and Zaragoza. *Journal of Experimental Psychology: General, 118*, 86–91.

Tzeng, O. J. L. (1973). Positive recency effects in delayed free recall. *Journal of Verbal Learning and Verbal Behavior, 12*, 436–439.

Underwood, B. J. (1957). Interference and forgetting. *Psychological Review, 64*, 49–60.

Underwood, B. J. (1961). Ten years of massed practice on distributed practice. *Psychological Review, 68*, 229–247.

Underwood, B. J. (1969). Attributes of memory. *Psychological Review, 76*, 559–573.

van der Heijden, A. H. C. (1981). *Short-term visual information forgetting*. London: Routledge & Kegan Paul.

von Wright, J. M. (1968). Selection in visual immediate memory. *Quarterly Journal of Experimental Psychology, 20*, 62–68.

Ward, J. (1893). Assimilation and association. *Mind, 2*, 347–362.

Warren, L. R., & Mitchell, S. A. (1980). Age differences in judging the frequency of events. *Developmental Psychology, 16*, 116–120.

Warrington, E. K., & Weiskrantz, L. (1968). New method of testing long-term retention with special reference to amnesic patients. *Nature, 217*, 972–974.

Warrington, E. K., & Weiskrantz, L. (1970). Amnesic syndrome: Consolidation or retrieval? *Nature, 228*, 629–630.

Washburn, M. F. (1916). *Movement and mental imagery*. Boston: Houghton Mifflin.

Watkins, M. J. (1974). Concept and measurement of primary memory. *Psychological Bulletin, 81*, 695–711.

Watkins, M. J. (1979). Modifying Waugh and Norman's primary measurement procedure: An alternative solution. *British Journal of Psychology, 70*, 445–447.

Watkins, M. J., & LeCompte, D. C. (1991). The inadequacy of recall as a basis for frequency knowledge. *Journal of Experimental Psychology: Learning, Memory, and Cognition, 17*, 1161–1176.

Watkins, M. J., & Peynircioglu, Z. F. (1983). Three recency effects at the same time. *Journal of Verbal Learning and Verbal Behavior, 22*, 375–384.

Watkins, M. J., Peynircioglu, Z. F., & Brems, D. J. (1984). Pictorial rehearsal. *Memory & Cognition, 12*, 553–557.

Watkins, M. J., & Sechler, E. S. (1988). Generation effect with an incidental memorization procedure. *Journal of Memory and Language, 27*, 537–544.

Watkins, M. J., & Sechler, E. S. (1989). Adapting to an irrelevant item in an immediate recall task. *Memory & Cognition, 17*, 682–692.

Watkins, M. J., & Todres, A. K. (1980). Suffix effects manifest and concealed: Further evidence for a 20-second echo. *Journal of Verbal Learning and Verbal Behavior, 19*, 46–53.

Watkins, M. J., & Watkins, O. C. (1974a). Processing of recency items for free recall. *Journal of Experimental Psychology, 102*, 488–493.

Watkins, M. J., & Watkins, O. C. (1974b). A tactile suffix effect. *Memory & Cognition, 2*, 176–180.

Watkins, O. C., & Watkins, M. J. (1975). Build-up of proactive inhibition as a cue-overload effect. *Journal of Experimental Psychology, 104*, 442–452.

Watkins, O. C., & Watkins, M. J. (1980). The modality effect and echoic persistence. *Journal of Experimental Psychology: General, 109*, 251–278.

Waugh, N. C., & Norman, D. A. (1965). Primary memory. *Psychological Review, 72*, 89–104.

Weinberg, H. I., Wadsworth, J., & Baron, R. S. (1983). Demand and the impact of leading questions on eyewitness testimony. *Memory & Cognition, 11*, 101–104.

Welch, G. B., & Burnett, C. T. (1924). Is primacy a factor in association formation? *American Journal of Psychology, 35*, 396–401.

Whitlow, J. W., Jr. (1990). Differential sensitivity of perceptual identification for words and pseudowords to test expectations: Implications for the locus of word frequency effects. *Journal of Experimental Psychology: Learning, Memory, and Cognition, 16*, 837–851.

Whitten, W. B. (1978). Output interference and long-term serial position effects. *Journal of Experimental Psychology: Human Learning and Memory, 4*, 685–692.

Whittlesea, B. W. A., Jacoby, L. L., & Girard, K. (1990). Illusions of immediate memory: Evidence of an attributional basis for feelings of familiarity and perceptual quality. *Journal of Memory and Language, 29*, 716–732.

White, M. J. (1983). Prominent publications in cognitive psychology. *Memory & Cognition, 11*, 423–427.

Wickelgren, W. A. (1965). Acoustic similarity and retroactive interference in short-term memory. *Journal of Verbal Learning and Verbal Behavior, 4*, 53–61.

Wickens, D. D. (1970). Encoding categories of words: An empirical approach to meaning. *Psychological Review, 77*, 1–15.

Wickens, D. D. (1972). Characteristics of word encoding. In A. W. Melton & E. Martin (Eds.), *Coding processes in human memory* (pp. 191–215). Washington, DC: Winston.

Wickens, D. D., Born, D. G., & Allen, C. K. (1963). Proactive inhibition and item similarity in short-term memory. *Journal of Verbal Learning and Verbal Behavior, 2*, 440–445.

Wickens, D. D., & Cammarata, S. A. (1986). Response class interference in STM. *Bulletin of the Psychonomic Society, 24*, 266–268.

Wickens, D. D., Moody, M. J., & Dow, R. (1981). The nature and timing of the retrieval process and of interference effects. *Journal of Experimental Psychology: General, 110*, 1–20.

Wickens, D. D., Moody, M. J., & Vidulich, M. (1985). Retrieval time as a function of memory set size, type of probe, and interference in recognition memory. *Journal of Experimental Psychology: Learning, Memory, and Cognition, 11*, 154–164.

Williams, K. W., & Durso, F. T. (1986). Judging category frequency: Automaticity or availability? *Journal of Experimental Psychology: Learning, Memory, and Cognition, 12*, 387–396.

Wingfield, A. (1973). Effect of serial position and set size in auditory recognition memory. *Memory & Cognition, 1*, 53–55.

Witherspoon, D., & Allan, L. G. (1985). The effect of a prior presentation on temporal judgments in a perceptual identification task. *Memory & Cognition, 13*, 101–111.

Witherspoon, D., & Moscovitch, M. (1989). Stochastic independence between two implicit memory tests. *Journal of Experimental Psychology: Learning, Memory, and Cognition, 15*, 22–30.

Woodward, A. E., Jr., Bjork, R. A., & Jongeward, R. H. (1973). Recall and recognition as a function of primary rehearsal. *Journal of Verbal Learning and Verbal Behavior, 12*, 608–617.

Wright, J. H. (1967). Effects of formal interitem similarity and length of retention interval on proactive inhibition in short-term memory. *Journal of Experimental Psychology, 75*, 366–395.

Yeomans, J. M., & Irwin, D. E. (1985). Stimulus duration and partial report performance. *Perception & Psychophysics, 37*, 163–169.

Zacks, R. T., Hasher, L., & Sanft, H. (1982). Automatic encoding of event frequency: Further findings. *Journal of Experimental Psychology: Learning, Memory, and Cognition, 8*, 106–116.

Zaragoza, M. S., & Koshmider, J. W. (1989). Misleds subjects may know more than their performance implies. *Journal of Experimental Psychology: Learning, Memory, and Cognition, 15*, 246–255.

Zaragoza, M. S., & McCloskey, M. (1989). Misleading postevent information and the memory impairment hypothesis: Comment on Belli and reply to Tversky and Tuchin. *Journal of Experimental Psychology: General, 118*, 92–99.

Zaragoza, M. S., McCloskey, M., & Jamis, M. (1987). Misleading postevent information and recall of the original event: Further evidence against the memory impairment hypothesis. *Journal of Experimental Psychology: Learning, Memory, and Cognition, 13*, 36–44.

Zechmeister, E. B., & Shaughnessy, J. J. (1980). When you know that you know and when you think that you know but you don't. *Bulletin of the Psychonomic Society, 15*, 41–44.

Zimmerman, J. (1975). Free recall after self-paced study: A test of the attention explanation of the spacing effect. *American Journal of Psychology, 88*, 277–291.

Author Index

C

D

E

F

G

H

N

O

P

Y

Z

Subject Index